THE ROYAL FAMILIES
OF EUROPE

Other titles from Constable by the same author

Saladin: a Biography
The Book of Magna Carta

THE ROYAL FAMILIES
OF EUROPE

Geoffrey Hindley

CARROLL & GRAF PUBLISHERS, INC.
New York

Carroll & Graf Publishers, Inc.
19 West 21st Street
New York
NY 10010-6805

First published in the UK by Constable,
an imprint of Constable & Robinson Ltd, 2000

First Carroll & Graf edition 2000

ISBN 0-7867-0828-X

Printed and bound in the EU

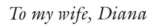

To my wife, Diana

CONTENTS

———•◦•———

ILLUSTRATIONS

———•◦•———

ACKNOWLEDGEMENTS

In addition to standard historical works a book like this, dealing with subject matter contemporary or near contemporary necessarily draws much of its information from the daily and weekly press. The reader will find references to the London Press, notably *The Times* and the *Daily Telegraph*, to *Le Figaro* of Paris, but also to specialist publications such as *Royalty Digest* and also to the French weekly *Point de Vue* which has been a useful source of information as to current events of royalist interest on continental Europe. I have also referred to websites maintained by members of the royal houses themselves and official publications from various embassies. A certain amount of the more purely historical narrative derives from reading done for my own earlier books and my script for the videogram *The Glittering Crowns*, narrated by Edward Fox and produced by the Electronic Publishing Company.

For the story of French monarchism over the past two centuries I relied heavily on the books by Jean François Chiappe and by Raoul de Warren and Aymon de Lestrange specified in the bibliography. For the story of King Michael of Romania the account to be found in his own book *Le règne inachevé: conversations avec Philippe Viguié Desplaces* was invaluable while Thierry Deslot's *Géraldine d'Albanie* ... had useful detail on the life of Leka of Albania. For the Balkans in general Guy Gauthier's *Les Aigles et les lions* provided important background information of more recent history while Juan Balansó's *Los reales primos de Europa* was an invaluable survey of the present generation of Europe's royal houses.

A note about names

The solution to this problem which I have decided to adopt will no doubt be disputed by some. It is neither consistent nor, I am bound to admit, a self evident compromise. Since the book's theme is monarchs both living and historical, a simple solution is not really possible. If one decides, for the sake of consistency, to adopt the spellings used in the language of the country (even given an acceptable convention of transliteration from the Slav languages), one is liable to be confronted by Frederick II the Great of Prussia, who can hardly be Friedrich der Grosse in an English language text and certainly cannot be Friedrich the Great. On the other hand, if one decides, again in the interest of consistency, to anglicize throughout, one finds the text infiltrated by that little known monarch of Spain, His Majesty King John Charles II, which is clearly absurd. The Queen of Spain instances another problem category of nomenclature, born Princess Sophia (Σοφια) of Greece she became Queen Sofia of Spain. This is modest compared with her husband's predecessor King Carlos I of Spain, otherwise known as Kaiser Karl V in Germany, Carlo V of Naples in Italy, Charles II Duke of Burgundy in France. In English he is the Emperor Charles V. Present members of the Houses of Habsburg and Hohenzollern and other former German ruling houses are given the German spelling of their names, historic rulers of these houses are anglicised where an acceptable English version of the name exists. For the Italian House of Savoy I have retained the Italian name Umberto (the anglicized 'Humbert' is hardly in common use).

In general, when speaking of monarchs or princes who are alive, I have aimed to adopt the version of the name they themselves use, or as it is listed in the *Almanach de Gotha*, but when speaking of sovereigns who are deceased, whether recently or in the historical past, I have used the common English form of the name. Thus Crown Prince Frederik of Denmark is the grandson of King Frederick IX while his mother Queen Margrethe II, takes her regnal number from Denmark's fourteenth-century queen regent Margaret I.

In the vast majority of cases, then, contemporary names will be in the language of the country, historical names in the anglicized version. The Netherlands Government Information Service adopts a similar system speaking, for example, of Crown Prince Willem and his ancestor William the Silent. But there are exceptions here also. In English, convention still generally dictates that William II Emperor of Germany be known as Kaiser Wilhelm II while, because the kings of Sweden commonly adopted double names of the type Karl XIV Johan or Gustav VI Adolf, I have followed Swedish practice as set out in the booklet *Kings and Rulers of Sweden* published in Stockholm in 1995. Even so there are exceptions to my rule, if it can be called that. Constantinos of the Hellenes and Mihaï I of Romania, both close family and friends of the Windsors, and among the royal guests at the centenary service for Queen Elizabeth the Queen Mother, are known world wide as Constantine and Michael. As I indicated at the beginning of this note, consistency and convention will not live together in this debate – I have done my best to find sensible solutions and in one or two extreme cases have resorted to parenthetical explications.

The full titles of French noblemen and women are given in French but the noun itself in English. Thus, 'For supporters of the claims of the House of Bourbon Orléans to the throne of France, Henri, Comte de Paris, is "Henri VII", but the Count himself rarely uses the title.' The Bourbon family itself has two main branches, the French Bourbons and the Spanish Borbóns, but there are also Italian branches of the French family who ruled in Italy designated by the state over which they ruled, and here I have retained the familiar English rendering of the Italian place name. Thus the family called Bourbon-Parme in French is rendered here as Bourbon-Parma. Because the royal house of Portugal has been familiar to English readers ever since Catherine of Braganza brought the city of Bombay (Mumbai) as a dowry to King Charles II I have retained the familiar English version of that name.

The book hopes to give a historical summary of the principal royal houses of Europe, some account of their present fortunes and also to argue the case for monarchy as an effective and practical constitutional formula in the modern world.

INTRODUCTION — PAST, PRESENT AND FUTURE

———•◦•———

Viewed objectively, hereditary monarchy today, when its powers are minimal, is the most trouble-free method available of choosing a head of state. The office is above politics – the sovereign is forbidden by constitutional clauses or by convention from intervening in political questions, and the succession is a simple matter of biological inheritance subject to parliamentary confirmation. Monarchies have the human interest of the family, and at their best they embody values of public service and a sense of communal and national identity. In addition, they quite simply offer an effective constitutional mechanism particularly well adapted to the conditions of the modern mass democracy where the increasingly exiguous but nevertheless still indispensable functions of a head of state should ideally be detached from the political process. As King Simeon Bulgaria's former monarch observed at a press conference in the early 1990s: 'What would one think of a football game where the referee belonged to one of the teams.'[1]

In this book my aim is to examine the present balance sheet of monarchy in continental Europe by describing first the personalities and traditions of those states where monarchy has been replaced by republics, but where monarchists still feature on the political scene and where family claims or individual pretenders still keep alive the dream of restoration. In the second half I look at the countries where monarchy still serves its constitutional function with a view to assessing the prospects for its future. In every case, the aim is also to set the present players – monarchs and their heirs – in the context of family and national history and traditions, for in this subject, as has been hinted, the ideas of family and nation are intertwined.

In April 1998 London's Greek Orthodox Cathedral of St Sophia provided the setting for a royal event on a truly majestic scale, which was also a European family event. The star was a somewhat startled baby, Prince Konstantinos Alexios, son of Crown Prince and Crown Princess Paul of Greece and grandson of ex-King Constantine II and Queen Anne Marie. And startled he might well be, surrounded by four royal godparents and a guest list to match. The British and Greek families were friends of long standing and, thanks to the royal network, the Danish and Spanish royal houses were closely involved in the proceedings, and – a memory of another Europe – a prince of the erstwhile Yugoslav royal house was also invited. For the London public, the most interesting of the sponsors was Prince William. The Prince was taking up for the first time a responsibility he would no doubt soon become familiar with; his father's godchildren, at the last count, numbered more than thirty, among them baby Konstantinos's sister, the two-year-old Princess Maria Olympia, and his father. William's mother, Diana, Princess of Wales, had been godmother to the baby's young uncle, the twelve-year-old Prince Phillipos of Greece. Standing by William were Crown Princes Frederik of Denmark and Felipe of Spain, and Crown Princess Victoria of Sweden. All three were from families related to the Greeks through the Danish-born Queen Anne Marie. And of course all the principal actors in this royal pageant are descended from Queen Victoria.

In Britain, according to conventional wisdom monarchy is an out-of-date remnant of bygone times. This is not the view in the world's second largest economy. Japan enjoyed decades of economic triumph under an emperor whose ancestors claimed direct descent from the sun god. And, of course, seven out of the fifteen members of the present European Community are monarchies, and

[2]

what may be considered the Community's principal institutions, the Commission and the Parliament, are based in the kingdom of Belgium and the Grand Duchy of Luxembourg. Monarchy can override as well as establish conventions. For generations in some European traditions monarchy has provided a few privileged women the greatest possible scope in government. Whether Boudicca, warrior queen of the Iceni, was an ancient British heroine or, as a modern writer suggests, merely a terrorist leader, she was a notable figure. In the fourteenth century, the first Margaret of Denmark ruled the union of the Scandinavian countries, and in the nineteenth Victoria of Great Britain made an indelible impression on her country's history.

Talking things over with her Prime Minister Lord Melbourne, on the evening of her coronation day, the eighteen-year-old Queen admitted that the heavy crown had hurt a good deal, while Melbourne conceded that the ceremonial sword he had been required to carry had been excessively heavy. The magnificent ceremony represented a unique life experience which once distinguished monarchs as a class apart from all other human beings. At the heart of the mystery was the ceremony of anointing with the holy oil. The spoon used at this ceremonial moment is the one item of the royal regalia of England which dates from the old Anglo-Saxon monarchy, having been used at the coronation of St Edward the Confessor, as King of England in 1042. The oil, like that used in the enthronement of a bishop, was thought to confer, if not divine power, then certainly divine approval upon the recipient. From that point on he or she had true 'charisma', potency today generally accorded only to pop stars or media personalities.

Things can change. Elsewhere in Europe the taking of the oath is central to the inauguration of a new sovereign rather than the act of crowning, while early in 1999 proposals were being aired in Britain that the historic Anglican ritual with its catholic elements such as the anointing, which date back to the tenth century, should be replaced with what was termed 'a multi-faith installation ceremony'. It was an interesting idea, which might have considerable repercussions, since in Britain, as in Norway, Sweden and Denmark, the monarch is constitutionally obliged to be a protestant Christian by religious confession. It was also, perhaps, somewhat premature since there was no reason to suppose that the time for considering future coronation arrangements was anywhere near at hand.

Royal women have made notable contributions in world politics and polemic. After more than 200 years the American republic has yet to produce a woman head of state – a rather sad record, perhaps, for popular democracy to set against Elizabeth I of England, Maria Theresa of Austria or Catherine the Great of Russia. And if in the twentieth century, by the nature of things, women royals have been denied opportunities for greatness on such a scale, they have nevertheless played a prominent part in the world's history. The Commonwealth remained at the dawn of the new millennium a thriving and expanding organization under the aegis of the Queen. The Netherlands were ruled by the women of the House of Orange-Nassau, among them the inspiring war leader Wilhelmina, for the whole of the last century. In the second half of the twentieth century even countries such as Belgium which formerly had excluded women from the succession decided to move with the times, and changed their constitutions accordingly.

Such adaptability to changes in the world should come as no surprise. Europe's surviving monarchies owe that survival to their willingness to remodel themselves to suit changing circumstances. Sometimes one may even catch a hint of royal networking and shared survival strategies. Outward show is important in most areas of life. Just as unelected life members of Britain's upper legislative chamber expect to be called Lord X and will probably go to the length of devising a coat of arms for themselves, even if before their appointment by the Prime Minister they deplored such flummery, so the Queen, as Head of State, with more justification expects the courtesy of a bow. It seems she has gentle ways of coercing the gesture. Writing in the *Royalty Digest* for July 1999, Piers Bressault reported a revealing exchange between a British cabinet minister and Crown Prince Willem of the Netherlands. The minister was recalling how, as a young Labour MP noted for his strident republicanism, he was to be introduced to the Queen with other members of an official reception committee. He had vowed that he would not make the bow. It seems the Crown Prince knowingly suggested how the story ended. When Her Majesty came face to face with the young MP, did she mutter something in a low voice, so that he had to bend forward to catch what she had said, and then, smiling, move on down the line, so that to onlookers the republican had seemed to bow to the monarch? Taken aback, the cabinet minister asked the Prince how he knew that that was exactly what had happened. For answer, the Prince winked.

In Sweden, where formalities are perhaps less important in all walks of life than in Britain, the motto adopted by King Carl XVI Gustaf when he came to the throne in 1973, *För Sverige i tiden* (For Sweden in keeping with the times) perfectly sums up the tradition of adaptability demonstrated by successful monarchies. In Spain, indeed, the institution was restored after an interregnum of four decades, the one symbol of political unity acceptable to a divided nation, and was to prove the bulwark of democracy. Astonishingly, in the 1990s some political commentators were not discounting the possibility of a restoration of the Romanov dynasty. After seventy years of the numbing and economically illiterate terror called communism, perhaps nothing could be truly absurd – but the return of an imperial monarchy?

And yet the vitality of this old regime of government has produced some equally startling effects. During the nineteenth and early twentieth centuries, which in the aftermath of the French Revolution should surely have seen the advance of republicanism at every opportunity, the birth of new nations or the rebirth of old ones was sanctified by the crowning of hereditary dynasties. Between 1815 and 1930, the Netherlands, where republicanism had been practised long before the French guillotine was even thought of, Belgium, Greece, Italy, Norway, Romania, Bulgaria, Serbia, Montenegro and, fatefully, Yugoslavia were all inaugurated or re-inaugurated into the ranks of the world's sovereign states by newly established royal houses. Germany first achieved united statehood in 1871 under the sovereignty of a newly recreated empire. But then, in the nineteenth century, not even the French had seemed to believe in republicanism. Re-established little more than a decade after the execution of King Louis XVI with the empire of Napoleon, than whom no more absolutist monarch had ruled in the country for half a century, monarchical regimes held power in France for more than sixty of the first eighty years of the post-revolutionary era.

In fact, in 1901, the year of Queen Victoria's death, only France, San Marino and Switzerland were outside the sway of monarchs. Perhaps, though, this is not so surprising. After all, the real revolution in human society, the explosive revolution which had transformed the means of production and so the basis of society itself, had been pioneered and presided over by the supposedly stultified and class-crippled monarchy over which she had wielded her sceptre. Today, the Continent still boasts nine reigning sovereigns, and in the Pyrenean state of Andorra there is a diarchy in which the president of the secular republic of France rather surprisingly shares the authority with the bishop of the Spanish diocese of Urgell. In addition there are the descendants of many royal houses now exiled from power who are country members, so to speak, of that elite club around whose members still lingers an aura of past majesty.

The appeal of monarchy for many has always in fact been precisely that it is rooted in the past. The challenge for monarchy is to survive in the present by adapting to the future. Reading the future can prove as difficult for royals as for anyone else. In no country is the difficult balancing act between love of tradition and the urge for trendiness more difficult than in Britain, and no royal house has been more assiduous in courting popular approval than the House of Windsor. For years the received wisdom was that the public liked a crowned head wreathed in mystery and majesty. The tabloid press jeered at the 'bicycle monarchies' of Scandinavia and congratulated Britain on having a regular royal queen.

The glorious and fervent girl who was crowned Queen in Westminster Abbey in June 1953 dedicated her life to her people and has lived by the letter and spirit of that oath ever since. Without, perhaps, the prickly insistence on protocol for which her sister Princess Margaret is notorious, the Queen has always expected the deference due to her office and her person, and for decades she was in tune with the mood of the mass of her people. Even so, she responded to advice and in 1969 agreed to the shooting of the television documentary *Royal Family*. A decade later the young royals participated in the hugely popular TV show *It's a Knockout*. As a young girl Princess Anne was a hate figure for Britain's press precisely because she was doing what today would earn her credit points – questioning traditional ways going her own way, indulging in unroyal behaviour and talking straight. And when she turned to the traditional work of royal ladies, the patronage of charities, she was unconventional again in her hands-on approach as president of Save the Children and patron of many other organizations. Like that other highly professional and hard-working royal, Princess Alexandra, her work did not attract much press attention from the media, nor, unwisely perhaps, did she seek it.

Standing in the opinion polls is, by the nature of things, variable. Apart from the Queen Mother, whose popularity in her centenary year nothing seemed able to dent, public figures must expect to take the rough with the smooth. It was always so. Late in his life, the vastly unpopular Leopold II of Belgium had no time for what he considered a mere manifestation of public caprice. Popularity, which he enjoyed for a time at the beginning of his reign, he compared to sea spray which disappears without a trace. In fact, as we shall see (though he seems not to have realized the fact), this misanthropic monster fully deserved his bad reputation. But even his hugely popular nephew and successor Albert I, whose death in a mountaineering accident in 1934 plunged the entire nation into mourning, could be a bit of a cynic on the subject. Once, when being welcomed by yet another cheering crowd, he turned to one of his aides to observe that the crowds would have been still larger if he were being led off to execution.

[7]

The hardened royal campaigner learns to weather press harassment and public criticism. A favoured few do not have to bother themselves on the matter. His Serene Highness, Reigning Prince Hans Adam of Liechtenstein, whose family receives not a penny by way of civil list and whose 30,000 subjects enjoy Europe's highest per capita income and pay Europe's lowest taxes, is liable, when the mood takes him, to show a positively lordly disregard for their views. Although one of his predecessors, Johann II, granted the microstate a constitution and fifteen-member diet in the 1920s, its powers and functions were minimal. Prince Hans Adam is said once to have threatened to retire from the country if that was the wish of the people, but he warned them that Bill Gates of Microsoft would probably buy the place.

The story may be apocryphal, but precedent would support it. The princely family's properties in Austria and central Europe cover territory some ten times more extensive than the principality of which Hans Adam is sovereign, while the first ruler to reside permanently in the country was his father Francis Joseph II who succeeded to the crown in 1938. The family's ancestral home is in fact the castle of Liechtenstein outside Vienna. The castle's name, which can be roughly translated as 'Stone of Light', was adopted centuries back by the family, one of the oldest and richest in the Holy Roman Empire. Its head was raised to the rank of Prince of the Empire in the early 1600s, and a century or so later when they acquired the two adjacent lordships of Schellenburg and Vaduz, lying in the mountains between Austria and Switzerland, the title became attached to a sovereign territory to which the family gave its name. At this time Prince Joseph Wenzel, who earned the emperor's gratitude for his services in the imperial army, embarked on a career as an art connoisseur which was to build what has been called perhaps the finest family collection in the world. Necessarily loyal to Austria, this miniature frontier territory was technically involved in the Austro-Prussian war of 1866. Since it had, as it still has, no army, this was a technicality which was overlooked, as indeed was the principality when the peace treaty was drawn up.

Diminutive in size, Liechtenstein is also, thanks to the scores of international holding companies with their head offices registered there and the prince's immense talents as a businessman, hugely rich. The family fortune is thought to exceed even that of Queen Beatrix of the Netherlands, generally reckoned to be the richest of Europe's royals. Prince Hans Adam, his wife Princess Marie, of an old Bohemian noble family, and their son HSH Hereditary Prince Alois belong by ancestry and sovereign status to a long-forgotten Europe where once there were Austrian and German empires which in their time had together comprised more than 300 independent princely states. A number of these states, as well as the emperors of Austria and Germany, survived into the second decade of the twentieth century, but the cataclysm of the First World War brought them tumbling down. For the most part, their rulers retained their fortunes but their occupation was gone. Surveying the ranks of deposed post-war royalty attending the celebrations of the marriage of his daughter Marie José to Prince Umberto of Italy (later King Umberto II) in 1930, Albert I, King of the Belgians, drily observed that he had no idea there was so much unemployment in the monarchy business.

1

THE PRETENDERS

From Russia in the East to Portugal in the West there are twelve European republics in which monarchists can point to candidates for the long-vacant thrones. The 1990s saw a resurgence in many of these countries of interest in monarchy as a serious political option. Even in Germany, where few imagine the former royal and imperial family of Hohenzollern will return to their thrones, either as kings of Prussia or as emperors of Germany, there is a strong interest in the traditions of monarchy and in the representatives of the many minor royal families which once ruled in the territories of the Federal Republic. In the first part of this book I want to look at the personalities involved, the claimants and their families, something of the history of the monarchies they represent, how they came to be established, the sometimes adventurous, often controversial careers of their predecessors, and to estimate as far as possible the strength of feeling for or against the institution they represent.

The fact that, at the turn of the millennium, Vittorio Emanuele of Italy's royal House of Savoy was still barred from entering his country by a provision of the Republic's constitution was, perhaps, evidence for fervent monarchists of republican nervousness. This was surely at odds with the human rights of a member of the European Union. In the summer of 1999 it was reported that the sixty-two-year-old prince was to ask the European Court of Human Rights to rule on the prohibition. For decades, the hostility of the Greek authorities to ex-King Constantine II and his family, amounting, it sometimes seemed, almost to a vendetta, could be thought to indicate apprehension about the continuing appeal of the former royals to a possibly significant body of public opinion. Late in 1999 Queen Sofia of Spain, born a princess of Greece, was permitted to return on a private visit to the scenes of her childhood at the Tatoï palace outside Athens, a sign perhaps of an easing of the tensions. And yet in Greece, as in Italy, the situation remained complicated.

In the countries of the northern Balkans by contrast, monarchy gained a more positive image during the 1990s. Both Simeon II of Bulgaria, where he is known as 'Tsar', and Michael of Romania reigned briefly in their countries in the mid-1940s (Simeon was a boy king with a regency council) before being ousted by communist manipulation, and thus they were the only surviving heads of state from the Second World War period. Both succeeded in returning to their countries in the last decade of the century, though both had some initial difficulties with the authorities. In the case of Michael these were considerable but as early as May 1991 Marie Louise of Bulgaria, King Simeon's sister, was welcomed on her appearance at a football match in Sofia with cheers and cries of 'Bring back the Tsar'. In Yugoslavia Alexander, heir to the royal house, let it be known that he was interested in helping his troubled country if he could be of service, hiring a public relations expert to promote his image. A cousin of Queen Sofia of Spain and connected with many of Europe's Royals, he was born in London in 1945 and numbered the then Princess Elizabeth, now the Queen, among his godparents. Educated, like his good friend Charles Prince of Wales, at Gordonstoun, the elite Scottish public school, before going on to Sandhurst, Britain's military academy, he developed an international business career in oil and shipping, and from his base in London's Park Lane was active in trying to find solutions to his country's problems.

For him, as for Belgrade, there was the added complication of the determinedly independent attitude of the constituent republic of Montenegro, which could look back on a brief episode as an independent monarchy in the early years of the twentieth century and to a living descendant of its royal house. Nikola Petrovic Njegos, a successful architect practising in Paris, is a man with a serious commitment to his ancestral country and his standing with its peoples. Broadcasting on Radio France International in December 1991, he made an appeal for peace and the cessation of the civil conflict in the territories of Yugoslavia, which he considered had been fomented by elements from the former communist order. It was his conviction that after a period of partition the states would inevitably return to federation because the diverse peoples had become so intermixed. What seemed like reason before the era of ethnic cleansing seemed an impossibility after it. For his part the Prince disclaimed any intention of working for an independent Montenegro, though there was a moment when this might have tempted a more ambitious man.

The Kingdom of Montenegro, proclaimed in August 1910 by the then Prince Nicholas, survived de facto for eight years before being annexed by Serbia, and de jure another four when the annexation was recognized by the international community and Montenegro found itself a province of the Kingdom of the Serbs, Croats and Slovenes. In fact the little country, thanks to its mountainous terrain, had been more successful than virtually any other region of the Balkans in retaining its independence from the Turks, and from the 1690s had been ruled by a succession of more or less warlike prince-bishops. Such ecclesiastical standing did not appeal to Prince Danilo I (d.1860), who changed the country's status from prince-bishopric to principality, nor to his nephew Nicholas, who succeeded him aged twenty and who, after forty years as a mere prince, adopted the honorific of 'His Royal Highness' in 1900. Finally in 1910 he proclaimed himself as King Nicholas I. A jovial despot, who according to Lady Salisbury in the 1870s looked like an elderly butler in search of a job, he boasted that his numerous daughters married out to neighbouring royals (among them Victor Emmanuel III of Italy) were his impoverished country's principal exports. He survived at least one assassination attempt and was forced to flee Montenegro for Italy in 1915 following defeat by the armies of Austria-Hungary. Three years later the country's assembly, the Skuptchina, declared him deposed – under the influence of Serbian troops, Nicholas claimed, though he made no attempt to return. He died at the age of eighty-one during a not unhappy exile on the French Riviera, his kingdom having been effectively integrated into Serbia.

However, the mountain clansmen of the country, undeterred by political realities, sent a deputation to seek out Danilo, his son and heir, in his comfortable Riviera retreat. These stalwarts appear to have been well armed, following local custom, and whether intimidated or merely out of politeness, the Prince agreed to be hailed as King Danilo II. After six days, he resigned his honours in favour of a nephew and Montenegro's brief regal episode faded out of the headlines. But while dynastic claims may cease for a time to be politics, they live on in a family's genes. When in the eventful year 1989 Prince Nikola Petrovic, recognized as the head of the royal house, made a much publicized trip to Montenegro's capital of Cetinje, it was estimated that some 200,000 people, or a third of the little republic's entire population, turned out to welcome him.

For centuries much of the Balkans was under the rule of the Ottoman Turkish empire, its capital of Constantinople (officially renamed Istanbul in 1930) formerly the metropolis of the Christian Byzantine empire. To the north, Ottoman rule faced the Habsburg family, emperors in Austria and kings in Hungary. The First World War spelt the end of both the empires but with the collapse of communism there was a resurgence of interest in the old monarchy in Hungary; and though Dr Otto Habsburg, the doyen of the former imperial family, adopted German nationality and won a seat in the European Parliament, there remained monarchists in Austria and Hungary who still looked to the family as the rightful heirs to government.

As a look at Europe's celebrity and society magazines will show, the world of royalty is still very much alive. In October 1999, Geneva's Hotel Intercontinental was venue to a glittering banquet in which the celebrities included HRH Emanuele Filiberto, Prince of Venice of the House of Savoy, and Natasha Andress, niece of the

American film star Ursula. Whether weekending together on the shores of Lake Geneva or touring on the Prince's Harley Davidson, or motoring in his immaculate Aston Martin, they were trend-setters for Europe's beautiful people. For his part, the Prince was a role model for hopeful young royals. Although barred from entry into Italy, he was frequently on the country's television screens, thanks to a three-year contract as a football commentator on Juventus games, and his book *Sognando d'Italia* (Dreaming of Italy), had enjoyed some success. Now, at the Hotel Interconti-nental, he was to add a new dimension to his career profile, being inaugurated as Grand Chancellor of the chivalric Order of Saints Maurice and Lazarus, of which his father was Grand Master. It was founded in the 1430s by Duke Amadeus VIII of Savoy – who ended life as a cardinal, having been for ten years anti-Pope Felix V after election by the schismatic Council of Basel, now in the third millenium of the Christian era the Order was to face, promised the Prince, 'modernization'. This was a destiny which many a tradi-tional institution, not least monarchy itself, had confronted and weathered over the centuries.

It is when the summer season of marriages comes round that Europe's nobility and royals, actual, ex- or would-be, are most in evidence, as they traverse the Continent to celebrate the weddings of friends and cousins near and distant. It may be a great set piece like a Habsburg ceremony in Budapest, or a minor fixture such as a lesser German princeling's nuptials in the onion-domed church of a Bavarian village. Here, depending on the importance of the event and, of course, the invitations issued, you are like to see the privi-leged progeny of quondam ruling houses – the Hanovers, the Württembergs, the Bourbon-Two Sicilies, whose forebears were the last dynasty to sit on the throne of the kingdom of Naples – as well as junior members of monarchies still in place. And in the 1990s it would be unusual not to find the family of Bourbon Orléans, regarded by many as the royal House of France, among those present. Commonly it was represented by the brothers Jean, Duc de Vendôme and Eudes, Duc d'Angoulême, grandsons of

[15]

Henri, Comte de Paris, then in their late twenties or early thirties. For transport they might share a modest saloon car, just as for accommodation they shared a less than palatial Paris flat. Following the precept of their grandfather, that 'the next generation must work' they led the lives of thousands of fellow Parisians, going by Métro to the office in the morning and in the evening perhaps to the theatre or a simple supper party with a few friends. But they seemed to feel a genuine sense, always old-fashioned, of obligation to live up to their hereditary pretensions. Sometimes, perhaps, they wished they had the income to maintain them more easily. For they had rivals.

Even in France, where monarchist regimes ruled for most of the nineteenth century, monarchist parties remained an active, if de-clining, force in the twentieth century. The standard bearer of the royalist cause was the head of the House of Bourbon Orléans, but in the summer of 1999 both its morale and its material fortunes were plunged into disarray. Following the death of the ninety-year-old Henri, Comte de Paris in June of that year, his will revealed that the family's once fabulous fortune which he inherited, along with the claim to the throne, from his father in 1940 had almost entirely disappeared. The man whom fervent supporters had re-garded as 'King Henry VI' of France, signed his final testament as 'Son Altesse Royale Monseigneur le Prince Henri' and made no mention of his political legacy. It was seriously suggested in some quarters that the Count had deliberately dissipated the family re-sources so as to deny his heirs the funds to maintain their preten-sions to the throne. Their chief rivals were members of the Spanish branch of the Bourbons, so that with the dawn of the millennium the fashionable favourite was Louis Alphonse, Duc d'Anjou, attrib-uted by devotees the title of 'King Louis XX'.

As for Portugal, although the last king to reign in Lisbon, King Manuel II, was driven out by revolution in 1910, eighty years later supporters of monarchy might nurse dreams that the royal house represented by Dom Duarte Pio twenty-third Duke of Braganza and his children might one day in some distant future return to the throne. Dom Duarte himself, who remained a bachelor well into his forties, had, exceptionally for a pretender to a throne, been allowed to live in his country – his home is a comparatively modest villa.

The revolution which overthrew the monarchy in Portugal was the outcome of decades of tension. The cosmopolitan and talented King Carlos, father of Manuel, was politically maladroit and extravagant to such an extent that he had to surrender certain palaces and royal yachts as a means of persuading parliament to settle his debts. A bon viveur and a gifted cultural dilettante, he had neither talent nor, it would seem, interest in the arts of government. His friendship with Edward VII of England provoked hostility in high Catholic circles from people who objected to King Edward's masonic connections and believed that he might 'infect' their king with Freemasonry. Other critics accused Carlos of financial corruption. Even in dynastic terms, the King's situation was questioned by some.

During the nineteenth century a rift had opened up between two lines of the House of Bragana: the one which occupied the throne and the other descending from King Miguel who was forced into exile in the 1830s and whose successors were barred by law from returning to the country. In the early 1900s a parliamentary bill to lift this prohibition had failed by only four votes. When in May 1907 King Carlos suspended the constitution, opposition intensified. The following February the King and his twenty-one-year-old heir, the Duke of Branganza, were assassinated in the streets of the capital. In 1910 his younger son, Manuel II, was forced to flee the country, finding refuge in England. The new constitution abolished the monarchy and disestablished the Church. Inevitably the republican regime which followed became the target of criticism in its turn, and monarchist parties began to find favour with the electorate. In 1932 the death of ex-King Manuel II without an heir left the claim to the throne with Duarte Nuno of the Miguelist branch. Talk of restoring the monarchy was overridden by the emerging strong man of Portuguese politics, António Oliveira de Salazar, who consolidated his authority as dictator and in 1933 nationalized the properties of the Braganza family.

[17]

However, family members were able to continue to reside in the country, though, as we have noted, in much reduced circumstances.

The Duke of Braganza has never made any move towards a restoration or countenanced any such move on his behalf by monarchist groups. And yet during the 1990s, perhaps because of his family's central role in the nation's history, perhaps by way of emulating the glamour and prestige with which King Juan Carlos and Queen Sofia had imbued the institution of monarchy in neighbouring Spain, the Portuguese state collaborated with Dom Duarte in some remarkable royal celebrations. In May 1995 the marriage of the Prince to Isabel Ines de Castro Curvello de Heredia was celebrated with great pomp and ceremony in Lisbon in the presence of the President of the Republic. In June the following year their first born, Alfonso Prince of Beira, was baptized in the city of Braga. In 1997 his sister Francisca was christened in the cathedral of Vila Vicosa. When it became known that the Duchess was expecting a second son in December 1999, it was decided that the child should be baptized in Oporto, next to Lisbon the country's leading city. The child was to be named Diniz, after one of Portugal's greatest rulers and a poet and patron of culture. The distribution of these various royal events, each in a different city around the country, seemed like a planned exercise in what can only be called royal propaganda; and since the baptism of Prince Diniz was scheduled for early 2000 in the city which had been designated European capital of culture for that year, for Portugal at least the dawn of the new millennium would very definitely have a royal glow.

Of course, the great monarchist event of the 1990s was the return of the Romanovs to St Petersburg and the ceremony of reinterment of the remains of Tsar Nicholas II and his family, murdered by order of the Bolsheviks in 1918. At the beginning of the decade, the *Royalty Digest* carried a lengthy article on the diverse and burgeoning monarchist movement in the Russian territory of the former Soviet Union. As the decade advanced there was increasing speculation which climaxed in talk of a restoration of the monarchy, and it was said that President Yeltsin considered the possibility. At the end of 1999, the confused state of affairs in Russia made almost any predictions as to the country's future hazardous in the extreme. A year later, despite the disaster of the nuclear submarine *Kutsk* and the ever parlous condition of the Russian economy the position of President Vladimir Putin seemed secure. The canonification of Tsar Nicholas II and the imperial family in August 2000 by the Russian Orthodox Church looked more like a gesture of nostalgic piety than the auguty of a tsarist revival.

Readers interested in further detail on the lives of claimants in exile up to the 1980s are referred to the books by Charles Fenyvesi and Jeremy Potter listed in the bibliography, both of which have provided me with useful material.

2

HABSBURGS AND HOHENZOLLERNS: EMPIRES AND POLITICS

<hr />

At about 10.30 on the morning of Saturday 18 October 1997, hundreds of thousands of Hungarians settled in front of their television sets to enjoy an extraordinary but traditional spectacle. Extraordinary because this was republican Hungary, traditional because the cameras installed in the great church of St Stephen in Budapest were awaiting the first arrivals for the wedding of His Imperial and Royal Highness George of Austria of the House of Habsburg and Duchess Eilika of Oldenburg. For churchmen the ceremony in prospect would have the rarity value of a combined ecumenical service. The groom was Catholic, the bride – descended from the Grand Dukes of Oldenburg in northern Germany, who lost their throne in the revolutions of November 1918 which broke up the German empire – Lutheran. But for the television audience, among them members of Hungary's small monarchist party, this was a mere detail compared with the stupendous celebration of European monarchy they were about to witness.

The body of the great church was packed. In addition to the royal guests seated in the pews to the right of the main aisle, room was also required for the nomenclatura of the Hungarian republican government in the pews to the left. Invitations were at a premium and overflow accommodation was provided in the gallery above the west door. The officials and their wives were, of course, there in their official capacities since the bridegroom, as well as being programme director for one of Hungary's television stations, was also Budapest's ambassador extraordinary to the European Union. He was the first of his family to live in Budapest since the failed attempt of his grandfather Charles I, the last Emperor of Austria and the last King of Hungary, to re-establish himself on the Hungarian throne in 1921.

The month following the wedding saw the eighty-fifth birthday of the bridegroom's father, the doyen of the family, Otto von Habsburg. Son and heir of the Emperor-King Charles, Dr Habsburg – to use the title he has for years preferred – was surrounded by his family for the celebrations, yet the keynote was not of royal and imperial pretensions but of European solidarity and extension. The star circle of the EU emblem was much in evidence among the flags in the background of the family group photographs. For many years the former heir to empire had been content to serve as a deputy in the European parliament. He had long been an active advocate of the expansion of the European Union, above all into the former communist states of eastern and central Europe. The Habsburg family, who established their power base as dukes in Austria in the thirteenth century, have a long perspective on matters European, and an eastward extension of the EU would chime well with the traditional Austro-German political involvement in central Europe, or Mitteleuropa. At the beginning of the twentieth century Catholic Croatia was a crownland of the Kingdom of Hungary under Habsburg kings. In the 1920s it constituted part of the new state of Yugoslavia under the Orthodox King of Serbia. On a visit to the region in 1991 Dr Habsburg criticized EU policy, then favouring the continuation of a united Yugoslavia, as amounting to a blank cheque for Serbia. Early in 1992, under pressure from Germany, the EU recognized Croatia's assertion of its independence.

For Otto von Habsburg himself, there was, too, an element of *noblesse oblige* in his sentiments for the historic family territory. As a twenty-six-year-old in 1938, when Austria was facing imminent amalgamation with Germany, he pledged that when Austria was threatened the Habsburgs were honour-bound to stand by her. In fact Austria succumbed to Hitler – to the satisfaction, be it said, of many Austrians proud that the Führer was Austrian by birth – and Otto was soon to emigrate to America as a refugee. American fascination with royalty embraced even this heir to imperial and kingly dignities: in a sentimental movie Freddie Bartholomew depicted the boy Otto being tutored in English by his mother Empress Zita in the correct intonation for an heir to empire to express the verb 'we com*mand*'.

From 1526 to November 1918 St Stephen's crown of Hungary with its famous crooked cross, the crown of István Arpád presented by the Pope and conferred upon the Magyar ruler on Christmas Day 1000, had been worn by successive members of the Habsburg family who had, of course, also been Holy Roman Emperors. 'Monarchy remains a force to be reckoned with', opined *The Economist* as late as December 1997, and while Dr Habsburg disclaimed all ambitions for a restoration of empire in Austria or kingdom in Hungary, as dreamed of by nostalgic monarchists in both countries, there is no gainsaying the ramifications of influence and loyalty available to a tradition reaching back more than half a millennium.

It was on Armistice Day, 11 November 1918, the Austrian empire having been defeated with its ally the German empire, that the Emperor-King Charles renounced the government of Austria. Two days later he officially relinquished his authority in Hungary, but in neither country did he abdicate his titular rights. He had acceded to the thrones two years previously on the death of his great uncle Francis Joseph I in November 1916. He decided against an inaugural ceremony in Austria on the grounds of expense but went through with the full traditions of coronation in Budapest. The ceremony over, Charles conformed to ancient tradition by mounting a charger while still crowned and robed, and riding to the top of the royal hill were he levelled his sword symbolically to the four points of the compass.

Over the next two years Charles tried to extricate his realms from the horrors of the Great War; nevertheless, the country was forced into unconditional surrender by the Italian army at Vittorio Veneto on 3 November 1918. In April the following year, Austria's new republican regime passed an act exiling all members of the house of Habsburg-Lorraine who refused to swear the oath of allegiance to the republic. (The dynastic name Habsburg-Lorraine was adopted by the descendants of Maria Theresa, Archduchess of Austria and co-Empress who married Francis, Duke of Lorraine in the 1740s.) Emperor Charles crossed into Switzerland with his dynamic wife Zita of Bourbon Parma and six-year-old son Otto. At thirty-two, Charles was still titular King of Hungary, and Zita urged him to plan a restoration there.

For a moment, events seemed favourable. In October 1919 the Hungarian communist regime under Béla Kun was succeeded by the right-wing Admiral Nikolaus Horthy who assumed the powers of head of state under the significant title of 'Regent'. In fact, whoever it was he thought he was regent for, Horthy evidently did not have Charles of Habsburg in mind. Late in March 1921 the King slipped across the Swiss-Austrian border in disguise. From Austria he smuggled himself into Hungary where he planned to 'take over' the government from the Admiral. Friends and supporters urged him to allow loyal regiments from the Hungarian army to march with him on the capital. But, wishing to avoid all possibility of bloodshed and armoured in the conviction of his legitimacy, the romantic claimant carried his gentlemanly gesture through to the final fiasco when he yielded to Horthy's persuasions and returned from whence he came. Decades later in an interview with Fredéric Mitterand on French television Otto Habsburg compared the uneasy ambivalence of Horthy, regent for a monarch to whom he denied restoration, to 'a character in Shakespeare', unable to wash his hands of the guilt of his betrayal. The allusion of course was to Lady Macbeth who had collaborated with her husband in the murder of King Duncan. Like her, Horthy had not actually killed the King, but his actions had effectively murdered the monarchy.

The Swiss government, uneasy that its friendly gesture of hospitality might impugn its traditional neutrality if any more sorties were launched from its territory requested that he and his family quit Swiss soil by January 1922. However, on 19 October, the royal couple, piloted by two loyal Hungarian airmen, crossed into Hungary in an old German Junkers warplane. Urged on by the unflagging Zita, this time the King was resolved on the use of troops. It made no difference. The amateurish *Putschists* were quickly dispatched, once more to their Swiss villa. There, finally, they packed their bags and left the country. They eventually found refuge at Funchal, Madeira. There, on 1 April 1922 the last of the Habsburgs to reign as monarch died of pneumonia.

The Emperor, in his life dedicated to the honour and cause of his dynasty, in death, like many another failed monarch, acquired a reputation for personal honour and piety. His tomb in the parish church near La Quinta da Monte, high above Funchal, soon became a place of local pilgrimage and it was said that the Roman Catholic Church was to institute a process for his beatification. In May 1991 Madeira was the scene of a papal visit and public Mass which was attended by, among thousands of others, the Archduchess Regina together with her sons Karl and Georg and her daughter Walburga, invited to attend the occasion by the regional authorities of Madeira.

For the Archduchess it was no doubt a time for thoughtful reflection on the difficult boyhood of her husband. One of eight children, like his brothers and sisters he had to help their mother with simple household chores, for the fugitive Emperor had left his wife in desperate financial circumstances; she had been banned from returning to the Habsburg homeland so long as she maintained the claims of the family to rule there. Even when in 1935 Kurt von Schuschnigg, Austria's Christian-Socialist Chancellor, lifted the ban on other members of the family, Otto and his mother were excluded. For the Empress Zita, Habsburg rule in Austria was part of the fabric of European history. In fact, for a historic moment in 1937, the conditions for a Habsburg restoration were actually the subject of secret, though fruitless, discussion between Schuschnigg and Archduke Otto. In later years, claiming, no doubt rightly, to be one of the few people to have read Hitler's *Mein Kampf*, Otto recalled that from that moment he had realized that war in Europe was only a matter of time. Interviewed by the Paris *Le Figaro* in February 2000 (some sixty-three years after the Schuschnigg meeting) on the subject of Jörg Haider, leader of Austria's extreme right-wing Freedom Party, Otto condemned him as a demagogue but rejected the prevailing European consensus of him as Nazi, xenophobe and anti-Semitic, observing that the two people then heading Haider's party list for the European Parliament were members of old Austro-Hungarian Jewish families.

Otto Habsburg's assessment of Haider's Nazi commitment had some interest, if only because in the year 2000 he was the only active European politician to have had personal dealings with Hitler's entourage in the 1930s. As the pretender to Austria's throne he had been approached by Prince August Wilhelm of Hohenzollern, the Kaiser's grandson and a devotee of the Führer. He may have been carrying out soundings on behalf of Adolf Hitler, at that time still an Austrian citizen making his first forays towards the eventual amalgamation, or *Anschluss*, of Austria with Germany. Just twenty years old, Otto had refused any truck with opportunistic politicians, particulary Nazis. Soon after the outbreak of the Second World War in Europe he joined the flood of royal and distinguished refugees, taking passage from Lisbon for the US where he tried unsuccessfully to raise an Austrian legion to join the other forces from occupied Europe, based in Britain and fighting against Hitler's Germany.

On 10 November 1918, the Emperor William II, the Kaiser, made his way to the Dutch frontier where he was requested to board a special train sent by the Dutch authorities. Eventually they agreed to grant him permanent exile and he made his home in a mansion near the town of Doorn. For some this ignominious shuffle from warlord to refugee was a betrayal of the nation's pride. One of his generals, General Groener, bluntly remarked that he should have gone to the front to look for death. The Kaiser himself blamed the manner of his departure on his advisers who had overridden his own inner convictions; but then he had blamed his advisers for forcing him to mobilize Germany for war in the first place. Even an autocratic warlord could find the conventions of constitutional monarchy convenient. After the war he made no attempt to intervene in German politics, but it seems that he never accepted his exile as final. There were many in Germany who shared that view. When in April 1921 the Empress died, the Republican authorities agreed that she should be buried in Berlin. It is said that the three dark green coaches of the funeral train bearing her body back from Holland were watched by silent crowds all along the route from the German border to the capital.

While the Kaiser had abdicated, his heir, Crown Prince Wilhelm, made no effort to promote his own claims to the throne and, after a period of internment in Holland, he was permitted to return to Germany. It seems that 'Willi', as he was universally known, was not only attracted to Nazi politics but even entertained the idea of himself as president with Hitler as chancellor. Hitler had no intention of sharing power with anyone, but it seems he would have welcomed the prestige that imperial endorsement would have brought to his movement. Before he was finally appointed chancellor, he twice sent Goering to Doorn as emissary. That flamboyant thug had no time for the courtly manner and got a disdainful reception. However, it was he who held the purse strings of the government's disbursements from the imperial fortune, and while the Kaiser never gave his endorsement to the Hitlerite regime, neither did he issue any public condemnation of its conduct. His sons, indeed, considered Nazism a patriotic movement founded by German heroes from the Great War.

The Crown Prince, who was happy to share public platforms with Hitler, appeared at Nazi ceremonies wearing full-dress uniform and all the insignia of his status, together with the swastika armband. His younger brother August Wilhelm ('Auwi' to the family) wrote effusive letters to Hitler, was proud to be invited as one of the party on board the Führer's official plane, and delighted to be seen in full uniform alongside brownshirt stormtroopers rattling his collecting box to raise funds for the party. Such public gestures

[27]

inevitably gave the regime respectability in the eyes of the many Germans who still revered the royal family. By contrast, Auwi's visits to his father were liable to slide into vaudeville as from time to time he inadvertently half-lifted his arm out of habit. These hurriedly aborted Nazi salutes provoked a series of withering rebukes; otherwise the haughty old exile treated him as if he did not exist.

The good name of the Hohenzollerns was redeemed by the Prince's younger brother, Prince Louis Ferdinand. By royal standards liberal in his attitudes, he was also, paradoxically, a favourite with the Kaiser and was in fact to become head of the family and, in the eyes of some, heir to the imperial title. This came about because Auwi contracted a morganatic marriage and so surrendered his rights in the dynastic succession. Between the wars, Louis Ferdinand spent much time in the US. His racy autobiography *Rebel Prince* chronicles his encounters with friends such as Charlie Chaplin and Henry Ford, and with a number of women. He got a job in the Ford organization, working his way up to a senior position in sales. Life in America was going well but the 'rebel' decided on the path of duty to the family dynasty. He returned to Europe and was lucky enough to find a woman of sufficient standing in monarchist eyes whom he could also love. In fact, the marriage between Louis Ferdinand and Princess Kira of Russia, daughter of Grand Duke Kyril of Russia, pretended successor to the last Russian Tsar, was outstandingly happy.

The Prussian prince had considerable standing on the political and society circuit. Britain's ageing former wartime premier David Lloyd George, one of the architects of the Allied victory in 1918, told the Prince that the Kaiser's abdication and the withdrawal of the imperial family from German affairs had been unfortunate for the country. Louis Ferdinand also met Mussolini and Hitler, whom he later compared to the Great Dictator as portrayed in the film of the same name by his friend Charlie Chaplin. Unlike the majority of his compatriots, Louis Ferdinand was a committed opponent of the regime and underwent a seven-hour interrogation by the Gestapo who were suspicious of his true affiliation. In fact, he became an active member of the underground resistance to the regime.

Between the wars, the idea of a Hohenzollern restoration hovered like a wraith in the murky atmosphere of German politics. Even as early as 1919 a rightist party believed to favour the idea won fifteen seats in the national elections. Six years later the Reichstag voted for a right-wing motion awarding a large financial indemnity to the Hohenzollerns for the loss of their property in the revolution which overthrew the monarchy. In November 1932, not yet Chancellor but with the scent of victory in his nostrils, Adolf Hitler, in conversation with the English journalist Sefton Delmer, asked him about a rumour in Berlin that the British government wished to re-establish the dynasty. In fact, as we have seen, Lloyd George had indeed hinted at some such idea to Louis Ferdinand. Delmer made some suitably anodyne response, that Britain was interested only in measures that were in keeping with order and stability in Germany. 'Quite right! Quite right!' came the reply. 'Germany would go up in flames if anyone tried to put the Hohenzollerns back. And I haven't the slightest intention of becoming a racehorse only for a royal jockey to jump on my back just as I am about to pass the winning post.'[2] Hitler never knew that at least one of those royal jockeys would rather have sent such a horse to the knacker's yard than touch him with a whip.

With the death of his father, ex-Crown Prince Wilhelm, in 1951, Louis Ferdinand, now head of the House of Hohenzollern, became for devoted monarchists the legitimate King of Prussia and German Emperor. He never contemplated activating his claim, though in extreme old age he could not bring himself to discount entirely the possibility, however remote, that with God's aid and the will of the German people he might one day be called upon to lead his country. And, at least, the stylish white residence he built in the suburbs of West Berlin after the war, had the right address: *Konigsalle* (King's Avenue). And there was, it must be said, considerable nostalgia for the monarchy, as was illustrated by the enthusiastic welcome given to his aunt, Princess Viktoria Louise, whenever she appeared in public. The Prince died in 1994 at the age of eighty-seven, leaving his claim to his grandson Prince Georg Friedrich. There may be some legitimists, looking into the uncertain mists of the twenty-first century, who hope to see a crown when the crystal ball clears, but this would surely be merely the optimism of nostalgia.

However, the Hohenzollerns possess more tangible assets than the shadowy prospect of a throne. In addition to a valuable collection of works of art, there is Berlin real estate, the ancestral family of Burg Hohenzollern in Baden-Württemburg, estates in Schleswig Holstein, and claims on properties elsewhere in Germany. Thus the senior member of the house is a man of considerable standing and influence – a fact which in 1998 culminated in a law suit which showed that some surprisingly traditional attitudes still flourish in republican Germany.

Before his death, Prince Louis Ferdinand saw his two eldest sons marry beneath them, as the saying once went, and thus, by these morgantic marriages, exclude themselves from all rights to the family succession. Accordingly in 1981 he designated as his heir his five-year-old grandson, Prince Georg Friedrich, child of his third son, who had died some years before on military manoeuvres, and his wife Countess Donata, daughter of the Prince of Castell-Rudenhausen, one of the fifty-eight 'mediatized' families of old imperial Germany, whose once sovereign territories had been merged into larger states but who continued to enjoy recognition as equal in rank and status to the pretenders to the imperial and other 'sovereign' states.

The issues at stake were not trivial. Indeed they had serious financial as well as dynastic consequences, and that is why Georg Friedrich's uncle, Prince Friedrich Wilhelm, oldest son of the late Louis Ferdinand, head of the House of Hohenzollern, took the case to court, to vindicate his rights of succession as the eldest child.

Two lower courts ruled in his favour, on egalitarian principles, accusing the family members who supported the dynastic protocol of being 'imprisoned in their traditional view of the world'. However, on 17 December 1998, Germany's Supreme Court gave final judgment, upholding the provisions of the family law. It also meant that the twenty-two-year-old Prince Georg Friedrich, educated at an exclusive Scottish boarding school and expecting to follow his father's example with a period of service in the German military, became proprietor of the eighteenth-century crown once worn by the kings of Prussia and restored to the family treasury after the Second World War. Should he in his turn marry a wife not of the requisite sovereign princely rank according to Hohenzollern tradition, he too would have to relinquish this heirloom along with headship of the family. However, one German expert on dynastic history estimated that the Prince would have a field of some 500 eligible ladies from which to select a partner. Any German woman descended from a number of petty princely families who lost their territories in the collapse of the Holy Roman Empire in the early 1800s in addition to thirty or so kingdoms, among them of course Prussia itself, grand duchies, margravates, or principalities etc which had continued in being up to the defeat of the German Empire in 1918, could claim to be of royal or of sovereign princely status. perhaps Georg Friedrich will arrange his life to ensure himself a potential, regular royal empress. With his red hair and, presumably his red beard, he might prove to be a (Georg) Friedrich Barbarossa worthy of German legend.

After the war the movements of Otto Habsburg were watched with wary fascination by Austrian politicians. Despite the concessions granted by Schuschnigg in 1938 the law of exile of April 1919 was retained at the insistence of the republican establishment. In itself this is testimony to the political potential attributed to the monarchic principle. Having briefly visited his native country in 1945 Otto Habsburg withdrew to Germany and after his marriage to Princess Regina of Saxe Meinigen in May 1951, he settled at Pöcking in Bavaria because it was conveniently near to the Austrian frontier. This did nothing to ease the speculation about his intentions. Admirers and Austrian monarchists were such frequent visitors to the exiled Habsburgs that the Bavarian press became intrigued by what might be going on at 'Pöckingham Palace'. In fact the heir to empire was developing more practical forays into the world of politics, cultivating a worldwide reputation as a lecturer and writer on international affairs and as a passionate advocate of the European Community.

Then, in May 1961, in a carefully worded statement, he renounced his personal title as a member of the House of Habsburg Lorraine and all the claims to sovereignty which it conferred. Since he had long wished to be free to visit Austria, it might seem puzzling that he had left the renunciation of his titles until he was in his fiftieth year. But in January 1961 Regina Habsburg, mother of five daughters, had given birth to her first son, Karl; at last the dynasty had an heir. Four months later the boy's father became, in name at least, plain Dr Otto Habsburg Lorraine, and his uncle Robert was deputed to discharge the functions of family head until he should come of age.

In 1966, the Austrian government decided to lift the ban on Otto's entering the country. Then in 1979, Austria not yet being a member of the European Union, he applied for German citizenship so as to be eligible to fight in the elections for the European Parliament, of which he in due course became a member. Soon after this Dr Habsburg, who never accepted the once fashionable identification of the word 'Europe' with the EU, became a vice president of the Pan-European Movement, explaining to all who would listen that the supranational character of the old Habsburg empire (which had embraced Bohemia, Slovakia, Slovenia, Hungary and Croatia as well as Austria) was the forerunner of a truly international political system. The political upheavals in communist East Europe of 1989–90 suddenly opened the prospect of a future return to this past. Perhaps a head of the House of Habsburg may one day become the elected head of a Federal Europe.

Probably Europe's favourite Habsburg joke is the one about Dr Otto's response on being told that there was an Austria-Hungary football match on television. 'Oh really,' he is said to have replied, 'who are we playing?' Sometimes called 'Mr Europe' and author of some thirty books on European questions, he has also written a biography of his great ancestor the Emperor Charles V. As ruler of Germany and Austria and much of northern Italy, as heir to the French Dukes of Burgundy and ruler of their territories in the Low Countries, and as King of Spain, Charles spoke all four languages fluently. His descendant, a still more proficient linguist, acquired mastery of no fewer than eight modern languages as well as Latin 'which is useful'. A devout Roman Catholic and devoted to the cause of a Christian as well as a united Europe, operating from homes and offices in Austria, Brussels, Munich and Strasbourg, his worldwide speaking engagements made him a globetrotter well into his eighties. His immaculate fluency in English was an accomplishment which would have seemed both quaint and unnecessary to his sixteenth-century ancestor.

At the Budapest wedding of his grandson, the trim figure and quizzical eyes of the venerable if somewhat owl-like patriarch received the deference of his own family, and that of the representatives of the numerous other royal families present, as his due. Among them was the present head of the House of Habsburg, his eldest son, His Imperial and Royal Highness, Imperial Crown Prince and Archduke Karl of Austria and his wife Francesca, daughter of Baron Heinrich Thyssen-Bornemisza von Kaszon. For all his own impressive-sounding titles, the head of the house in all but name remained for him, as for the nobility and royals and ex-royals of Europe, Dr Otto Habsburg. As Archduke Karl explained, his father's renunciation had been necessitated by Austrian state regulations if he was ever to be able to return to the country, but had changed nothing within the family.

A revered dynast turned democratic statesman, Otto Habsburg achieved a notable accolade in his political career in 1989 when a small group of Hungarian politicians seriously sounded him out on the possibility of his standing for the presidency. Firm in his refusal, he nevertheless warmed to the idea that such a development might help the people to reaffirm their national identity by rediscovering

[33]

their age-old traditions. Reflecting perhaps on the example of Juan Carlos of Spain, he confided to the Spanish writer on monarchy, Juan Balansó that he had seriously considered the possibility. In fact, he apparently concluded that he could be of more use to the Hungarians, as to other central European members of the old Habsburg Empire still outside the European Union, through his position and contacts in the corridors of the European institutions. He may well have been right, for it seems certain that, through a long career as statesman and political theorist, Otto Habsburg established himself as a figure of consequence and influence in European affairs.

3

QUESTIONS OF LEGITIMACY FROM ROME TO ST PETERSBURG

———

> God bless the king, I mean the Faith's Defender,
> God bless, no harm in blessing, the Pretender,
> But who Pretender is and who is king,
> God knows that's quite another thing!

One of the many quips, double entendres and secret signs and practices current among supporters of the Stuart dynasty in England after the exclusion of King James II and his descendants by act of parliament, the jingle, tongue in cheek through it may be, puts the point concisely. History is the record of the victors and as such there is no appeal – until the victor is displaced by another. Imperial China raised the pragmatic acceptance of the facts to an almost religious principle with its doctrine of the Mandate of Heaven. The Emperor of the day ruled by that mandate and as such was the Son of Heaven – rebels were thus by definition impious traitors meriting the cruellest and most ruthless penalties should they be defeated. Successful rebellion, however, was proof that the Mandate of Heaven had passed from the old regime. For legitimists such acts of naked force have no validity at the bar of history. For them there is always a true successor descended by right of birth who will one day come into his own. It is a romantic world they inhabit but also quite often a muddled one.

Few legitimist traditions have lasted longer than loyalty to the Stuart family, whose last king to rule in Britain, James II, left London in 1688, without a shot having been fired in anger, never to return – but also, never to be forgotten by supporters of his family. In the early 1700s Britain's closet Jacobites (from Greek, *Jacobus*) adopted the White Rose of York as their emblem. Exquisitely engraved wine, ale and cordial glasses, many of them produced at Newcastle near the border with Scotland, carried the innocent flower which to the knowledgeable could be read as the badge of Stuart legitimism against usurpation. Unfortunately, what neither the originators of the mysterious rebus nor the members of the Order of the White Rose, who revived it in the 1880s, seem to have allowed for is that the Stuart claim to the throne of England, and hence of the United Kingdom of Great Britain, derived precisely from the usurper Henry Tudor who made himself king by defeating and killing the lawfully anointed King Richard III of the House of York at the Battle of Bosworth Field. Henry married his daughter Margaret Tudor to James IV of Scotland and, in due course, their great-grandson was able to claim an hereditary right to the English throne, the right from which all Stuart claims subsequently derive. If, however, the true succession to the English throne lay with the White Rose of York, then no claims derived from the Tudor usurpation could have validity.

In fact, birth is only one of the varied qualifications vaunted by candidates for monarchy to establish the legitimacy of their pretensions to the crown. Assent by the governed is of equal importance. In Anglo-Saxon England a candidate for the crown had to be able to show relationship to the blood royal; the approval of or nomination by his predecessor; and acceptance by the community of the realm, represented in the choice of the royal council, or witan, and the acclamation of the people. In no modern monarchy is mere proximity to blood enough to establish a claim. On the continent of Europe where written constitutions are the norm, all have a clause specifying the conditions on which a person may lose his or her rights of succession, and in every case the sanction is permission either from the head of the royal family or from the national assembly or from both. Even so, legitimacy once established has traditionally conferred upon the occupant of a throne an aura and a constitutional authority which can be real and potent.

[36]

Early in 1943, a small group of leading fascists in Italy were contemplating the removal of Benito Mussolini. After more than twenty years of supreme power, the Duce held a seemingly unassailable position. There was one figure who, in constitutional terms at least, held the authority to order the deed and that was King Victor Emmanuel III of the House of Savoy. Little more than five feet in height, unimpressive in style, he nevertheless represented legitimacy in the Italian state. In the view of one of the conspirators, the situation had to be handled under the aegis of the dynasty since that would give it a legal character and the troops would obey their orders. It was, perhaps, one of the most remarkable tributes to the office of monarch in the twentieth century. As we shall see, the King did play an important role in the coup which toppled the fascist leader. But he was unable to exploit the initiative and when, after the war's end, on 9 May 1946 he abdicated in favour of his son Umberto II, it was too late to save his dynasty which in the public mind had been heavily implicated in the Mussolini years. Italy's new Republican National Assembly passed a constitutional law banning the head of the house of Savoy or his male heirs entry to the country.

In 1998, despite numerous proposals for new legislation, that law had still not been repealed and the injustice of this denial of his human rights was a constant grievance with Umberto's son, Vittorio Emanuele, fourth of that name. In protest he and his son Emanuele-Filiberto, Prince of Venice, both enthusiastic scuba divers, breached the prohibition with a gesture as witty as it was illegal. Operating out of their villa on the French island of Cavallo, half way between Corsica and Sardinia, on 13 October they dived from a vessel anchored outside Italy's territorial waters and then swam underwater towards the Italian coast, touching their native soil several metres below sea level. In fact, it was said that Vittorio Emanuele had made a number of gestures before that time, having visited Turin as a simple tourist, skiied across the frontier between Chamonix and Courmayeur, and violated Italian airspace by flying over Naples, his birthplace, in a helicopter.

Much more interesting than such schoolboy pranks was the Prince's decision in 1999 to challenge the law of exile in the European Court of Human Rights. As if to forestall such action, in December 1997 the Italian Parliament had voted by 276 to 150 in favour of abrogating the law. For the decision to take effect, a positive vote in the senate was required, followed by a second reading in both houses. By the middle of 1999, these formalities had still to be completed. There were those who saw a combination of inertia and calculated blocking tactics by the communists behind the delay. For his part, the Prince of Venice, interviewed by Eric Jansen for *Point de Vue* in May 1999, claimed to have no political axe to grind, but he likewise objected that he might be required to take an oath of loyalty to the Republic. A television survey had shown a sizeable majority of those polled in favour of lifting the ban; a referendum, however, was for constitutional reasons not possible. If the ban were not lifted, the result would be that the claimants to the Italian throne would possibly be the world's only Roman Catholics barred from making the pilgrimage to Rome in 2000, the year of the Jubilee. Given Europe's open frontiers following the Schengen agreements, there should be nothing to prevent a prince in a fast car from joining the crowds to receive the Pope's blessing.

When in 1957 the six founder members of the then European Common Market signed the inaugural treaty in Rome, the choice of city with its echoes of the Roman empire seemed obvious enough – after all the long-term objective was political union. However the one-time imperial city had been part of a modern unitary state for less than a century. In 781 Charlemagne conferred the title 'king of Italy' on his four-year-old son Pepin, but it never carried connotations of real power and soon lapsed. Over the centuries the real Italy blossomed into a multitude of independent republics, duchies, grand duchies and even kingdoms which largely ignored the Holy Roman Emperors, successors to Charlemagne, their supposed overlords. By the 1850s the peninsula boasted the following independent states: the kingdom of Sardinia, comprising the island and the mainland territory of Piedmont-Savoy, the duchy of Modena, the duchy of Parma and Piacenza, the kingdom of the Two Sicilies (ie, Naples and Sicily), and the grand duchy of Tuscany (capital Florence) – northern Italy from Lombardy and Venice remained subject to the Austrian empire. The first king of a united and independent Italy was proclaimed on 17 March 1861 in the person of Victor Emmanuel II of the House of Savoy, King of Sardinia, after years of struggle. His name and title, in Italian Vittorio Emanuele Re D'Italia, had been a slogan for patriots who, to the fury of their music-loving Austrian oppressors, chanted it concealed as an acronym in the name of their great contemporary the composer Giuseppe Verdi.

In fact, Victor Emmanuel and his chief minister Cavour connived with the nationalist leader Giuseppe Garibaldi in the overthrow of the Bourbon rulers of the Kingdom of the Two Sicilies and openly encouraged the populations of the central duchies of Modena (represented today by the d'Este branch of the Habsburgs) Parma (ruled by a branch of the Bourbon family) and Tuscany, to revolt against their rulers … Rome, an autonomous state under the pope, had to be subdued by invasion. Victor Emmanuel II was succeeded by his son Umberto I who died, aged fifty-six after a troubled reign, at the hands of an assassin in July 1900, to be succeeded in his turn by his son Victor Emmanuel, the Prince of Naples.

The title for Italy's crown prince was redolent of southern Italy's independent past under the medieval kings of Naples and then in the nineteenth century under a branch of the Bourbon family. At the turn of the millennium pro-monarchist sympathies were still strongest in the south of Italy, even though the royal house of the united Kingdom of Italy had been the northern family of Savoy and Piedmont. Thirty-one at the time of his father's death, Victor Emmanuel III spoke Italian with a heavy Piedmontese accent, but was shrewd and well prepared for his position. His schooling had indeed been princely, with lessons delivered in the boy's own rooms in the palace by professors from Rome's top institutions. The prince's exams, were conducted orally, in the presence of the

King and Queen, following a printed programme secured in ribbons of Italy's national colours. The board of examiners comprising the minister of war, the head of the army staff, the first adjutant field general and other worthies, was seated at a long table facing a much smaller table at which sat the candidate. Each topic on which he was to be tested – from geography and languages to military tactics was represented by a coloured ball and the proceedings were opened by the minister of war who placed the balls in a linen bag closed with draw strings. This was then presented to the prince who pulled out one of the coloured balls and the questioning on that topic then began. The procedure apparently produced results. When Victor Emmanuel visited Windsor in the 1880s, Queen Victoria pronounced her magisterial approval of him as the most intelligent prince in Europe. Some sixty years later he proved himself intelligent enough to outwit one of the Continent's most brutal and powerful men.

As the year 1943 opened, things were going badly for the Italian war effort. It seemed that Germany's reluctant ally was facing the prospect of almost certain defeat. The seventy-four-year-old King could look back on a reign as old as the century. His country had fought bravely in World War I, and thanks to fascist military adventures added the crown of Albania and the empire of Ethiopia to his titles. But the King's failure to authorize martial law at the pleadings of his ministers in 1922, had assured the triumph of the Fascists' 'March on Rome' and Mussolini's seizure of power.

There had been whispers of an anti-fascist coup back in 1942. Even some 'moderate' members of the party itself, among them Count Dino Grandi considered that the national plight demanded a change in the regime. However, the King would have to be involved for such a move to have any hope of success. It was the Count's view that only action by the King, acting at the right moment, could restore the right order of things. But the King knew that he would get no second chance if he miscalculated or faltered – a successful counter coup would spell the end of the monarchy and with it any chance of a peaceful transition away from the dictator.

In the summer of 1943 the allied invasions of Siciliy put Mussolini under pressure from his generals to negotiate a separate peace.
At a meeting with Hitler in a secluded villa near Treviso in northern
Italy on 19 July the suggestion was brusqely dismissed by the
Führer. Returning to Rome a few days later, Mussolini called a
meeting of the Fascist Grand Council. The Duce used to boast that
there was never never any question of voting at these meetings.
This time, however, things were different. The meeting stretched
into the small hours when Count Grandi proposed a motion critical of 'the regime'. It was not only voted on, but approved by the
majority of those present. Mussolini appeared unconcerned. He
prepared for his usual five o'clock audience with the King, unaware
that the latter had decided to move in conjunction with a close
group of courtiers and military men. At three o'clock that afternoon
he gave orders that the Duce be arrested as he left the audience.
However, he asked his household military adviser to mount guard
outside the room where the meeting was to be held and to intervene if called for.

Mussolini arrived punctually and began his report. The King interrupted him and, in a few disjointed sentences – with characteristic
lapses into the Piedmontese dialect – he demanded the dictator's
resignation. The Duce saw that the game was up. He knew his
king well enough to realize that, if he dared make such a demand,
he already had the backing to enforce it. He resigned. None of the
Fascist Grand Council intervened or attempted to contest the royal
verdict.

Perhaps, reclining in the limousine as he was driven away under
escort, he mused on the blunder he made years ago when at the
height of his power he had not disposed of the monarchy and so
had left in place a source of legitimacy superior to his own. At all
events, a new government was installed that evening and many a
dazed fascist was left to come to terms with the fact that the fascist
regime in Italy had blundered to collapse in the course of a single
day without a shot being fired in its defence. The defence of the
national interest had fallen not to the political representative of

[41]

modernismo and the futuristic forces of the twentieth century but to the most antique of all possible powers, a king.

However, Victor Emmanuel III was tarnished by decades of association with the dictator. Too late he delegated the royal power to his son Umberto as regent in 1944, and only formally abdicated on 9 May 1946 when he went into exile in Egypt. Within weeks, with a referendum vote of 59 per cent in favour of a republic, the nation turned its back on the house of Savoy and on 13 June Umberto II, accompanied by his wife Maria Jose of Belgium and his nine-year-old son Vittorio Emanuelle, Prince of Naples, left the country.

Inevitably the results of the referendum had been disputed, but feelings were running high and Sandro Petrini, a future socialist President of the Republic, had warned the King that he would be lynched if he showed his face in Milan. In the south of the country, by contrast, there was talk of establishing a separatist monarchy in the traditionally royalist regions of Naples and Sicily. In fact, Umberto's prospects had never been bright, though he granted a number of titles to petitioners in the hope of buying support. With the reputation of a playboy, dubbed 'entirely insignificant' by the great historian Bendetto Croce and 'stupid', 'weak' and 'dissipated' by a government minister, he had served as lieutenant of the realm in the shadow of his unpopular father for the two years before coming to the throne in his own right, for a reign of just thirty-four days.

Umberto II did not renounce his claim. In fact for many years before his death in 1983 he was closely involved in Italy's major monarchist organization, the Unione Monarchica Italian, though he did not approve of monarchist political parties. Debarred from Italy by the constitutional law, he eventually established himself in a property he named Villa Italia at Cascais, near Estoril in Portugal. The Count of Barcelona and his family, including of course his son Juan Carlos, the future king of Spain, were among his neighbours. People spoke of a court in exile and it is true that the King was liable to create new titles of nobility – more than one hundred and fifty, it is said – each duly attested by a diploma of authentication. One candidate conspicuous by his absence from this galaxy of exiled titles was Umberto's grandson, Prince Filiberto, whom we joined earlier in this chapter with his father on their dive off the Italian coast in 1998.

According to some they are the pretender and heir apparent to the royal title. According to others who would style themselves the true legitimists, the claim to the crown in fact passed to a distant cousin, Prince Amadeus of Savoy, Duke of Aosta, on the day in 1970 when Vittorio Emanuele, Prince of Naples, married without his father's prior consent. By a family statute or patent of 1780, any claimant to the titles of the House of Savoy who marries without the permission of the head of the House loses all entitlement for himself and his descendants. In January 1970, the Prince married his companion of some years' standing, the Swiss-born Marina Doria, by civil ceremony in Las Vegas, Nevada. King Umberto certainly withheld his permission, though without giving a reason. Whether it was that the lady was a commoner, or that the ceremony was a civil one, is not clear. The decision of the Prince and Princess to go through with a religious ceremony in Tehran in 1971 made little difference to King Umberto's attitude. But he did attend the baptism of their son Filiberto and pronounce him 'Prince of Venice'. However, since there was no diploma of title and since, in any case, the title in question had only ever been previously borne by Eugène de Beauharnais, Napoleon's stepson, it was not entirely clear what the distinction might signify.

At the time, 'King Victor Emmanuel IV' as he was wont to style himself, even during his father's lifetime, was living in Switzerland as a business consultant for an aircraft company, thanks to an introduction from the Shah of Iran. He had been brought up in Switzerland where his mother moved after breaking with King Umberto on grounds, it was said, of physical incompatibility. Brought up on the kind of permissive principles then in vogue, he was to earn a reputation for over-the-top eccentricity and worse, even among his jet-set cronies. In the late 1970s an unfortunate scuffle with a group of tourists in Corsica, which led to his being incarcerated for more than a month before being acquitted, seemed to mark the end of his madcap years. But for some monarchists, more serious than such antisocial escapades were the 'royal decrees' issued by this self-styled 'king in exile'. In one of these, 'Victor Emmanuel IV' accused Umberto II of having acted illegally when he accepted the result of the 1946 referendum, since monarchy could not be subjected to jurisdiction by the people. He also charged that his father's leaving the country was tantamount to abdication, whether or not he had formally abdicated. It followed that he, Vittorio Emanuele, was king even before his father's death. Whether King Umberto ever learnt of these legalistic manoeuvres by his son is not known. Certain it is that his last lonely years in his residence in Portugal were often unhappy; that in his will he left his archives to the Italian state; and that the royal seal which he had taken with him into exile and which, since he had never abdicated, he had never destroyed was buried with him. For the last king regnant of Italy, at least, the legitimate succession to the crown in the House of Savoy was one of history's closed chapters.

On Friday 17 July 1998, with great pomp and ceremony, the remains of the last Romanov tsar and his family were laid to rest in the chapel next to the dynasty's mausoleum in the cathedral of the St Peter and St Paul Fortress in St Petersburg. It was eighty years to the day since the murder of the imperial family in the basement of the house in Ekaterinburg where they had been held by orders of the local soviet. At the time of his death Nicholas Romanov was no longer Tsar Nicholas II since he had abdicated more than a year earlier. It was for this reason, apparently, that the family were not buried in the imperial mausoleum itself, and that the remains of Nicholas were honoured with a nineteen-gun salute instead of the twenty-one accorded to a defunct head of state. Nevertheless, the coffin was honoured with a bow from President Yeltsin and his wife Naina while the symbolic handful of earth was thrown by Prince Nicholas Romanov. He was recognized by most as head of the family of which some fifty members were present at the religious ceremony conducted according to the rites of the Russian Orthodox Church. According to *Time* magazine reporter Paul Quinn-Judge 'those who spoke Russian did so in an archaic St Petersburg accent'. The ceremony was attended by many distinguished people from all over the world, among them, the cellist Mstislav Rostropovich and, representing Britain's royal family, Prince Michael of Kent. The genuine sentiments of the average citizen were difficult to assess. Vincent Meylan, reporter for the French weekly *Point de Vue* reported a crowd of 50,000 at St Petersburg airport the day before to give a solemn welcome to the truncated coffins containing the remains; the actual service was televised in its entirety; and for weeks after the ceremony queues of people waited to pay their respects. And yet many observers felt that, along with feelings of compassion, there was a large dose of curiosity about the fate of one whom generations of Soviet schoolchildren had known as 'Nicholas the Bloody'.

Before 1991 such a ceremony could not have been contemplated since the bodies of the imperial family had never been found. It was known that the family had been held in the Ipatiev house in Ekaterinburg, renamed Sverdlovsk by the Soviets, and that they had been killed in or near that building. Then in 1977 the Communist Party chief in Sverdlovsk, Boris Yeltsin himself, had ordered the destruction of the site. Only four years later the government of the Soviet Union had authorized excavations in a nearby wood where, according to recently opened records, it was believed the remains of the bodies had been buried. In 1981 human remains were indeed found in the wood, but it was not for another ten years that the Russian authorities agreed that they might go for scientific examination. Thus the last Tsar to wear the crown of all the Russias was to be subjected to the ultimate test of hereditary legitimacy – comparative DNA tests.

The tests were done on samples from the bones themselves and samples supplied by Prince Rostislav Romanov and other family members, and by Prince Philip, Duke of Edinburgh, descended like the Tsarina from the ducal family of Hesse. Together these showed that the Tsar, the Tsarina and their four daughters were among the remains. The body of the Tsarevich was not found at this time, which inevitably prompted accounts of his having survived the shooting – a remarkable achievement for a haemophiliac. In fact the body was later discovered and solemnly laid to rest.

But although the religious service was according to Russian Orthodox rites, it was not conducted by the Patriarch. The Church refused to accept the DNA tests as final, despite the fact that they had been conducted independently in laboratories in Russia, the US and Britain where the whole technique of DNA 'fingerprinting' had been developed. The Muscovite patriarchate had its reasons for refusing to acknowledge the identification. There was, for example, a question over the possible saintly status of the dead Tsar, in which case even the remotest possibility that the remains were not his would be a cause of scandal. And there might have been a political calculation. For the Russian Orthodox Church, the 1990s represented a rare historical moment of independence. Traditionally a state Church, its patriarchs, under the Tsars had recognized themselves as the spiritual arm of the autocrat; under the rule of the Communist Party secretaries, they had, perforce, continued the tradition of subordination with a policy which to many seemed little better than collaboration. With the collapse of communism and the destabilisation of all the organs of the state, the Church was enjoying a position of unparalleled influence and independence. While the cathedral service was conducted by Father Glebov, a rival commemorative ceremony was held by the Patriarch Alexi II in the monastery of Saint Serge at Zagorsk. In neither ceremony did the congregation hear mention of the names of the dead. In the cathedral, where each one of the nine coffins had a brass plate screwed to its lid inscribed with the name of the person whose remains it contained, Father Glebov concluded by asking God's blessing 'on the spirit of these assassinated servants of God whose names, oh Lord, thou alone knowest'.

Before 1981, not only had the bodies not been found; it was not

[46]

even certain how many of the family had perished. A rumour persisted that one of the children, the youngest daughter Grand Duchess Anastasia, had escaped. From the 1920s to her death in 1984, a mysterious German woman called Anna Anderson claimed to be the missing Anastasia. Her story was so convincing and circumstantial that the imperial family itself could not conclusively disprove it and Hollywood made a film, starring Ingrid Bergman as the claimant, which convinced millions of movie-goers. But with the evidence of the 1993 tests that all four daughters had been shot at Eekaterinburg, it was decided to make comparative tests on DNA tissue from Anna Anderson's remains. The results demonstrated beyond question that Anderson had been the 'False Anastasia' the family had always claimed.

Obstinate pretenders were not unknown in Russian history. Fifteen years of turmoil, still known as 'the Time of Troubles', led to the establishment of the Romanov dynasty in 1613, when Michael Romanov displaced an impostor styling himself Dmitri II. This was the second 'False Dmitri'. The first, who had claimed to be a supposedly murdered prince of the blood royal and had contributed to the downfall of the usurping Boris Godunov, met his end when supporters of his (successful) rival had him fired from one of the cannons in Moscow's main square. At the time this must have seemed an irrefutable method of exploding a pretender's pretensions but just six years later, according to the historian Norman Davies, an adventurer known to history as the 'Thief of Tushino' managed to inveigle his way into the widow's affections as the resurrected form of her (literally) disembodied husband. Others apparently did not believe the yarn, or his regnal number would, presumably, have been 'Domitri I: part ii'.

In fact, the Russian succession had been in dispute for some thirty years, ever since the death of Ivan IV, the Terrible, the first Russian ruler to adopt the title of Tsar and the requirements for legitimacy itself were ill-defined. The nearest Michael Romanov could approach to the blood royal was, apparently, that he could claim to be a great nephew of Ivan's first wife. Romanov dynastic history itself offers a few oddities. Peter I, the Great, having ordered his son and heir to be flogged to death, possibly for cowardice, was succeeded by his second wife, and she by Peter's grandson. In 1762, the murdered Peter III was followed not by his eight-year-old son Paul but by his wife, who came to the throne under somewhat irregular circumstances, not as regent but as Empress Catherine II and reigned until her death. Only then did her forty-two-year-old son succeed to the throne. In the late twentieth century the Grand Duke Vladimir Kirillovich, the nearest surviving relative of Tsar Nicholas, without consulting other family members and ignoring the laws of succession prohibiting the passage of the crown through the female line, created his daughter Maria Vladimirovna Her Imperial Highness and Grand Duchess of Russia and designated her head of the imperial house.

Grand Duke Vladimir himself was about a year old when the world learnt about the killings at Ekaterinburg, and his father Kirill, the Tsar's cousin, was acclaimed in certain emigré circles as Tsar in his turn. Most of these refugee aristocrats had escaped with very little of their former riches and were ill-adapted to work. Setting out to make new lives for themselves in London or Paris or Madrid or in America, some were able for a time to exploit the snob value of their princely titles to acquire directorships or other sources of largesse. Prince Rostislav Romanov, who was born in Chicago in 1938 and died in 1999 after a career in London banking, recalled a childhood in which the exiguous family budget was eked out by occasional free dinners at the city's smarter hotels and restaurants, when Prince Rostislav Romanov (senior) and his wife the Princess Alexandra Pavlovna Galitzine were handsomely wined and dined as table hosts to fee paying diners flattered to eat with royalty.

When his father died, in 1938, Grand Duke Vladimir was recognised by most of the emigré community, as head of the family. Indeed, according to ruling after ruling by his father and later himself disqualifying other family members from the succession on grounds of their morganatic marriages, there were few others worthy of consideration. Inevitably his own marriage in 1948 came in for critical comment since, although his wife claimed connection with the ancient royal family of Georgia, the cognoscenti of Europe's royal pedigrees discounted the idea. However, thanks in part to her private means, they were able to make their principal residence, complete with custom built Orthodox private chapel in the grounds, in Franco's Madrid where, along with Simeon of Bulgaria and Leka of Albania, they numbered themselves with that little coterie of royals with which the dictator liked to flatter his self esteem.

For their part, these monarchs in waiting took their responsibilities, others might say their pretensions, seriously. It is said that when his daughter was in her teens the Grand Duke arranged a religious ceremony in his private chapel, attended by selected members of emigré families, during which she took a solemn oath of succession. But what others may have considered play acting took on the aspect of a more realistic scenario with the discovery of the imperial remains at Ekaterinburg.

Then, in the autumn of 1991 came the official invitation from the mayor of Leningrad for the Grand Duke and Grand Duchess, to attend the ceremonies marking the restoration of the city's original name of St Petersburg. There was nothing particularly 'imperial' about the Grand Duke's arrival by charter flight. 'Just like a tourist', grumbled a Russian monarchist from the industrial city of Voroneszh. But the Russian crowds were enthusiastic and a massive portrait of the dead Tsar rode confidently among the tsarist banners and Russian tricolours sporting a cartouch showing a gold imperial eagle on a black background.

Born in Finland, it was the first time that the Grand Duke had set foot in Russia. He and his wife were drawn through the streets of the city in the principal state coach, accompanied by an escort of outriders and they opened a gala night at the opera, the first time the royal box had been occupied by a member of the imperial family since the Revolution. Like all modern pretenders, the Grand Duke necessarily pledged that he would not contemplate a restoration, without the expressed will of the people; however, like a true heir to the autocrat Nicholas II he insisted that should the call

[49]

come, he would expect a more decisive share in political power than that accorded to the restored King Juan Carlos of Spain. He died, while visiting America, in a Miami hospital in April 1992. The funeral obsequies celebrated in St Isaac's, St Petersburg by no fewer than sixty clergy seemed, to onlookers, worthy of a tsar and there were some who recognized his daughter as titular Tsarina. However, at a Romanov family council in Paris, in the June of that year, the seventy-year-old Prince Nicholas Romanov, the eldest son of the senior line of the imperial family, made an oration of solemn farewell to Grand Duke Vladimir as the family's oldest member, 'our doyen, nothing more'. Now, the Prince concluded, this honour had passed to him.

Be that as it may, when plans began to be laid with a view to the ceremonial reinterment of the remains of the imperial family, it was with Grand Duchess Maria that the Russian government first consulted. This set the world of monarchists and legitimists in an uproar. Holding Grand Duke Vladimir's unilateral decision on the succession law to have been outrageous as well as invalid, seven of the senior male members of the family threatened to boycott any ceremony if Maria Vladimirovna were to be given precedence. For them the principal family member at any such ceremony would, of course, have to be Prince Nicholas Romanov, since 1992 accepted by the majority as doyen of the imperial house. For her part, the Grand Duchess refused to attend. She gave as her reason that the service was not sufficiently grand to honour the memory of a Tsar: gossip said she was indignant that she had not been invited to attend in the capacity of head of the family. When the patriarch withheld his blessing, and then the Duma refused its sanction, it seemed that plans for the ceremony were beginning to unravel and that the president himself had decided not to attend. In fact, not only did he do so; there were even rumours that he had at one point considered lending his authority to a full-scale Tsarist restoration.

Should such a thing ever happen, the question of who should assume the crown would seem likely to provoke controversy and conflict beside which the infighting habitual in Russia's presidential politics would appear mild. For outside viewers of this world of virtual royalty, the prospect with the most intriguing resonances would be Tsarina Maria Vladimirovna descended through her father from the Romanovs and, if her genealogists are to be believed, through her mother Princess Leonida Bagration de Mukhrani (born in Tiflis, Georgia in 1914), from the Bagratid dynasty who claimed descent from St Joseph and who ruled the medieval Christian empire of Georgia in the Middle Ages. (Georgia was, of course, the home country of Russia's most terrible communist tsar, Joseph Stalin.)

Born in December 1953, the Grand Duchess took her degree at Oxford and in 1976 married the thirty-three-year-old Prince Francis William of Prussia, who converted to Orthodox Christianity and adopted the baptismal name of Michael, being created a Russian Grand Duke by her father (they divorced in 1987). Their son, born in Madrid in 1981 and known as Prince Georgy of Prussia, was designated by his grandfather His Imperial Highness Grand Duke George, and is considered by followers to be the next heir to the imperial Russian crown. He was said, in his early teens, to be learning the language: but as indicated, such an accession would likely be contested. Perhaps it will never happen.

4

GREEK ODYSSEY

———•◦•———

With the approach of the year 2000, the family of Constantine II, former King of the Hellenes, and his Danish-born wife Queen Anne Marie, were, though living in exile, a model of the cosmopolitan aspect of monarchy. Londoners of long standing, the royal couple were, so to speak, neighbours of the King's second cousin Prince Philip Duke of Edinburgh, and close friends of the Windsors. The Prince of Wales had stood godfather to their eldest son Crown Prince Pavlos, a successful investment consultant based in the US. Their daughter, Princess Alexia, for some five years a resident of Barcelona, was to marry an architect of that city. Exiled from her mother country, living in another country from her parents, Alexia was not far from family since the Queen of Spain, King Constantine's sister, and King Juan Carlos are her aunt and uncle. At the beginning of the 1990s, indeed, the Spanish royals had cancelled an official visit to Greece when Madrid learnt that the Greek authorities, fearing the popularity of the former Princess Sophia of Greece, were preparing for it as if for a private and not a state visit. Yet even as a private person making the kind of nostalgic pilgrimages to places of sad and happy memories normal to family members returning to old haunts, Queen Sofia would surely have attracted the kind of attention which the Greek authorities at that time did not wish to revive. Monarchy embodies the old-fashioned values of family at the centre of the political process, and so can still pose conundrums for republicans. Agreement was finally reached between the Greek and Spanish protocol officials so that in November 1999 Sophia of Greece was able to make a private visit to the graves of her forebears in the grounds of the former royal palace of Tatoï on Corfu.

Inevitably the Spanish royal couple were among the guests at Alexia's wedding, held in the Greek Orthodox cathedral of St Sophia in West London in July 1999. In fact, some sixty European royals were there, among them Queen Elizabeth II and the Queens of Sweden, Norway and Denmark, the King of Sweden and the Crown Princes of Spain, Norway, Belgium and Denmark, as well as Alexander of Yugoslavia and the Prince of Preslav, second son of Simeon II of Bulgaria. All were descended either from Queen Victoria or King Christian IX of Denmark or both.

Despite the royal family's acrimonious relations with the Greek government, the ceremony was screened live by two Greek television stations. Four years before, another Greek wedding in St Sophia, that of Crown Prince Pavlos to an American heiress Marie-Chantal Miller, had been transmitted direct to Greek viewers by a private television station owned by a committed monarchist. This had caused furore in Greek government circles who accused Right-wing deputies attending the event of exploiting it to undermine the republican regime. Also in the congregation dressed in his uniform, an officer in the Greek airforce was accused of irresponsible behaviour by the Greek minister of defence who said he should appear before a disciplinary court. Such reactions on the part of the authorities signalled their continuing sensitivity on the issue of monarchy versus republic, nearly thirty years after Constantine had been ousted by a group of colonels and then rejected in a referendum organized by those same colonels. But then Greek kings have made something of a tradition of exiles and comebacks.

In December 1922, Prince Philip of Greece, future consort of Queen Elizabeth II and captain in the Royal Navy, made his first voyage in a British man-of-war. He was eighteen months old and travelling in an orange-box. He was, in short, a refugee. It was a not uncommon plight for members of the Greek royal house in the twentieth century: some anonymous wit is said to have observed: 'He who would be King of Greece should keep his bags packed.'

The events surrounding the export of baby Philip as a piece of boxed fruit epitomized many such a Greek exodus. In the August of that year, the Greeks had been routed by a Turkish force under Mustaph Kemal, later Atatürk, and forced to abandon historic territorial claims in Anatolia. The campaign had been launched to popular acclaim by King Constantine I; its disastrous outcome prompted a military coup and he duly abdicated and went into exile in September 1922, his thirty-three-year-old son acceding as George II. Furious public opinion and a mutinous army demanded scapegoats, and in the ensuing trials five politicians and one general lost their lives. Then on 2 December Philip's father Prince Andrew, a senior officer during the war, faced a court in the chamber of deputies with little hope of a better fate. The trial ended at midnight; the sentence, death. Fortunately for him, the light cruiser *HMS Calypso* was in Phaleron Bay. Early the following morning the Prince, having agreed to surrender his Greek nationality, was driven with his wife Princess Alice to the dockside by a government minister.

This denouement was thanks to the determined intervention of the Princess, a great granddaughter of Queen Victoria. When her husband was arrested, she first appealed to the hapless new king desperately hanging on to a precarious throne. Then Alice turned to her influential family connections and wrote direct to King George V of Great Britain. For his part, in an almost certainly unconstitutional exercise of his royal authority, possibly remorseful over his failure to help his Russian cousins, Tsar Nicholas II and his family four years earlier, the King called the Admiralty and ordered a ship to be sent at all speed to Greek waters. From the Athens waterfront *Calypso* steamed to Corfu to pick up the royal children.

The story of the modern Greek monarchy began at the London Congress of 1832. In that year, after a long struggle to gain their independence from the Turkish empire and four turbulent years of an attempted republic, the Greeks, at the instigation of Europe's great powers, turned to the conventional form of constitution – a monarchy. There being no Greek royal family, they equally conventionally recruited a minor German royal, the seventeen-year-old Otto of the Bavarian royal House of Wittelsbach. The teenage Otto rapidly attracted the antipathy of his subjects by his evident approval of the regency council of haughty Bavarian aristocrats. Ten years did nothing to soften his attitudes so he was forced by military coup to promulgate a constitution. When he attempted to annul the constitution that he had been forced to adopt, Greece's first king was, in 1862, deposed by a military coup to popular acclaim. It had been a turbulent reign but the Wittelsbach colours, white and blue, remain those of the Greek national flag.

In June 1863, the Greeks found a successor in the person of William of Denmark, whose sister, Princess Alexandra, had recently married into the British royal family to become Princess of Wales, and whose father succeeded to the Danish throne as Christian IX later that year. A veritable patriarch of European monarchy, in addition to his son the King of Hellenes, Christian also numbered Tsar Nicholas II of Russia, King George V of Great Britain and King Haakon VII of Norway among his grandsons.

Before his reign was two years old, the new king of Greece, who had adopted a Greek name 'Giorgios' in honour of Saint George, one of the principal saints of the Greek Orthodox Church and also a new royal title 'King of the Hellenes' in place of 'King of Greece', introduced a constitution. For fifty years George I ruled as an exemplary progressive constitutional monarch, but he and his queen, the Russian Grand Duchess Olga, with their seven children seemed to live to the full the carefree and privileged life of late nineteenth-century aristocratic Europe. The wedding of King George I's second son Andrew to Princess Alice of Battenberg, in Darmstadt in October 1903, had been a frolic out of a fairy tale, but in March 1913 this model of constitutional monarchy was murdered only months before the golden jubilee of his reign.

The great issue in Greek political life was the seemingly endless struggle against Turkey. To this day there are some Greeks who look back on the Turkish conquest of Constantinople in 1453 as an historic injustice and the Turkish state as an occupying power usurping the rightful position of the Greek Byzantine empire. The events under debate may have happened more than 500 years ago but, for committed believers, the return of a Jewish state on Palestinian territory after close on two thousand years is a heartening precedent. Even for less fanatical Greeks, national pride demanded the recovery of ancient Greek territories from the crumbling Ottoman empire. During George's reign the country extended its frontiers to something like their modern shape. Britain, which had won a protectorate of the Ionian islands from the Ottomans, returned them to Athens (and with them the Corfu Cricket Club). The Greeks themselves forced the Turks from the territory of Thessaly in the north and, in 1913, formally annexed the island of Crete. On 18 March, the event was celebrated with a military parade headed by King George riding in an open carriage. National jubilation turned into mourning when a bullet from the gun of a deranged assassin killed the unprotected monarch. He was followed by his son Constantine I whose Queen, Sophie, was sister of the German Kaiser, Wilhelm II.

The scramble for control of the territories of the collapsing Turkish empire was the cause of two Balkan wars (1912–13) and intervention by European powers. The London Conference of 1913 recognized an independent Albania despite objections from Serbia. Within her own borders Orthodox Serbia faced the discontent of her Roman Catholic Croatian population, who looked for support to Austria. It was largely because he appeared to favour an independent Croat state that Archduke Franz Ferdinand was assassinated by the nineteen-year-old Serbian fanatic Gavrilo Princip on 28 June 1914.

From this point events moved ineluctably towards European and then world war. Minor powers now had to determine their allegiances. In Greece, Constantine I was believed to favour the German-Austrian central powers. His prime minister, Venizelos, on the other hand favoured alliance with Great Britain and France.

Venizelos had to go. As the war progressed the western Allies found Greece increasingly necessary to their war plans in the Balkans. They found a willing ally in Venizelos who organized armed resist-ance to the royal regime. As a result, Constantine and his family woke up one morning in June 1917 to find their palace being bombarded by warships. In response to this ruthless hint, the King packed his bags. Forced into exile he sought refuge in Switzerland.

Venizelos returned as head of government while Constantine's second son Alexander came to the throne, his elder brother George being considered too pro-German in his sympathies. The Allied victory in 1918 brought Greece accessions of territory. The reign of Alexander I ended when he died of blood poisoning after a bite from a pet monkey. Once again Prince George was passed over and this time Venizelos offered the crown to his younger brother Prince Paul. The offer was firmly declined. Soon after this Venizelos himself was thrown out in an election and after a plebi-scite Constantine I was recalled from exile. His triumph was short-lived. In September 1922, in the wake of defeat in the Greco-Turkish war of 1921–22 over the newly acquired territories in Turkey, he was again forced to leave his throne. As we have seen, his brother Prince Andrew and family were rescued by the Royal Navy, and as they sailed away into exile King Constantine's eldest son George finally made it to the throne as George II. Constantine himself died in exile in Palermo in January the following year.

George II and his wife Elizabeth of Romania were destined to continue the itinerant traditions of the monarchy. Within two years of his accession to the throne, he was again on his travels, forced into exile by a coup which established Greece's first twentieth-century republic. The royal couple went first to Bucharest where, a few years earlier the heir apparent, Crown Prince Carol, had been obliged to dissolve a love match with a commoner and enter a dynastic marriage with Helen of Greece, King George's sister. Almost immediately on the birth of their son Prince Michael, Carol had deserted the family home to live with a new mistress. For a time, Princess Helen had the company of her brother and the sympathy of her embarrassed sister-in-law. But the exiled Greeks soon moved on to London and, later, Florence. In Greece the republic seemed as well established as any regime in that country and as the years went by it seemed that the see-saw story of the monarchy in Greece had become a thing of the past.

But there was conspiracy afoot and in October 1935 the president was forced out of power in a pro-monarchist coup engineered by the new prime minister, General Giorgios Kondilis. In November he held a referendum which showed a 98 per cent vote in favour of a return of the monarchy, and George, comfortably ensconced though he was in Brown's Hotel in London, could hardly refuse the invitation. Greek affairs were in a critical state and the King, after an absence of twelve years, was expected to put things right. He introduced more liberal constitution but following indecisive election results in 1936 he concurred in the establishment of the near-dictatorial regime of Ioannis Metaxas. Early in his reign, hoping perhaps to secure the place of the monarchy once and for all, he ordered the bodies of his mother and father and his grandmother Queen Olga to be exhumed from a Florentine cemetery, and taken to Athens. There they lay in state for six days before being ceremoniously reinterred in the dynasty's burial ground at Tatoï, to the north of the city. Virtually the entire royal clan descended on Athens, and the capital's largest hotel was taken over for the occasion.

Three years later the family convened again. This time it was to celebrate the marriage of the King's brother, Prince Paul, to Frederika of Hanover and Brunswick-Lüneburg. By reason of her descent, the bride was subject to the Royal Marriages Act of 1772, requiring any member of the family to get the consent of the head of that house, the King of Great Britain, before marrying. King George VI duly obliged with notifications of his assent in the Court Circular. At the wedding itself, celebrated according to the rites of the Greek Orthodox Church, Prince Philip of Greece stood behind the bride and groom as his cousins Michael of Romania and David Mountbatten held the ceremonial golden crowns over their heads.

[59]

This same year General Metaxas, who had dissolved parliament in 1936, was proclaimed premier for life. Unswervingly royalist in his political credo and economic reforms, he was also harsh and reactionary. King George did little to defend the human rights of his subjects against his dictatorial first minister, a fact which was to have consequences in the years ahead. Paradoxically, Metaxas was able to salvage something of his reputation through his resistance to Italy's attack on Greece on 28 October 1940. Even his political opponents regretted his death in office in January 1941. The German invasion of Greece on 6 April, from their bases in Bulgaria, was a very different affair. King George and his advisers knew that the country faced almost certain defeat. He and his family escaped to Alexandria and thence made their way to London, where the King was to be head of the government in exile throughout the war.

In Greece, despite ruthless reprisals, the Germans and their puppet governments faced dogged resistance from rival royalist and communist guerrilla bands who controlled large areas of the country. But from early 1943 the resistance was weakened by sporadic fighting within its ranks and when in the September of the following year the British had driven the last German troops from Greek soil, these sectarian skirmishes widened into a civil war. During the war years in London, King George, like other heads of state in exile, had been flattered by the attentions of London and Washington, where he was received by President Roosevelt, while keeping in touch with developments at home as best he could. In the turbulent condition of Greek politics compounded by civil war and intervention by the great powers, only one thing was clear – that the country was still, officially at least, a monarchy. Though popular sentiment towards the monarch himself was far from clear, a plebiscite in September 1946 showed a clear majority in his favour. King George II decided to return but lived barely six months, troubled by the continuing civil war and the challenge from an alternative communist 'government' established by guerrillas in the mountains. He was succeeded as king by his brother, Paul I.

Over the next twenty years, from the death of King George in April 1947 to the coup which forced his nephew Constantine II into exile in April 1967, the monarchy was a central factor – one might almost say *the* central factor – in Greek politics. For most of this period the dominant figure was the controversial Queen Frederika. Know to her friends as 'Freddie' and considered by her more hysterical enemies as a crypto-Nazi, Frederika of Brunswick was undoubtedly a passionate anti-communist and threw all her considerable energies into the fight against the communist insurgents. Superficially her intervention followed the pattern of charitable patroness prescribed by tradition for royal ladies. But her Royal Welfare Institute, conceived as 'a home for the rescue of children from the communists', was not content to open its doors and wait for victims of the fighting to arrive. The Queen and her numerous women volunteers, many of them wealthy Americans whose contributions largely funded the institute, went into the mountains in the wake of the army to bring back children orphaned in the fighting or said to have been abandoned by parents who had gone to join the guerrillas. The communists claimed that the Queen's mission was little better than a mass propaganda and indoctrination campaign, promoted by kidnapping. But there can be little doubt that a bed in the Welfare Institute had many advantages for its young clients over the precarious life in the mountains in a civil war conducted with outstanding viciousness and brutality on both sides. The Queen herself revelled in the element of danger as she pushed forward with front-line troops to beleaguered towns in communist-held territory. Physical courage has its own charisma and Freddie, who loved dancing with the locals in village festivities, was frequently jostled by villagers eager to see and touch her.

Her husband's regime, however, was far from charismatic and was at first deeply unpopular for its economic stringency, derided for its incompetence and hated by many for its restrictions on political freedoms. Nevertheless, by 1950 the communist threat had been largely contained and stability of a sort restored. Two years later the royal couple broke one of the taboos of traditional

Greek politics; in June 1952 they made a state visit to Turkey, including Istanbul. What appeared to the outside world a remarkable gesture of goodwill and international statesmanship seemed to many Greeks little better than betrayal. Tradition held that no Greek ruler should set foot in Constantinople (renamed Istanbul by Atatürk only in 1930) except as conqueror. There were those who saw the influence of the German-born queen behind the visit, Turkey and Germany having been traditional allies for much of the century.

Queen Frederika had always had a subversive streak. She liked to boast that as a schoolgirl in England she had forced the school authorities to abandon cricket as the school game. It was under her influence that she and her husband sent their son Constantine (later King Constantine II) to boarding school and Athens University as a move towards democratizing the monarchy. But if King Paul boasted the monarchy's liberal credentials to his western allies, opponents pointed to undoubtedly oppressive aspects of the regime and to the influence of the maverick queen.

Paul died in March 1964, to be succeeded by his twenty-four-year-old son, Constantine, the Prince of Sparta, traditional title of the Crown Princes of Greece. That September Constantine II married the 18-year-old Princess Anne Marie of Denmark. The following July their first child arrived, Princess Alexia, who, since the Greek law of succession admitted women, was Crown Princess until the birth of her brother Pavlos in May 1967. Both months were ominous in the history of the King's relations with his people.

Following what at the time was a democratic education for a prince, the young Constantine had gone on to become a world-class sportsman, making the Greek Olympic sailing team and achieving a judo black belt. But he had no real preparation for the responsible job of monarch, in a country where the court was a major element in the political system. In July 1965, as if to confirm the worst fears of his critics, King Constantine dismissed the Left-wing administration of premier George Papandreou. For many it was yet more proof of the malign influence of the Queen Mother.

[62]

A woman of extremes and, it was said, given to intrigue, Frederika easily made enemies not only among the press but within the government. Whatever the reason, the consequence was to destabilize the delicate fabric of Greek democracy. The usual succession of ministries followed until the King himself announced plans for a new election in May 1967. the plan was forestalled by a coup, ironically enough from the right, by a cabal of colonels. In December the King's attempt at a counter coup failed miserably and he went into exile. At the time, it seemed that Constantine was merely observing a traditional rite of passage within the conventions of the Greek monarchy. He was convinced that he would in due course return as his ancestors had always done.

Constantine and Queen Anne Marie and their two children began their exile in Rome. Constantine had not abdicated nor had the monarchy been abolished. Technically speaking, in constitutional terms, the regime of the colonels was a regency. At first the King was allowed an annual pension but he had few other resources. The ceremonial carriages, the thousands of paintings in the royal collection, the yachts and all the other trappings of royalty which Constantine might have hoped to be able to sell remained in situ. Nor was the official pension as generous as it at first appeared, since the running costs and maintenance charges on the royal palace as well as incidental expenses of the regency were deducted at source. In any case, the pension was discontinued after a year. There remained the Tatoï Palace estate, the royal family's personal property. It seems that the sale of some 450 acres could raise a sum equivalent to about ten years' pension. Currency controls prevented long-term expatriates permanently resident abroad from exporting capital, but the King's advisers reasoned that since Greek government decrees continued to be promulgated over his seal, his expatriate status could hardly be permanent. Then in May 1973 the Colonels declared the abolition of the monarchy and the establishment of the Hellenic republic. Later that year there was a failed coup in the King's favour, mounted by a group of admirals. The King made no attempt to capitalize on the event at the time or subsequently, but the Colonels claimed to believe that the Queen Mother had been the moving spirit behind it with the King's participation. George Papadopoulos, the leader of the junta, denounced the King as collaborating with foreigners and murderers with the aim of becoming a political leader – an ambition with which, perhaps, not even a king should be charged in the absence of persuasive supporting evidence. The Colonels organized a 'popular' plebiscite shortly afterwards. Not surprisingly it showed a large vote in favour of a republic. Finally, in November 1973, Papadopoulos was ousted in his turn. The following year the exiled sixty-seven-year-old Constantine Karamanlis, who had served three times as Prime Minister under the monarchy between 1955 and 1963, was invited to return to head what became an interim government. Elections in November 1974 gave him 57.4 per cent of the vote – hardly an overwhelming result.

Karamanlis nurtured bitter memories of interventions by the Queen Mother during his premierships. Indeed Queen Frederika, who by this time was involving herself in the fashionable world of Indian mysticism, was called the Marie Antoinette of the Greek monarchy, a *bête noire* held responsible for everything wrong with the system. It has been said that Karamanlis had nothing against King Constantine except that he was her son. At all events he told the King not to return to the country until he was called for. This squared with Constantine's sentiments. Inexperienced in the ways of politicians but well versed – perhaps too well versed – in the conventions of constitutional monarchy, he held himself in readiness.

It seemed to some observers that Constantine, now established with his family in London, had made a mistaken analysis of how things actually stood. Since the situation in the country was by definition in a state of flux, and since the nature of the new political establishment had yet to be finally decided, Karamanlis could be considered as no more than provisional head of government, whose recommendations did not, as yet, have the binding quality of constitutional advice. The King had influential and enthusiastic supporters and they urged that he had as much right to take the initiative as had Karamanlis. There was, of course, the danger of a humiliating rejection by the public but that was a risk that had to be taken. Unless the Colonels' plebiscite was to be accepted as constitutionally valid – and that would surely be preposterous – Greece was still technically a kingdom and Constantine had the right, possibly even an obligation to his supporters, to return to the country and put his fortunes to the test. Constantine made public statements welcoming the development of events in his country and made formal visits to Buckingham Palace and Number 10 Downing Street but, punctilious to a fault, preferred to await the call. It never came.

Instead, to the King's bitter disillusionment, in December 1974, just one month after the general elections, Karamanlis held a referendum on the issue of the monarchy. The public were not to be given time to reflect and the King and Queen with their winsome children were certainly not to be allowed to return in the interim. In the campaign that ensued the King's supporters pointed to his attempted counter-coup of 1967 as evidence of his bona fides as a democrat; his enemies retorted that he had agreed numerous measures of the right-wing oligarchy before making his move. However, the single most devastating weapon in the opposition armoury was a poster which proliferated across the billboards of the capital. It portrayed the single smiling figure of Queen Frederika, her arms flung wide as if to embrace the observer, with a caption bubble containing the words 'I'm coming back'. In desperation, the King's campaign issued a formal refutation, to the effect that his mother would not be invited to return should the vote go in favour of the monarchy. Constantine issued a personal statement apologizing for mistakes he had committed during his reign and begging the forgiveness of his people. It was all to no avail. In a poll verdict, which for the monarchist cause was uncomfortably close to that achieved under the Colonels, the Greek public voted by seven to three in favour of a republican constitution.

There was no arguing with the result. Hurt and bitter though he might be, Constantine determined to get on with the rest of his life. From now on his home would be in England. He took a degree in constitutional law at Cambridge University and kept the lowest of profiles in public life. He was often seen in company with his relations, the royal family, but refused press interviews and lived the life of a private citizen as far as possible. Some twenty years later, Karamanlis, at the launch of the twelve-volume collection of his personal archive, charged that in 1975, the year following the pro-republican referendum, the former King had attempted to mobilize a coup in his favour. In fact Constantine maintained a low public profile in all things relating to political questions. Living in comfortable exile in London, a sailing partner of Prince Philip and frequent companion of the British royals at horse trials and social occasions, he and Queen Anne Marie seemed to have retired entirely from the political arena. But the transformation of the Balkans, with the fall of its communist regimes and the revival of interest in their former monarchies in Bulgaria, Romania and Yugoslavia, seemed to suggest possibilities to the Greek monarchists too. At any rate in 1991 Constantine II, former King of the Hellenes, let it be known that he would like to return to Greece, if only as a private citizen. Broadly speaking, the left-wing press derided the idea as hypocritical while the right wing press virtually ignored it as not worthy of consideration. Supporters of the monarchy muttered that the corrupt Greek political class was afraid that the King or his son might win popular support from the electorate.

In the summer of 1993, as if to probe the public mood on the possibility of a royalist restoration, Constantine chartered a yacht for a cruise of the Greek islands. Perhaps the Greek government was justified in seeing it as a provocation. Whether it was justified in stalking the royal party with gunboats and air force planes is another question. The king called it panic reaction – Greek government ministers viewed even his slightest remarks on Greek matters as unwarranted intrusions into domestic affairs. In short they expected Constantine to live in the kind of political purdah imposed for generations on the British royal family.

In March 1994, the socialist government of Andreas Papandreou proposed to strip the king of his passport, his property and his citizenship, asserting that he had no right to use the royal title as a means of identification. At one of his rare press conferences held in his London home the following month, Constantine observed that to deprive a person of their citizenship was the first gesture of totalitarianism. A right-wing deputy charged that the proposed bill would be unconstitutional, and ministers who liked to refer to him as Mr Glucksburg, supposing that to be the dynasty's name, modified their position. He might keep his citizenship on condition that he renounced his title and abandoned his 'political interventions'. To receive a Greek passport he would also – not surprisingly, perhaps – be requested to recognize the Greek constitution, while he and his family would be required to register themselves by first name and family name with the authorities of a municipality. They were to choose which one.

There was no sign that Constantine planned to avail himself of the permission, having refused during his April press conference to rule out a return to the throne if the Greek people should ever decide to overturn the 1974 referendum. In August the authorities on Corfu moved to take into public ownership the royal summer palace of Mon Repos, home of many happy memories for the Greek royals and birthplace of Prince Philip. Built in 1831 as the residence of the then British High Commissioner, the pleasant if unremarkable neo-classical structure had become dilapidated over the years of royal exile and it was planned to turn it into a museum. The Corfiotes cited the government's bill passed that year as their justification. The King issued a statement the same week, denouncing the action as illegal since he was appealing against the legality of the government bill.

This affected among much else, the royal estate of Tatoï to the north of Athens. The King was permitted to pursue his case through the Greek courts, until in June 1997 a special high court – responding, many claimed, to government pressure – handed down a majority decision which confirmed the 1974 judgment.

Constantine refused to accept the ruling and announced his intention to take his case to the International Court of Justice.

At the dawn of the twenty-first century, more than thirty years since a king last sat upon the throne of Greece, it might seem improbable that monarchy would see a restoration there. The country is, after all, integrated into the European Union where the balance is just in favour of republics. And yet there is always the example of Spain as a precedent for restoration. It would also seem equally clear that the regime was uneasy about public opinion while the conservative opposition party, New Democracy, had despite its name a sizeable pro-royalist fraction. Crown Prince Pavlos, the Duke of Sparta, looked forward to the day when he and his family might return to the homeland he left as a baby. His wife, Marie Chantal, following in the footsteps of countless royal women, was devoting her energies to a hospital charity to benefit the children of poor families in all parts of the world, particularly Greece ... Nothing is ruled out if nothing is also ruled in.

5

BLACK GEORGE AND THE EAGLES

Asked for his comments on the problem of a 'Yugoslav' Kosovo in an interview with the Spanish writer and journalist Juan Balansó, Leka, pretender to the Albanian crown, summed up all the simplicity and all the complexities of the situation with a simple affirmation of his regnal title. 'Looking proudly down from his full height,' Balansó recalled, 'he replied: "I am King of the Albanians, not of Albania; that is to say I am not the king of a country but of a people".'[3]

As all the world knows, and as a glance at a population map will confirm, the national boundaries of modern Albania enclose a much smaller territory than the land actually occupied by ethnic Albanians. Not only Yugoslavia – in the 1990s reduced to Serbia, Kosovo and Montenegro – but also Macedonia and Greece have sizeable Albanian populations, and the concept of a 'Greater Albania', like that of a 'Greater Serbia' has been a shadow over Balkan politics since at least 1911 when an Albanian uprising put an end to the Turkish imperial presence in the area. According to Norman Davies, the historian of Europe, it also 'accelerated the creation of the Balkan League made up of Albania's Christian neighbours [who were not prepared] to see a Greater Albania in which all Albanians would have been united.'[4]

At six foot eight (a healthy metric 2.06) a giant of a man and known in Spain where he lived for some years as '*el Rambo de los Balcanes*' (the Balkan Rambo), His Majesty King Leka I of the

Albanians, was born at 3 am in the morning of 5 April 1939 (his name is the Albanian equivalent of Alexander). Accused by some of being a gunrunner, he certainly had a passion for firearms. Perhaps, as he claimed, his was the simple enthusiasm of the collector; either way it would hardly count as a fault in the claimant to the throne of a country where, in the mid-1990s, it was calculated that the ratio of guns to people was running at three to one. The statistic represented a venerable tradition. The *Encyclopaedia Britannica's* entry on Albania for 1875 observed that 'the manufactures of Albania are few and unimportant, being almost entirely confined to embroidered cloaks, cutlery to a limited extent, firearms and gun and pistol stocks – all for home consumption... . The Albanian goes constantly armed ... and his whole delight is in arms and plunder.' While Leka was not born with a gun actually in his hand the defect was quickly remedied. His father put a brass pistol by the bed, placed his son's tiny hand on the stock and intoned the once customary Albanian invocation to a newborn boy: 'Be strong and brave as were your forebears.'[5]

The child's ancestry was remarkable enough. His father, Ahmed bey Zogu, was descended from a distinguished Albanian family of hereditary provincial governors, but his mother, the American-Hungarian Countess Geraldine Apponyi, could claim descent through her father back to the time of Attila the Hun in the fifth century, and relationship through her mother's family to ex-President Richard Nixon in the twentieth century.

She was born in Budapest in August 1915, the daughter of a Hungarian noble, Gyula Count Apponyi, and an American million-aire's daughter, Gladys Virginia Stewart. A society photographer duly recorded her début in society at a Hungarian monarchists' ball in Budapest in 1932. At this time Geraldine was effectively an orphan. Her father had died when she was nine, and shortly after-wards her mother had set herself up in the fashionable resort of Menton, in the south of France. Geraldine and her sisters returned in due course to live with their grandmother in Hungary. After the ball, unaware that anything important had happened in her life, she found a suitably ladylike job as an assistant librarian in the Budapest National Museum where her uncle was the director. Four years later, just after her twenty-first birthday Geraldine received an invitation to visit the court of Albania. It came from a sister of the king – a man looking for a wife who should be beautiful, of a noble family and, above all, not recommended or sponsored by Mussolini, the Italian dictator who had designs on his kingdom.

For many a royal consort hoping to win popular approval, learning about her new country was a priority. For Geraldine of Albania, breakfast was to be followed by a history lesson. The history of the Albanian monarchy, restored by her husband little more than a decade before their marriage, was short indeed, but the history of the Albanian people was long, contentious and obscure in its origins.

The Albanians are one of Europe's more ancient peoples, whose traditions of independence are a subject of intense national pride. The 1875 *Britannica* speaks of 'a fierce and haughty race' whose bearing was 'erect and majestic to a degree which never fails to strike the traveller'. The country, known to its people as Shqiperia, the land of the eagles, maintained, thanks to its mountainous terrain, a degree of autonomy for long periods. In the fifteenth century, under the national hero Iskander Bey (Scanderbeg) they fought a heroic rearguard guerrilla action against the Ottoman Turks led by Mehmet II, conqueror of Constantinople, as they established their empire in the Balkans. In the ensuing centuries most Albanians adopted Islam. Though the uprising of 1911 had finally forced the end of Turkish rule, it had also alarmed neighbouring Christian Balkan states who had large populations of ethnic Albanians within their borders and feared the loss of territory to a Greater Albania. In 1913 the Treaty of London recognized the sovereignty of an Albanian state, its borders to be fixed by an international commission, its constitution to be a Western-style monarchy. The first 'King', a German prince of the house of Wied, left the country after barely six months, defeated by the prevailing state of anarchy. During the First World War the Western Allies, of which Italy was one, secretly agreed that after the war Italy should have Albania as a protectorate.

In the country itself political upheaval and civil war agitated the constitutional kaleidoscope from regency to kingdom to republic until in January 1925 Ahmed Bey Zogu, Moslem by religion, president by title, autocratic in style and ambitious by nature, inaugurated a period of comparative order. On 1 September 1928 he proclaimed himself king. He descended from a prominent family which for much of the nineteenth century had been hereditary governors of central Albania, and if he was despotic it was through necessity not by nature. Thanks to him, Tirana graduated from a rambling township towards the status of a capital city; the country acquired a school system (after her history lesson, Queen Geraldine was accustomed to receive leading figures in the fledgling educational sector as well as advisers on the hygiene programme the King was anxious to install in the country's remote mountain villages) and even a standardized language, derived from a diversity of regional dialects; the beginnings of a road network and, inevitably, a police force.

At the end of December 1937, accompanied by a friend, the future Queen Geraldine embarked at Bari on Italy's Adriatic coast for a voyage which, in her own account as told to the French writer Thierry Deslot in his *Géraldine d'Albanie, reine du pays des aigles*, to which this chapter is much indebted, would take her to a twelve-month romance before twentieth-century reality closed round her, hard and unrelenting.

The two friends disembarked at the Albanian port of Durrësi (Durazzo), a stage-set of steep mountains and plunging cliffs, the ancient walls of its fortifications, founded by the Romans, enhanced when the place was a Venetian colony and backed by a scatter of domes recalling the centuries of Turkish conquest. Geraldine was driven to a villa decorated in every room with a profusion of red roses. Late that evening she was presented to King Zog, whom she described as a tall, handsome man with piercing blue eyes impeccably dressed in the white uniform of colonel-in-chief of the army.

Zog also had a small jet-black moustache of which he was inordinately proud. They talked into the small hours and the following day Geraldine woke to find that an immense heart made of roses had been delivered from the palace. Four o'clock that afternoon the King proposed and she accepted.

Zog insisted that she have ten days in which to think over her response. Every morning and evening a superb bouquet was delivered and every day some expensive present was sent to her villa. Confirmation of her acceptance was never really in doubt, but she was showered with jewels and her engagement ring was a diamond reputedly of 40 carats. Presented to the jubilant crowds outside the villa on the day of her betrothal, she followed tradition by scattering breadcrumbs and silver pieces from the balcony.

Vatican approval of this marriage between a Catholic noblewoman and a Moslem ruler was slow in coming. Nor was Italy's dictator Mussolini best pleased. Determined to realize the terms of the 1915 secret accord which had awarded Albania in protectorate to the Italian crown, he had hoped to see an Italian princess on the consort's throne in Albania. When in April 1938 the ceremony did take place, Zog was obliged to accept Mussolini's son-in-law, Count Ciano, as one of the witnesses. The proceedings, awkwardly bridging the gap between the religions of bride and groom, were brief and to the point. In a wedding dress created by Worth of Paris, the bride stood by the groom while the president of Albania's parliament read the relevant clauses from the civil code. He then declared them man and wife, they signed the register and the proceedings were over. After the cheering crowds and the ten-foot-high wedding cake cut by the queen with the king's sword, the Hungarian gypsy band and all the other splendours of the wedding reception, they left for Durrësi where a pavilion had been built for the honeymoon.

Ciano presented himself the next morning – it was clear that the Duce was determined to force Italian protection on the unwilling Albanians. In June, it appears, there was even an attempt to kidnap the royal couple under the pretext of a yacht cruise down the Adriatic coast, and in September there were reports of an imminent Italian invasion. In February 1939 Zog heard that Italy was planning to divide his country with Yugoslavia. Queen Geraldine was now expecting her first child and her apprehensions were naturally intensified. In the morning of 5 April she was safely delivered of a healthy boy. She had played her part in securing the future of the dynasty, but the future of the country over which it ruled was less certain. On the 6th the people of Tirana were dismayed to find that the Italian community were evacuating the city under instructions from their embassy. Meanwhile an Italian general had been to the palace to present the King with an ultimatum: if he wished to retain even the semblance of his royal status, he would have to make concessions which would in effect transform Albania into an Italian province. Late in the afternoon of the same day, the general was followed by the Italian ambassador, come to present his government's congratulations on the birth. With the conventional formalities out of the way, the diplomat demanded a reply to the ultimatum of the morning. Only one outcome was possible. The royal family prepared for flight. Astonishingly, although the danger had been looming for weeks, the queen, we are told, had not cleared her bank account. It was too late now. In the early hours of the 7th news came through that the Italians had launched an attack on Valona in the south of the country. With only her jewels and a few personal possessions and accompanied by her grandmother, the queen was carried down to a waiting limousine. A doctor and nurse installed themselves with the infant Prince in the back of the car which swept out of the palace grounds into the night. The vehicle was a red Mercedes Benz, a wedding present from Adolf Hitler. Thus the Führer helped cheat Mussolini of his prey. Ten days later Victor Emmanuel III of Italy was proclaimed King of Albania.

A long drive over winding mountain roads faced the fugitives as they headed for the Greek frontier. Before leaving her adopted homeland, Queen Geraldine made the gesture of many an exile before her and scooped some of the soil into a little bag in which she had packed some of her jewels. From that point the jewel bag with its precious dust accompanied the queen on all her travels. She was soon joined in Greece by her husband but, rather than expose their host King George to reprisals from Mussolini, they made their way to France. This was easier said than done. The direct route through Italy was obviously impossible, so they travelled via Romania – where they were briefly received by King Carol – central Europe, Sweden, and finally the Netherlands and Belgium and so to Paris. But in those troubled times France herself was hardly a safe haven. News of the German invasion of Belgium drove them from their lodgings in the Paris region. They and their court of some three dozen headed south in a convoy of six limousines, usually travelling no faster than the farm carts and laden family cars of the refugees hoping to find safety around Bordeaux, briefly to be the country's seat of government. At one point the convoy was straffed by German fighter-bombers, and for a time the royal group was split up. Reunited at Bordeaux they were among the fortunate few, in late summer 1940, to embark on the last boat to sail from that beleaguered port for England. They were surely more fortunate than most of their fellow travellers, for on arrival in Liverpool they soon entrained for London and the Ritz hotel. Within the week the Luftwaffe started its Blitz of the capital, but a mattress in the basement of the luxury hotel was better accommodation than was enjoyed by many a Londoner.

Later, the Queen established a family home in a spacious property not far from Windsor, the King stayed in London hoping to persuade Churchill to send him to the war front in the Balkans, only to find that British policy in the area increasingly relied on communist partisan forces. In Albania, these were led by a group including Enver Hoxha. As the war drew to its end, it was obvious that neither the British nor the American government had any intention of sponsoring the royal couple's return to Albania where Hoxha was laying the preparations of his baleful tyranny.

The following year, with the return of peace in Europe, the Albanian royals left England for Egypt. There they were welcomed by King Farouk. They took rooms in a hotel at Giza, near the pyramids until they could find a comfortable villa in the smart Ramleh district of Alexandria. It was here that Leka began his education, receiving private tuition from a Swiss governess, who was also Queen Geraldine's personal assistant, and attending Victoria School. For those with the resources – and the Albanian royal family seem to have been very well off – post-war Alexandria was a haven of the good life. In addition to his secretary King Zog employed a minister of court to handle matters of protocol. The family was looked after by a sizeable personal staff, including numerous domestic servants in addition to a bodyguard and a driver. The coterie in which they moved included the young King Simeon of Bulgaria, his mother Queen Ioanna and her father King Victor Emmanuel III of Italy. For some seven years they joined the round of tennis parties, dinners and cards enjoyed by the clique of ex-royals in and around the city. Ioanna of Bulgaria, mother of King Simeon II, became one of Geraldine's closest friends, and she was even reconciled with the deposed Victor Emmanuel of Italy whose armies had driven Zog from his kingdom and who had usurped the title 'King of Albania' from April 1939 until September 1943. In a minor triumph of drawing-room diplomacy a truce was patched up between the two ex-monarchs and the peace of Alexandrian high society preserved. But if Zog and his entourage relaxed over the card table, they played only for token stakes, except on the monthly visits of King Farouk when real money was involved. They devoted most of their time to planning for the eventual liberation of Albania.

Briefly, in the early 1950s, Zog and Geraldine were able to talk about return and restoration. Belatedly, Britain mounted a commando operation to infiltrate Albania with a view to ousting Hoxha. The plans were betrayed to Moscow by Kim Philby who held a watching brief on the Balkan desk of Britain's intelligence services. At the time it was known only that the enterprise had failed. It was a dark shadow over their Egyptian exile but in any case the time had come to move on. A military coup in July 1952 ousted King Farouk and soon after Zog moved his household to the less hazardous ambiance of the French Riviera. But he was a sick man. For years he had suffered from a series of ailments and finally, on 9 April 1961, he died of cancer. The funeral was attended by hundreds of Albanian exiles (it is estimated that there were more than 80,000 in the US alone) and with the dead king was buried the little bag of Albanian soil, treasured by his wife from the moment they had crossed the Greek frontier twenty-two years before. Later that same year, in a ceremony at the Hotel Bristol in Paris, Leka was acclaimed 'King of the Albanians' by a 'National Assembly' of exiles. Soon after he moved to Madrid.

Spain was at that time governed by Franco, Europe's last old-fashioned right-wing dictator and in Leka's opinion, the last bastion against creeping communist socialism. Better still, the Spanish ruler was prepared to grant him, like King Simeon of the Bulgarians, rights of extra-territoriality which would enable him to travel on a unique passport issued by his own chancellery which was, in effect, sovereign territory. In Spain Leka maintained regular contact with the leaders of Albanian communities in Spain and elsewhere in the world, and in Madrid in 1972 he presided over a congress of exiles. Having been trained at Sandhurst, Britain's prestigious military academy, Leka had a strong grounding in the skills of professional soldiering, and these he seemed determined to devote to preparing for the liberation of his country. In October 1973, aged thirty-six, he married Susan Cullen-Ward, the daughter of a rich Australian entrepreneur, in a private civil ceremony conducted in the Mairie of Biarritz. It was followed by a ceremony of blessing held at Illescas, near Toledo, in which Moslem, Catholic, Orthodox and Anglican clerics participated just five weeks before the death of Franco. The VIPs who attended included, as well as Queen Geraldine, radiant in an elegant little tiara and a powder-blue gown, Queen Farida of Egypt and Queen Margarita of Bulgaria, as well as the Grand Duke and Grand Duchess of Russia. Among the immense throng of guests were numbers of Albanian exiles. The bride wore traditional Albanian marriage costume, the King the uniform of the Royal Albanian Army, with the sash of the order of Skanderbeg. It was a brilliant and happy occasion but for the members of this right-wing court, the death of Franco the following month did not augur well for the future. Some four years later, in January 1979, a detail of four Spanish police officers presented themselves at the residence of the Albanian royal family. Despite the diplomatic immunity granted by Franco, they had a warrant to search the place.

Leka had installed himself in an old fortress which he had had refurbished in authentic style and where a body of heavily armed Albanian vigilantes mounted guard. Photographs showed him clad in camouflaged battle fatigues inspecting a commando of troops, or at least volunteers, clad in combat dress and balaclavas and armed with up-to-date combat rifles with fixed bayonets. According to Spanish sources, these 'troops', despite the superficial resemblance to the vicious hardmen of IRA cadres, were eager young Albanian exiles who attended summer training camps, returning to their civilian lives in the hope that one day the liberation army would be called on in the national struggle. Leka's strategy of return was based on two fundamental assumptions: one, that Albania had more nationals outside than inside its borders; and two, that he alone of the exiled Balkan monarchs had been able to unite virtually all his country's exiles, republicans included, under his flag. He had always said that he would ascend the throne only if a referendum or plebiscite showed a clear majority in favour. Presumably his 'liberation army' volunteers would have been the first stage in establishing the conditions in which the referendum could be held.

The full extent of Leka's activities do not seem to have been fully appreciated by the Spanish authorities. The police search revealed a small arsenal which, despite the king's protestations that it was merely the private collection of a military enthusiast, prompted the Spanish authorities to take further action. Together with his paramilitary activities the suspicion, or at least the accusation, that the expatriate royal was a gun-runner was enough to have him expelled from the country. He believed that the real cause was pressure from the Spanish communist party, now in favour with the democratic regime of the young King Juan Carlos, and the wish to mollify the Yugoslav communist president, Marshal Tito. According to her biographer, Queen Geraldine believed – significantly enough in the light of later events – that the ageing Marshal was angered by her son's desire to see the Yugoslav province of Kosovo integrated into Albania. It may at first seem unlikely that Tito really believed that the expatriate sovereign, who had not lived more than three days in his claimed kingdom, presented a more serious threat than did Hoxha. But then, from the moment he won power, Hoxha had done much to disarm the hostility of his Balkan neighbours, chronically concerned by the possible resurgence of ambitions for a Greater Albania. He shrewdly renounced all interest in the ethnic Albanian minorities in Kosovo, Montenegro and Macedonia, while there were rumours rife in the 1960s and 1970s that Leka was gun-running for the CIA.

After the collapse of the communist regimes in the Balkans, Leka's known sympathy for ethnic Albanian causes seems to have upgraded his image from that of embarrassingly anachronistic Ruritanian right-wing strong man to that of a factor to be taken into account in the real political world. Whatever the reason for his expulsion from Spain, Leka did not blame King Juan Carlos, for whom he professed a great affection. After a brief interlude in Rhodesia (now Zimbabwe) and an offer of asylum in Egypt by President Anwar Sadat, Leka and Queen Susan found refuge in Johannesburg, South Africa, where on 26 March 1982 their son and heir, Prince Leka Anwar Baudouin, was born, being named after his father, Anwar Sadat of Egypt and King Baudouin of Belgium. Queen Geraldine, who had remained in her Madrid home after her son left Spain, finally joined him and his family in South Africa in 1992. In a boyhood photo, taken when he was about eight, Prince Leka Anwar sits in dazzling white sailor-suit holding an ancient muzzle pistol rather more than half as big as he is. Antique it may be but, if it came from his father's collection, we may be sure that it was fully operational.

For King Leka, the 1990s opened as a decade of possibilities. In September 1990 he and his wife and heir attended a ceremony at a French château which accommodated the Royal Albanian Foundation. As the Albanian flag was run up, the royal party arrived to a fanfare played on hunting horns in the French manner. Leka a self-confessed 'militant', declared himself ready, when the time came, to return to his native country and take his chances. In April 1997 he was able to make his first visit there since he was three days old, and was mobbed by thousands of enthusiastic supporters on his journey to his father's birthplace in the family's home province of Mat. As reported by Tom Walker in *The Times* for 21 April, the scenes were extraordinary. Travelling in five black Mercedes of 1960s vintage, the royal party of king, bodyguards and Albanian police took three hours to cover the 100 kilometres from Tirana the capital, to Burrel, the chief town of Mat. Joined by the vehicles of delirious supporters, the motorcade was greeted by volleys of small arms fire all along the route. Overcome by the beauty of the country and the upsurge of enthusiasm for his cause, Leka Zogu, as he is known to Albanians, urged his 'brother and sisters' to work to build the future of their wonderful land.

He evidently remained actively involved in their cause from his home in Johannesburg, South Africa, for President Mandela was to withdraw his diplomatic privileges. In February 1999, the house was raided by police who seized a number of weapons and the ex-king was held in police custody over the weekend. The experience did nothing to lessen his warlike spirit and in April he was reported by Reuters 'from his heavily guarded home in Johannesburg', commenting on the Nato air strikes in Yugoslavia. Quoted in *The Times* of 14 April 1999, Leka is reported as saying: 'You cannot hold ground with air power ... The only way to hold ground is a seventeen-year-old with a bayonet.' And the self-styled 'King of the Albanians' went on to call for self determination by ethnic Albanians as the only solution to the problems of Kosovo.

[80]

Things appeared differently from the perspective of Crown Prince Alexander of Yugoslavia, Leka's younger contemporary who decided not to activate his claim when his father ex-King Peter II died in 1970. His decision is entirely understandable in view of the troubled and eventually tragic evolution of his father's career, but Alexander's own situation was in any case rather complicated. When he was born, his father had been in exile since 1941. In November 1945 the kingdom effectively ceased to exist when the country's ruler, Marshal Tito, proclaimed the People's Republic of Yugoslavia and the international community recognized the new state. Alexander's very claim to the now non-existent kingdom depended on a legal fiction.

The constitution had stipulated that monarchs of Yugoslavia had to be born on Yugoslav territory. Alexander was born to King Peter and his wife Alexandra of Greece on 27 July 1945 in the family's suite in Claridge's Hotel, London. In anticipation of the event, the British parliament had declared the hotel suite to be Yugoslav territory until the child should be safely delivered. Given that every embassy throughout the world is considered to be extra-territorial to the host country, the fiction was no doubt acceptable. It was, moreover, important since, as Alexander once pointed out, his dynasty, unlike those of Romania, Bulgaria or Greece, is native to the Balkans and not imported from Germany. In fact, as the Republic of Yugoslavia shrank to Voivodina, Serbia and Montenegro, Alexander himself, descended from the Karageorgevich kings of Serbia and, through his great grandmother Princess Zorka, from King Nicholas I of Montenegro, had excellent credentials in the event of a restoration of the monarchy.

Under Stephan Dushan in the fourteenth century Serbia briefly ruled a sizeable Balkan empire comprising Bosnia, Albania and much of modern Macedonia (which still has a large Serbian population). It quickly fell apart after his death and the Turkish victory of Kosovo in 1389 (a catastrophe still celebrated in bardic epic tradition) ensured Ottoman domination until the late eighteenth century. During this time there were pogroms against the Serbian nobility – the ethnic cleansing of an elite – and population movements of hundreds of thousands, both enforced deportations and voluntary emigrations, notably to Hungarian territory. Dreams of a return to the days of the 'Greater Serbia' were nurtured and were not dead when Turkish power began to be rolled back in the nineteenth century. At that time too, dynastic feuds and clan rivalries, inhibited by Ottoman imperial government, revived. Chief among these were the hostilities between the family of the peasant pig-breeder turned guerrilla fighter George the Black (Karageorge, from Kara, Turkish for 'black') and the family of one of his lieutenants, the Obrenovich. Modern Serbia's independence was given international recognition by the Treaty of Berlin of August 1878 which formally recognized the principality then ruled by Milan Obrenovich. Four years later he proclaimed Serbia a kingdom but, although he made territorial acquisitions, he also made many enemies and was forced to abdicate. Another four years passed, and his twenty-seven-year-old son and successor Alexander and his Queen were butchered in their palace during an army revolt which brought the sixty-year-old Peter Karageorgevich to the throne as King Peter I.

From that point on, the position of the Karagoergevich dynasty was not seriously contested in Serbia, and when the Treaty of Versailles created a new Balkan state, the Kingdom of the Serbs, Croats and Slovenes, Peter was recognized as its king. True, he was the only king available but his elevation was a dubious formula for national unity. The new state also comprised Bosnia-Herzegovina (including Sarajevo), Dalmatia on the Adriatic coast and parts of southern Hungary as well as Croatia and Slovenia. In addition the principality of Montenegro, a self-styled kingdom since 1910 and now faced with the occupation of the country by Serbian troops, opted to join Greater Serbia.

The distinction between the territories ruled by King Peter as King of Serbia and those ruled in his capacity of King of the Serbs, Croats and Slovenes was not carefully maintained by the monarch. The regions were in any case divided by religion; by language (Slovenian, Serbo-Croat and Hungarian); and even by alphabet (Cyrillic, Roman and Arabic). Moreover, the Roman Catholic Croats who look back to their medieval hero Prince Tomislav and had long chafed under Austrian rule as former members of the Austro-Hungarian empire, boiled with anger at now having to submit to Slav neighbours who were Orthodox by religion and, in Croatian eyes, peasants in their mentality. For their part, the Serbs vaunted the virtues of their peasant past. King Peter himself liked to boast that his grandfather had been a peasant, and claimed to value his ancestry more than his throne. The lot of the true peasantry throughout the new kingdom was, of course, dire and in the first elections the communists with fifty-eight deputies were the third largest grouping in the Parliament.

The approach to some kind of social balance was deceptive, for this would be the last parliament with communist representation before the coming of Tito. The rivalries of the nationalities would prove still more difficult to deal with. Alexander, who succeeded his father in August 1921, seemed willing to try. With a neat diplomatic sleight of hand, he refused a coronation on grounds of expense and so sidestepped a ceremony which should have been a symbol of unity but in a country of three religions could only have been a symbol of division. As it was, the Croatian party began the reign rigidly opposed to the royal government, and when its leader began to look for rapprochement in June 1928, he and four Croatian colleagues were shot down on the floor of the chamber of deputies. The Croatian representatives decamped in a body from Belgrade to Zagreb. However good his intentions, King Alexander had an image problem. While his father had boasted to be himself a man of the people, the son was unsettled by the bustle of city life surging round the walls of the palace and irritated by the raucous badinage of drinkers at the pavement cafés across the street. He also objected to the seemingly endless stream of unofficial petitioners who queued outside his gates. Commonsense security considerations no doubt supported his position, but his aloof public posture did nothing to ameliorate the autocratic nature of his regime.

Alexander began his reign by building a new royal palace in the hills outside Belgrade, and a new summer palace at Bled in distant Slovenia. Officially the site, so far removed from the capital, was chosen as a way of bringing the royal family into contact with the people of the Slovenian region of the multi-ethnic kingdom. For the King it seems to have been a reclusive retreat. It was also something of a centre of life in the English style. The King's cousin Prince Paul of Greece took a villa nearby and his relations – Prince Nicholas and Princess Helena and their daughter Princess Marina, later Duchess of Kent – were frequent house guests. Alexander's Queen, Marie of Romania, known to one and all as 'Mignon', was a granddaughter of Queen Victoria and Crown Prince Peter, born in September 1923, was educated in England. A somewhat timid boy, he held his father in awed respect.

Then King Alexander was assassinated together with the French foreign minister Louis Barthou in the streets of Marseille at the beginning of a state visit to France on 9 October 1934. On learning that he was now King Peter II, the 11-year-old was horrified at the prospect which confronted him. 'Only papa can be king!' he is reported to have cried.

Peter was right to be worried. In 1990 the French historian Edouard Calic adduced evidence to show that Barthou, motivator of the Little Entente with the Balkan powers by which France hoped to restrain Hitler's ambitions, was the primary target of the killers. At the time most people assumed that the murders were the work of Croatian terrorists gunning for Alexander and that Barthou was, so to speak, collateral damage. Alexander's response to the 1928 liquidation of the Croatian deputies had been to establish a personal dictatorship which was intended, among other things, to curb corruption and achieve national unity. In a country where corruption was institutionalised and nationality the most vaunted badge of identity, such a policy, even if well-intentioned, must seem provocative. Serb opinion was outraged when the King honoured the Roman Catholic archbishop of Zagreb with a high Serbian order of chivalry and disgusted when the flying of Serbia's national flag was discontinued. This was in conformity with the renaming of the state as the Kingdom of Yugoslavia (ie, of the South Slavs). The elections of 1931 had returned an overwhelming majority of deputies in favour of the King's government and an overwhelming majority of Serbs.

With the murder of Alexander I, the administration of Yugoslavia passed to a regency council headed by his brother Prince Paul. It was this regime that on 26 March 1941 decided to sign a pact with Hitler's Germany. King Peter was told that the Yugoslav armed forces stood no chance against Germany and that the pact would hold the position until he came of age on his eighteenth birthday in September. In fact, in the small hours of the next morning, a coup overthrew the regency council and proclaimed King Peter II the country's acting ruler. It was a harsh initiation and barely a week later, on 6 April, Belgrade came under attack from the Luftwaffe.

On 13 April, little more than a fortnight since the proclamation of his reign, Peter II of Yugoslavia took off, on the first stage of a circuitous itinerary, from a meadow in the Montenegrin mountains. Eventually early in June he arrived in London. There he and his advisers set up a government in exile. Even before the end of the war it was becoming an irrelevance as British policy-makers turned increasingly to support for the Croat communist leader Josip Broz whose *nomme de guerre* was Tito. Peter would never return to his home country.

Even in the face of the barbarous Nazi enemy, the ministers of the government in exile in London continued their old ethnic sectarianism. In Yugoslavia the Resistance was split between royalist Serb Chetniks under General Draza Mihailovich, Peter's Minister of War, and Tito's communist partisans. The Croat terrorists, who had been responsible for King Alexander's death, collaborated in the breakaway puppet state of Croatia, set up by the German occupying power.

Chetnik atrocities gave Churchill leverage as he pressured the student King (Peter was at Cambridge) to support the Allied pro-Tito policy. This pro-Tito stance seemed to Peter to be an act of betrayal – the more so because of the happy anglophile associations of his own childhood (King George VI and Queen Elizabeth, then

[85]

Duke and Duchess of York, had been guests at his christening). In England he gained his wings with the RAF, and he had friendly meetings with Churchill and made many a happy visit to the family of his 'Uncle Bertie' (King George). He managed to persuade the British government to organize commando training for Yugoslav officers who had escaped from German prison camps. But on the question of Tito the British government was unyielding. Peter also found himself seriously short of funds. He had to abandon his luxury accommodation at Claridge's, finding temporary accommodation in London's Yugoslav embassy-in-exile. After the war he moved first to France and then to America. For a time he worked as a consultant on international affairs. Speculation on the currency markets deepened his financial problems. Increasingly he turned to alcohol and died in California almost destitute, at the age of forty-seven, in 1970.

His son Alexander, now twenty-five and in the Brigade of Guards, had also taken British nationality and, as we have seen, refused to adopt the phantom title of Yugoslavia. With the death of Tito it seems he may have reconsidered his position. It was reported that he believed that in monarchy lay the country's only hope of survival. If so, it would not be a Serbian monarchy. It is true, as he boasted, that the Karageorgevich are a native, not an imported, dynasty like the Hohenzollern Sigmaringen of Romania or the Saxe-Coburg-Gotha of Bulgaria. Perhaps it would have been better if the southern Slavs had been able to adopt a foreign dynasty in the hope of suppressing their own rivalries in common allegiance to an impartial crown. Karageorgevich and Obrenovich only resolved their differences over the rule of Serbia by butchery. And if during the forty-seven years of Tito's regime the Serbs were prepared to be managed by a Croatian, there was no chance that in time of peace the Croats would ever again accept a Serbian king as head of state.

During the mid 1990s Alexander sometimes called himself 'a Serb for peace', and during the brief flourishing of the liberal opposition to Milosevich, he won approval with his comment that, though he might not speak Serbian very well, he understood the language of democracy perfectly. Even a kingdom of a lesser Yugoslavia comprising Serbia and Montenegro would, like the other new south Slav states, find survival a competitive business. In late 1989 a ceremony of remembrance for Alexander I was held in the Muette quarter of Paris near the statue of the murdered king. It was attended by some three hundred and fifty, among them the heads of the royal houses of Serbia and Montenegro, Alexander and Nicholas. As the Nineties advanced, the relations between the two Balkan homelands moved too often into discord, without clear ways to resolution. The Montenegrins, effortlessly absorbed by Serbia in the 1910s, still maintained a penchant for genuine independence. The royal option seemed ambivalent. Visiting Montenegro in June 1999, on the 610th anniversary of the Battle of Kosovo, Alexander of Yugoslavia was welcomed enthusiastically by politicians opposed to the regime in Belgrade and had talks with the leader of the republic, President Djukonovic. And yet monarchists could reflect that the former Montenegrin royal family still had a representative, however reluctant, in the person of Nikola Petrovic, directly descended through the male line of King Nicholas I, should they want him – and should they be able to persuade him to abandon his successful Parisian architectural practice.

6

BULGARIAN TSARS

———•◦•———

When King Paul and Queen Frederika of Greece were visiting the USA in 1958, their eighteen-year-old-son Crown Prince Constantine met Simeon of Bulgaria, a few years his senior and a student at Valley Forge Military Academy in Pennsylvania. Out for a drive, with Constantine at the wheel, they were flagged down for speeding. The traffic cop began his notebook routine. 'What's your name?' he demanded. 'Crown Prince Constantine of Greece,' came the reply. 'Oh, yeah! And who's your friend?' 'King Simeon of Bulgaria.' The officer responded: 'And I'm J. Edgar Hoover.'⁶

In fact, King Simeon II of the Bulgarians – he preferred this title to the old-fashioned Tsar – long nurtured the hope of once again leading his people as their monarch. Born in 1937, he was the second child and only son of Tsar Boris III and his Italian spouse Ioanna, daughter of King Victor Emmanuel III and Helena of Montenegro. Descended through his father from the German princely house of Saxe-Coburg-Gotha, Simeon also has French blood through his paternal grandmother Marie-Louise of Bourbon-Parma. His childhood was overshadowed by the outbreak of the Second World War when he was just two, and he came to the throne some four years later when his father died in mysterious circumstances a few days after returning from a meeting with Hitler in Berlin.

Germany had long been a threat to the Balkan states. For Tsar Boris (he adopted the title used by the medieval monarchs of Bulgaria in the days of the country's greatness), the facts of geography and military inferiority were compounded by conflicting allegiances among his people and advisers. 'My generals,' he is said to have remarked, 'are pro-German, my diplomats are pro-British, my queen is pro-Italian and my people are pro-Russian.' He wanted to save his country from all military involvement if at all possible, but guessed it was a forlorn hope. He had little choice but to ally with the Rome-Berlin axis for the duration of the Second World War. In 1939 Russia had signed a non-aggression pact with Germany; with the collapse of France in June 1940, Britain was alone in Europe, fighting for her life; Boris had family ties with Fascist Italy (his wife Ioanna was daughter of the Italian King Victor Emmanuel III); and finally a rapprochement with Germany could mean the recovery of Macedonia which every Bulgarian government for sixty years had dreamed of. Boris agreed to lease airbases to the Luftwaffe. Then, at Hitler's insistence, in December 1941, the month in which Germany declared war on the United States, he made a formal declaration of war on Britain and the US. But he was to refuse Hitler's later demand that he go to war against the Soviet Union. Not only was the Slav superpower uncomfortably close to his country, but most Bulgarians still looked on Russia with gratitude for the part she had played in the nineteenth century in liberating their country from the rule of the Turkish empire. Determined to hold out as long as possible, Boris continued to wriggle through the dangerous jungle of wartime diplomacy even if he wryly compared himself to a caterpillar under the raised foot of an elephant. Then, in August 1943 Hitler peremptorily ordered him to come to see him. The details of the meeting are still unclear but, almost certainly, Hitler demanded a more whole-hearted Bulgarian commitment to the war.

On 17 August Boris arrived back in Sofia from Hitler's mountain retreat at Berchtesgarten aboard a Luftwaffe airplane. In those days of non-pressurized cabins, high-altitude flying meant breathing equipment. It seems that the Tsar had complained of a malfunction in his oxygen mask, but nevertheless, soon after landing, he left the capital for the family's summer residence at Tzarska Bistritza for a week's holiday. He even did some mountain-climbing. Perhaps this was unwise. Four days after his return from Germany, he was complaining of repeated attacks of dizziness. Back in the royal palace he described his encounter with the Führer to a member of his personal staff. Apparently it had been 'a terrible meeting' lasting for hours, during which he was under unrelenting pressure to agree to substantial German intervention in Bulgarian affairs. When the gruelling interview finally came to an end, Boris was convinced that he had managed to keep the Nazis 'paws' off his country, but he was beginning to wonder whether his resistance might not have cost him his life. On the afternoon of 23 August Boris told his Private Secretary that he had never felt so poorly, and broached the suspicion that he might have been given a slow-acting poison during his German trip. According to one account he had his first bout of vomiting soon after this and died some three days later. Mystery certainly surrounds his death. The official announcement was made by the prime minister Bogdan Filov on 28 August. 'His Majesty Tsar Boris III, "the Unifier", died at 4.22 pm today from a short, severe illness.' The official cause of death was given as 'a thrombosis of the left artery to the heart, double pneumonia and a cerebral congestion'. The Tsar was not the only Bulgarian to suspect the hand of German agents, whether in Germany or in Bulgaria itself.

Simeon II, the six-year-old boy who succeeded him, was named after one of medieval Bulgaria's great monarchs, but could hardly look forward to a reign to match that of his namesake. The omens were bleak. He, his sister and their mother Queen Ioanna were effectively the prisoners of the Germans in the royal palace in Sofia. Then, with the reverse of German arms at the battle of Stalingrad, Soviet victory on Germany's eastern front seemed only a matter of time. Queen Ioanna contrived to leave the country with her children, travelling via Turkey to Syria, while the government was conducted in Simeon's name by the pro-German regency council headed by his uncle, Prince Kyril. There was fierce opposition from the Agrarian Party, the Communists and pro-Russian elements in the lower ranks of the army. When in 1944 the Red Army crossed the Bulgarian frontier, opposition groups seized power. They gave token loyalty to Simeon and for a brief period Prince Kyril headed a coalition government but in 1946 this fell to a communist coup, and Simeon's uncle along with some 200 other members of his regency regime were executed.

Still the eight-year-old monarch remained nominal head of state and another regency council was appointed to maintain appearances. Tsar Simeon and the Queen Mother, who had returned to Sofia after a two-year absence, were held under comfortable house arrest. But the charade could not last much longer. It was less than thirty years since Soviet Russia had murdered its own Tsar and his family and it was not possible that Russia would tolerate another such regime. Accordingly, in September 1946, Bulgaria's Communist Party stage-managed a referendum which returned a majority of 92 per cent against the monarchy. On 16 September, just three years, five weeks and three days after his accession, the boy monarch and the Queen Mother left Sofia for exile. No doubt the Communist government was pleased to be rid of the old regime. Compared with the butchers of Ekaterinburg they had proved humane; but it would perhaps have been tidier for them if the Tsar had abdicated. Apparently, in the rush, no one thought to ask him to go through with the formalities. Thus while the verdict of the referendum was as suspect in the eyes of monarchists as it was inevitable in the eyes of Moscow, this caterpillar had not been crushed by the elephant's foot of international politics. According to the technicalities of protocol, on achieving his majority Simeon could assert the standing of a reigning monarch.

Queen Ioanna chose Egypt for the family's new home. It was here that her father had retired to after his abdication from the Italian throne in May 1945. Simeon went to Victoria College, an

English school in Alexandria. The death of his grandfather in 1947 would also mean changes in the life of the little family, as the Italian government eventually permitted Queen Ioanna to draw on the sizeable legacy of her father. Four years later their life in the anglophone world of Egypt in the last years of the British mandate came to an end and the Queen Mother, with her son and his sister the Princess Marie Louise, moved to Spain where Ioanna was able to buy a sumptuous mansion in one of Madrid's most select residential districts. Later Queen Ioanna would settle at Estoril in Portugal, near her brother the exiled Umberto II of Italy. Simeon continued his education at the Lycée Français in Madrid and then in 1956 he left Spain for the United States where he entered the Valley Forge Military Academy in Wayne, Pennsylvania.

The oversight on the part of the Bulgarian authorities in the matter of abdication had, from his point of view, some useful as well as some strange results. Because Spain's ruler, the right-wing Franco, did not acknowledge or maintain diplomatic contacts with communist regimes, Simeon was accorded a degree of recognition as King of Bulgaria by the Spanish state. His coming of age in 1955 was marked by a solemn religious ceremony in Madrid attended, on behalf of the Spanish government, by three senior cabinet members: the foreign minister, the minister for the army and the minister of justice. He was also able to establish his own chancellery in Madrid.

In the world of diplomacy, formalities are significant and the dignity was important for a monarch dedicated to returning to constitutional power in his own country. One of the first acts of his majority was to swear to serve his people and to fulfil the constitution of his country – by which, of course, he meant the monarchical constitution.

Admitted to Valley Forge as Cadet No 6883, Simeon, although describing himself as King of Bulgaria for the discomfiture of traffic cops, adopted the incognito of a Mr Rilsky (the name of a Bulgarian saint, Ivan Rilsky) among his fellow cadets. However he had not abandoned a belief in his royal destiny. Graduating from Wayne in 1959, he married three years later Doña Margarita Gómez-Acebo y Cejuela, daughter of a distinguished Spanish aristocrat. The wedding was celebrated in three ceremonies, together redolent of the world of an exiled monarch obliged to conform with the laws of his host country but determined to respect the traditions of his homeland. The first was a Roman Catholic ceremony in the diocese of Madrid; in the second, on 21 January 1962, Simeon and Margarita were united in a civil ceremony in the town hall of Lausanne, in republican Switzerland, in the presence of guests who included Albania's Queen Mother Geraldine and her son, King Leka, and also King Farouk of Egypt who had been exiled following a military coup. It was Farouk who famously and mistakenly quipped 'Soon there will be only five kings left: Spades, Hearts, Diamonds, Clubs and England'. Perhaps he was mulling it over that day in Lausanne. Certainly the young couple whose union he witnessed were not, for on the following day they were joined in an Orthodox ceremony conducted in Bulgarian by an exiled priest. On that day the bridegroom rededicated himself to reestablishing the monarchy in his country. The eldest of their four sons, Prince Kardam of Saxe-Coburg, was, according to his passport, born on 2 December 1962. He was to be recognized as his father's heir to the Bulgarian crown with the historic title of Prince of Tirnovo. Over the next six years King Simeon and Queen Margarita had four more children, three sons and a daughter – Kyril (born in June 1964), Kubrat (November 1965), Konstantin-Assen (December 1967), and Kalina (January 1972).

Living in Madrid, from his royal chancellery in the city, assisted by a small and loyal staff, the king kept up active contacts with Bulgarian exiles throughout the world. Even during his country's communist years, he was convinced that there were many enthusiasts for a restoration of the monarchy in Bulgaria. And he may well have been right. In September 1974, more than twenty-five years after Simeon's expulsion, a Bulgarian court sentencing one Boris Arsov Iliev for 'counter-revolution-ary activities' described him as 'an inveterate monarchist'. Just possibly the man had been baptized in honour of Simeon's father; Boris, a common enough name in Slav countries, had particular resonance in Bulgaria.

Modern Bulgaria takes its name from Turkic tribes from the Volga region who crossed the Danube in the seventh century AD and subjugated the Slavic people who then inhabited the region. Under their khans these Bulgars continued a career of conquest against the Byzantine empire in the Balkans. Early in the ninth century Bulgarian forces took the Byzantine city of Sofia (still the country's capital) and even forced the Byzantine emperor in Constantinople to pay an annual tribute. Some fifty years later Khan Boris I adopted Orthodox Christianity and Sofia became an archbishopric subject to the patriarch in Constantinople. By this time the Turkic conquering minority had merged with the culture and language of the local Slavs (thus Bulgarian belongs to the Slavic family of languages). Bulgarian power reached its zenith under the younger son of Boris, Simeon I who abandoned the title of Khan in favour of that of Tsar. By the time of his death in 927 he had conquered most of what is today Serbia and had raised the archbishopric of Sofia to the status of an independent patriarchate. In addition to territorial conquest his reign also witnessed a golden age of culture and literature. It was with these ancient glories in mind that Boris had named his son Simeon. For in the decades which followed the death of Simeon I, this first Bulgarian empire succumbed to counter-attacks from Constantinople.

A second Bulgarian state, with its capital at Tirnovo where the ruins survived into the twentieth century, flourished from the late twelfth to the early fourteenth centuries but this in its turn succumbed first to the Serbia of Stefan Dushan and then to the Ottoman Turks. The Turkish empire was to rule in the Balkans for the next 500 years until, during the course of the nineteenth century, its power was severely eroded, thanks to the intervention of imperial Russia. At the Treaty of San Stefano in 1878 Russia forced Turkey to agree terms which confirmed an immense increase in Russian influence in the Balkans and which also defined the borders of a 'Greater Bulgaria' which included not only what we understand as Bulgaria today, but also most of modern Macedonia, parts of Serbia and large areas of northern Greece; it almost matched in extent the first Simeon's empire. It was recognized as an autonomous province within the Ottoman empire with its own prince. In fact, the great powers of western Europe forced a revision of the terms at the Congress of Berlin in July the same year. In 1999, 121 years later, it seemed to have settled nothing – perhaps not surprisingly. The conflict which had led up to these treaties had been sparked by Turkish atrocities against the Balkan Christians in which, it was reckoned, some 20,000 people were slaughtered. But in the event the Balkan peoples most concerned were treated dismissively by the Congress. The Turkish province of Bosnia and Hercegovina was given over to the protection of Austria; the Greater Bulgaria was split in two; Serbia and Romania were declared independent but denied the territories they considered most important to their interests. Russia even took Bessarabia from her 'ally' Romania. The Balkan states, independent or autonomous, would thenceforth seek their own solutions.

The 'Greater Bulgaria' proposed at San Stefano was to provide the rulers of the newly autonomous province a mark to aim at. The first Prince of Bulgaria, Alexander of Battenberg, a German by birth but a favourite nephew of the Russian Tsar, proved unequal to the manoeuvres of Balkan politics and, having angered St Petersburg, was removed and sent into exile. In 1887 he was replaced by another German prince, Ferdinand of Saxe-Coburg-Gotha, related through his mother to the French royal family of Bourbon Orléans and through his father to the family of Queen Victoria.

Born in 1861, King Simeon's grandfather, Prince Ferdinand of Saxe-Coburg-Gotha, was just twenty-six when he acceded as Prince of Bulgaria at the invitation of the Bulgarians and to the indignation of Russian and Turkey, neither of which were consulted. He was a tall, imposing figure even if, for most people, the first impression seems to have been a nose 'permanent like a cathedral' according to Princess Pauline Metternich. But Ferdinand, with an un-German sense of humour and an immense fortune thanks to an ancestor's marriage into a rich Hungarian noble family, never concerned himself with the opinions of others. Able, thanks to his wealth, to ameliorate the somewhat basic amenities of late nineteenth-century Sofia, and thanks to his cunning to navigate the currents of domestic politics and international diplomacy, he finally won St Petersburg's acceptance, even if the price was to have his baby son and heir, shrewdly named Boris with an eye to his adopted country's heroic past, confirmed also in the Orthodox faith. Tsar Nicholas II stood godfather to the child; Pope Leo XIII excommunicated the father for apostasy from Roman Catholicism; Ferdinand's outraged and pious consort, the French Princess Marie-Louise of Bourbon-Parma, left the court. She was to die three years later at the age of twenty-nine.

For his part, 'Foxy' Ferdinand as he was known in Europe's fashionable spas for his wit, and in its chancelleries for his deviousness, pursued his ambitions undeterred. His first aim was total independence from Constantinople and in 1908 an opportunity presented itself. That year was the sixtieth anniversary of the accession of the Austrian Emperor Francis Joseph II, whose chief minster Aehrenthal decided to honour the event by painlessly adding a new province to the empire, that of Bosnia Hercegovina. This was, of course, a part of the Turkish empire and came under Austrian administration merely as the result of the international mandate granted by the Congress of Berlin. It was also largely Muslim in religion and it was regarded by Belgrade as historically part of Greater Serbia. Austria's act of expropriation from an enfeebled Turkey not only prepared the ground for Sarajevo in 1914; it also more immediately helped provoke the revolt of the 'Young Turks' in Constantinople. As far as Ferdinand of Bulgaria was concerned, it was a godsend. Assuring Vienna of his support if needed and taking advantage of the turmoil in Turkey, in September 1908 he declared Bulgaria's full independence, adopted the title of Tsar in imitation of his ancient Bulgarian predecessors, made a triumphal entry into Sofia, and went in solemn procession to the medieval ruins at Tirnovo.

To his mind, all this was only a start. For this German princeling whom fate had brought to a Balkan throne believed his destiny was to recapture Constantinople itself, the ancient capital of Orthodoxy, for the Christian faith. For a time a fantasy portrait of him attired in the robes of a Byzantine emperor and entitled 'The Emperor of the East' hung in the cathedral of Sofia. But his dreams came to nothing and even the recovery of Macedonia proved beyond his machinations. When he joined Germany in the First World War in a last attempt at gaining the province, and when his imperial ally lost that war, the great game was over for Ferdinand. In October 1918 the Bulgarian royal train, more luxurious than even that of the Russian Tsars, steamed out of Sofia carrying into exile the eccentric, often ruthless, monarch accompanied by his younger son Kyril.

He was succeeded by the twenty-four-year old Boris who, unlike his father, spoke fluent Bulgarian, and who if he inherited a streak of ruthlessness and deviousness, was popular in a way his father had never been. His passion for railway engines meant that on occasion the citizenry found itself greeted by its monarch from the footplate. He hobnobbed with the leader of the Agrarian Party and seemed even to share its objectives. Its burly leader Stambolisky was moved to declare jovially: 'If we make the republic, we must keep Boris, for he would be the best of presidents.'[7] But, despite his easygoing image, Boris presided over an often repressive regime, and on 14 April 1925 he was the target of a determined attempt on his life. As the royal car negotiated a mountain defile a hail of bullets killed a passenger and immobilized the chauffeur. Seizing the steering wheel, King Boris ground the gears into reverse and backed off at speed down the narrow, dusty road. Then when the car rode up the stay cable of a telegraph pole, he flung himself into the roadside ditch. Round the bend came a post office bus. As the King ran on to the road, there was another burst of firing; but while the driver and passengers ran for cover, the King commandeered the bus, drove to the next township where he ordered the telegraph wires to Sofia to be cut, and hurried on to reach the capital before the news of the attempt could spread.

A few days later another attack on the royal regime caused one of the most horrific catastrophes in the history of political terrorism. As a distinguished congregation awaited the arrival of the royal party for a solemn commemorative service in Sofia cathedral, an immense explosion shook the huge building and the dome came crashing down killing some 200 people. Government reprisals approached terror proportions and Boris's visits abroad over the next two years were thought by some to be intended to evade revenge killers. In fact his regime seemed to some to be developing into a royal dictatorship.

The marriage in October 1930 of King Boris to Princess Giovanna (Ioanna, in Bulgarian) of Italy, daughter of King Victor Emmanuel III, seemed to link him with the dictatorial regime of Benito Mussolini. It was also to cause consternation in the Vatican. The pope approved the match on the express condition that any children be brought up as Catholics. In fact, the Catholic wedding ceremony in the church of Assisi was followed within the week by an Orthodox marriage in Sofia, and both children of the union, Princess Marie Louise born in January 1933 and Crown Prince Simeon born in June 1937, were baptized according to Orthodox rites.

In addition to his Bulgarian internal opposition, there was the festering problem of Macedonia – a continuing cause of contention with Yugoslavia since the 'freedom fighters' who for decades had virtually controlled the territory on the Bulgarian side of the border were suspected of being secretly supported by Yugoslavia. Boris had no wish for war but he wanted some kind of a settlement, if possible through private discussion with King Alexander of Yugoslavia. The choice of venue was the first hurdle but an ingenious solution was suggested by, of all people, King George V of Great Britain, when Boris was on a visit to Balmoral in 1933. The apparently bumbling, bearded patriarch was respected by those who knew him for his solid common sense. Why could not the two Balkan monarchs meet, as if by chance, as Boris travelling on the luxurious Orient Express, interrupted his journey to Sofia at the first-class waiting room on Belgrade railway station? King Alexander was wary. Yet the meeting was a success. Queen Ioanna embraced him at the unofficial welcome and her affectionate greeting struck the right note of informality. Such encounters do not, of course, change state policies but there was at least a thaw in relations between the heads of state, and the following year King Alexander made a state visit to Sofia.

The outbreak of war in Europe in September 1939 would engulf both Balkan monarchies in disaster. Neither his personal diplomacy nor his coolness under the fire of the assassin's carbine were sufficient in the firestorm that was in preparation for Boris. In his manoeuvrings to maintain his country's independence, the Tsar's courage and strength of will was to be seen in his dealings with Hitler. But it was not enough to save his dynasty or his country from the realities of geopolitics.

In the end these same realities forced the nine-year-old Simeon into exile. He, his mother and sister left Bulgaria with just $200 in cash, but the future was not unkind to them. Following his cosmopolitan education King Simeon became a successful citizen of the world – in his own words 'a jack-of-all trades, primarily interested in business, banking and politics'.[8] He made a successful career in the first two, with residences in Madrid and Switzerland. At an age of retirement for the average businessman the King remained hopeful of a third career in his third primary interest, politics 'which', as he once observed to the author, 'some call statesmanship'. He has never lost faith in the possibility of a restoration. In 1979 at a banquet held in his honour in London he declared: 'We Bulgarians look confidently to the future, convinced that freedom, justice and welfare will finally triumph in our land.' Just ten years later, with the fall of the communist regime, it did not seem impossible that the fulfilment of that dream might come under the royal aegis.

But Simeon's responses to the sensational turn of events in 1989–1990 were uncertain. He was honest enough to admit that he was as astonished as anyone else. During the long years of the communist establishment, he had once confessed that he saw no hope of returning. Now his first reaction was a wish to return to the multi-party, republican and democratic Bulgaria as a citizen. A year later he was speaking of terminating his exile in Madrid to return to Bulgaria with the prospect of resuming the crown. In June 1991 it was announced that he was planning to visit Bulgaria in the wake of the constitutional referendum. Apparently the authorities in Sofia could see no objection and were quite prepared to issue a new passport. The foreign ministry went out of its way to emphasize that the King had not been stripped of his citizenship at any time and a passport was issued the same month. In fact this visit did not take place. No explanation was given, but that may have been because at that time the authorities were not prepared to issue passports either to Queen Margarita or to Crown Prince Kardam until they applied for Bulgarian nationality (both were Spanish by birth). Probably, like any other tourist, they could have had their passports stamped with a visa. But this, according to Juan Balansó, was the whole point. At that time the King could not adjust to the idea of returning as a tourist.

But times move on. Years of communist abuse of the monarchy could not be erased overnight. Queen Margarita had a happy and successful life in Madrid society. Their children had good careers in medicine and banking, which they no doubt saw little reason to abandon on the chance of an uncertain future in a near-bankrupt country with unstable constitutional prospects. Crown Prince Kardam, Prince of Tirnovo was based in the United States and was an expert in agricultural science, yet to his father's delight he found time to learn something of the Bulgarian language. For his part, the King averred that he was too patriotic and too convinced of his historic role in the divine plan, and moreover too law-abiding, to contemplate any kind of dubious stratagem to regain his throne. At this time he was even arguing against a referendum on the monarchy in favour of a rigorous constitutionalism. Should the parliament as the organ of the popular will issue an invitation, then that would be the time to consider the option of restoration. There were too those, it must be said, who wondered whether in truth he might not in fact be quite content with his life as it was.

In 1990 a solemn Mass in memory of Boris III was celebrated at the St Ivan Rilsky monastery by the Patriarch of the Bulgarian Orthodox Church in the presence of a huge crowd. King Simeon, former 'Cadet Rilsky', was also present in spirit through a message which he had sent to be read at the ceremony. It ended with words that sum up Simeon's credo as to the place of an historic monarchy in the life of a nation: 'A country that has no past has no future.' The ceremony concluded with the restoration to its place of honour of a portrait effigy of the King's father, which had been erected in the monastery forty-seven years previously and had lain hidden from the eyes of the authorities during the communist years. In 1990 the return of the King in person seemed unacceptably premature, but in May 1996, all problems over visas and passports having been at last resolved, he did return and this time he did visit the Rilsky monastery where his father's heart had been solemnly interred in the presence of his mother, Queen Ioanna three years previously. Reports on the three-week visit conflicted. The official Bulgarian media downplayed the event, refusing the King even the courtesy of a royal title, referring instead to 'Simeon Saxe-Coburg-Gothsky'. Foreign press reports which took their lead from the Bulgarian news agency spoke of hundreds of people lining the route from the airport, whereas eyewitnesses reported hundreds of thousands; and at least one photograph of the welcome in Sofia's main square showed it packed with thousands of ecstatic supporters with, at their head, a banner portrait of the King.

The attitude of the international establishment was ambivalent. While Russian TV news seemed favourable, referring throughout its reports to 'His Majesty King Simeon', the visit of an official of the International Monetary Fund to Sofia during the first days of the visit, to announce details of a financial package of aid to the Bulgarian economy, detracted from the impact of the royal presence. The government media and government ministers were able to divert attention from the royal news story and some commentators speculated that the IMF intervention was not merely the result of confidence. Most intriguing of all was the summary of the eventful visit to 'our country' given by the King in his open 'letter to the Bulgarian people' republished 'in reply to numerous requests' on the King's Internet website (simbul@mad.servicom.es) in 1998. From this it is clear that it was a very emotional time for Simeon and Queen Margarita but the subtext of this highly diplomatic account is of an immensely successful royal progress.

Similar scenes occurred elsewhere in the country during the three-week tour which followed. The chaotic royal entry into Sofia was heralded by the pealing of the cathedral's bells for most of the day. The following day King Simeon and Queen Margarita were the guests of the president at lunch and of the mayor of Sofia at dinner. However, many government ministers seem to have avoided the various functions and receptions staged to honour the royals, and the prime minister tended to field rather than answer questions on the visit. The republican establishment had some grounds to be wary on the monarchy issue. The country's prospects were uncertain, a sizeable body of opinion distrusted both the motives and the competence of their politicians, and many more were looking wistfully for a national saviour. It is the context in which pretenders have traditionally flourished, but Simeon of Bulgaria, a shrewd man of the world, had no intention of adopting the role of white knight. Later he was to reveal that there had been half a million people in the streets of Sofia. To some it seemed an opportunity of restoration had been presented which had been missed. Simeon, who described monarchist parties as 'a nonsense' preferred to stress unity and consensus and rejected the role of what he called in an interview with Neal Ascherson of the *Observer* 'a rabble rouser'.

The authorities had some difficulty in controlling the demonstrations of enthusiasm which in some cases, to the King's regret, resulted in the kind of 'disorder, even injuries which are inevitable when huge crowds gather'. This is as far as the King himself went in referring to what were clearly at times ugly incidents, but on at least one occasion, according to eyewitnesses, he vaulted out of the official car to stop a security man beating up a too enthusiastic spectator who was old enough to remember the days of the monarchy. It is also clear that, despite his meticulous respect for the conventions of protocol and his care not to lay himself open to the charge of interfering in Bulgarian affairs, he was equally determined to give the impression of a constitutional sovereign expressing the proper and traditional sentiments without infringing the conventions that govern relations between a government and a constitutional monarch.

This was, indeed, the impression conveyed with some skill in King Simeon's website message. The references to a 'constant stream of goodwill' etc seem to express more than the formalities of royal graciousness, while the claim that the streets were filled with many cheering people and that he and Queen Margarita were deluged by flowers and bouquets were verifiable to anyone who was present or knew people who had been present. (At one provincial centre it was estimated that 20 per cent of the population had turned out to welcome the royal couple, while the gifts they received during the three-week visit were so numerous that a plane had to be chartered to transport them to the family home in Madrid.) The opening 'thank you's' to the president, to the Bulgarian Orthodox Church and its Patriarch, and the warm welcome extended by the clergy wherever the royal party went, to the local authorities and the organizers of the various receptions, all sound banal to anyone familiar with the pronouncements of royal heads of state, but there were telling and unexpected details and emphases. The goodwill shown helped to erase the sad memories of 'a half century in exile' – an exile during which he was the target of at least one assassination attempt and was traduced as a traitor to the people and a CIA agent.

The King thanked those of his fellow Bulgarians who came 'from near or afar' and so helped make his homecoming a significant event which impressed the whole world. That conventional word 'homecoming' was, in this context, unwontedly vibrant. These and other such textual details produced a cumulative effect of a conventional piece of upbeat royal morale-raising – no small achievement for a monarch who was not recognized as such by the government of the country. In fact the skilfully drafted open letter even managed to suggest that the King's itinerary was subject to unwelcome restrictions. Given the limited time he had in the country, there were, of course, 'many towns and places' the King 'so much wished to visit'. But there was a hint of some factor other than mere pressure of time when the King said that it had proved 'impossible' for reasons which those 'who had followed the tour closely' would understand.

A celebration does not make a restoration. In the meantime, Simeon of Bulgaria maintained the presence and dignity of his office in the context of the late twentieth century. Inheriting his father's wry sense of humour, he did not allow formalities to interfere with the efficient conduct of business. However, as a monarch he recognized the importance of protocol. Perhaps for that reason it was his son Prince Kubrat and his wife who attended the wedding of Archduke Georg of Austria to the Duchess Eilika of Oldenburg in St Stephen's basilica in Budapest in October 1997.

The ceremony itself was surely among the most telling examples of the revived enthusiasm for monarchy in the former communist world, as well as a notable and significant event in the centuries-old epic of the Habsburg family. The following month Kubrat's parents attended the royal occasion of the decade when they joined a host of other crowned heads to celebrate the golden wedding anniversary of the Queen and the Duke of Edinburgh. Themselves married for some thirty-five years, did Simeon and Margarita perhaps speculate on the possibility that they might hold their own golden anniversary as the restored constitutional monarchs of Simeon's homeland?

Probably such thoughts would remain in the realm of nostalgia rather than anything more practical. In interview with Juan Balansó in the early 1990s, Simeon admitted to something of a Jekyll and Hyde personality. In the United States, which he used to visit on business, he tended to be Mr Saxony-Coburg, senior executive in a major European hotel group; the same was true even in Madrid and Switzerland where he has residence. And yet he had never abandoned his title and, as the decade progressed, he continued assiduously in the service of his country, making a number of visits rather like a politician nursing a constituency. On a visit to Pernik, for example, some thirty kilometres from the capital, he took time off to go down the coal mine there, wearing the regulation hard hat and pressing the proffered flesh.

Over the Orthodox Christmas and New Year holidays of 1998–99 Simeon, accompanied by Queen Margarita and their daughter Princess Kalina, made a private visit to Sofia. Once more the crowds where enthusiastic and on this occasion the King had a meeting with President Petar Stoyanov. He took the opportunity to expand on his constant theme since the fall of communism: that his only wish was to 'calm and unite people' and to cooperate in promoting a positive image of Bulgaria in the world at large. After the long decades of exile King Simeon must have been particularly happy to be able to pass the holiday period at the palace of Sitniakovo in the southwest of the country which, in accordance with the Bulgarian government's policy of restitution to exiles and expatriates returning to the country after the overthrow of the communist regime, had recently been restored to the King for his personal use, together with the Urana palace in Sofia and the nineteenth-century Tzarska Bistritza summer palace.

There was little doubt as to the King's personal popularity. At the beginning of the 1990s opinion surveys had shown almost 30 per cent in favour of a straight restoration of the monarchy and more than 50 per cent who said, according to the king's own report, that they 'wouldn't mind Simeon coming back'. An opinion survey in 1996 had shown as many as 40 per cent of the sample in favour of his standing in the next presidential elections.

The results of the 1997 election were, in their way, flattering to royalist hopes. A respectable minority of the members of the winning coalition, the Union of Democratic Forces, was said to be interested in the idea of restoring the monarchy as an institution while the monarchy party, campaigning on a straight restoration ticket, polled 8 per cent of the total vote. The King himself was less interested in party politicking, more in practical participation. To most voters, President Stoyanov seemed a safe pair of hands and the problems posed by a major change in the constitution too great a risk. Even so, observers did not write off royalist chances; in a country with a decade of change behind it, and where few options seemed closed, traditionalist solutions too deserved to be considered.

The Bulgarians themselves seemed to have an ambivalent attitude to the man many call 'Simeon'. Abroad, like others of his species, he continued to exercise his skills at official public functions. In July 1999, for example, he and Queen Margarita, who also speaks Bulgarian fluently, assisted Queen Beatrix of the Netherlands at the opening of an exhibition of modern Bulgarian sculpture as part of the cultural exchange between the two countries. At home, whether in his Spanish residence in Madrid receiving members of parliament or other prominent figures in Bulgarian public life, or on his visits to Bulgaria itself, he continued to play an active role in the national life. In the autumn of 1999, he took advantage of an invitation to participate in a symposium on 'Religion, Science and the Environment', focusing on the ecological disaster being created on the Danube and held on a Romanian river cruiser, to make an unofficial private visit to various riverside Bulgarian townships. The trip was reported in London's *Observer* newspaper by journalist Neal Ascherson. At each stop the King was showered with gifts as he had been during the 1996 visit, and bundles of petitions – some perhaps from the unemployed simply demanding that he find them work since the authorities had failed to do so, others perhaps asking for his good offices in arranging treatment abroad for a sick child. Bulgarian journalists came on board with questions on the main political and economic problems facing the country as well as foreign policy issues. His private comment on the economic sabotage caused by Nato's bombing of the Danube bridges that April was 'wanton stupidity and arbitrary destruction'. At the town of Lom, where more than a century earlier his grandfather had taken possession of the principality as it then was, local elections had returned a pro-Simeon politician as mayor. More than seven hours behind schedule, the river boat did not arrive until an hour before dawn; roused from his sleep by his jubilant supporters Simeon gamely went ashore to join the party.

In Sofia, together with his sister Princess Marie Louise, he announced the family's donation to the Bulgarian people of a magnificent estate near the capital, among the properties restored by the democratic regime. Developed by King Ferdinand as one of Europe's great botanical gardens, it was to be opened after renovation and restoration work in the year 2000. The visit was extensively covered in the Bulgarian media, but perhaps yet more interesting were the King's meetings with leading politicians. Both sides were anxious to reduce the ideological spin surrounding such encounters in the past. Both wished to encourage a perception of 'business as usual' in a normal democratic context. Relations between the monarch and his country seemed to be warm and mutually approving as the dawn of the new millennium approached.

Variously known as 'Simeon' or 'the King' by his compatriots, he was happy to be able to serve his country as a kind of hereditary first citizen, so to speak. Reluctant to regard himself as an 'ex' king, he admits to adopting the Boy Scouts' motto of 'Be Prepared'. Courteous by nature, almost deferential in manner, his receding hairline, high forehead, keen blue eyes and trim designer beard give him the aspect of a wise, friendly but inquisitive elf. Continuously interested in every aspect of life, his natural modesty of manner concealed a diversity of talents. Fluent in Bulgarian and English as well as Europe's four principal languages, together with some Portuguese and Arabic, he had had a successful international business career before becoming, to use his own words, the 'moderator' or 'father confessor' of his people.

In his professional life, using the name Simeon Saxe-Coburg-Gothsky or Count Rilsky, he always regarded the name of 'Bulgaria' as something sacred and in no sense his own personal possession; if he made mistakes, then they went no further than the private citizen Simeon Borisov. Allowing himself only five and a half hours sleep, in his mid-sixties at the turn of the century he kept up a punishing schedule of travel, reading and official engagements with a constant commitment to keeping abreast of events in Bulgaria. During the 1990s it was not unusual for Bulgarian parliamentary deputies to seek his opinion and advice on contemporary issues and problems. He is a king without a crown but most definitely with a function – an instance of the ancient institution of monarchy once more demonstrating its capacity for adaptation and innovation.

7

ROMANIAN EXILE

In April 1992 King Michael of Romania returned to his native country to attend Easter Mass; he was cheered by a crowd of more than 200,000 people. The visit was not unprepared. In September 1990 the king's daughters Sophie and Margarita had toured Moldavia and Romanian Transylvania to see for themselves the extent of the deprivations and suffering left by the horrors of the Ceausescu tyranny. Michael himself, who had always said he would not return without the assurance that Romanians wished him to, seems to have felt that the mood in the country was sympathetic to the royal family, and he made a flying visit there in 1990. Romanian public opinion on the question of monarchy proved difficult to read. The National Liberal Party urged him to stand in the presidential elections; the King refused; the party won no seats in the national assembly. Whether its failure was to be attributed to its approach to the monarch, or to his refusal, was difficult to decide. During the long communist years King Michael had always maintained that he would return to constitutional office only as king. It seemed clear that he would not compromise to accept a presidency, even if it were to be offered to him. This fact alone made the restoration of the Romanian royal house to a place in the country's constitutional life distinctly problematical. A sadness for the King and for the country for, since the proclamation of the independent kingdom of Romania in 1881, Michael could be described as the best head of state the country never had.

The serious-minded monarch, whom photographers almost always most caught with a characteristic look of harrowed introspection on his handsome face, had the interests of his country close to his heart from boyhood. On the rare occasions that king and subjects met, they reciprocated his patent honesty of intent with rapturous demonstrations of affection. For despite his taciturnity, King Michael is a man of deep warmth with, in the words if Ileana, Princess of Romania, Archduchess of Austria, 'a most enchanting smile. It brings with it deep dimples that are almost disconcerting in the face of a man so serious and given to so few words.'[9] The enthusiastic crowds of Easter 1992 must have numbered among them a few of the King's generation who remembered and had perhaps participated in the manifestations of loyalty which greeted him as a young man in the streets of Bucharest. In those months of hope between the end of the Second World War and the onset of the communist regime, the twenty-four-year-old king embodied for many Romanians the possibility of a future. But in January 1948 he was forced into exile after a reign of seven years. It was in fact his second reign, inaugurated by a right-wing coup which had ousted his father King Carol II, and it is impossible to understand the hectic and unhappy early life of Michael without a look at the career of his playboy parent.

The origins of the Romanian monarchy were somewhat erratic. During the Middle Ages the territory of modern Romania was occupied by the principalities of Moldavia and Wallachia and parts of Transylvania; it was conquered in the fifteenth century to become part of the Turkish empire. In the late sixteenth century Prince Michael the Brave defied Turkish rule and briefly united Wallachia and Moldavia as an independent fiefdom. After his death Transylvania came under the Austrian Habsburg rulers of Hungary, while the other two provinces reverted to rule by Turkish-appointed governors. In 1812 tsarist Russia forced the Turks to cede Bessarabia, a border province of Moldavia, which has remained a bone of international contention ever since. Defeat in the Crimean War in the 1850s meant that Russia had to concede southern Bessarabia back to Turkish Moldavia. In 1861 Wallachia and Moldavia proclaimed themselves as the 'United principality of Romania' within the Turkish empire. Five years later they elected as their ruler Prince Karl Eitel of the German princely house of Hohenzollern-Sigmaringen. Romania's powerful neighbour Austria-Hungary was not happy about the development. Prince Carol (the Romanian form of his name) had to travel incognito to Bucharest from Vienna on a Danube steamer, adopting the identity of a Swiss businessman complete with passport.

In 1877 he allied with Russia in a war against Turkey, achieving the important victory of Plevna and so saving the Russian forces from a humiliating defeat. At the Congress of Berlin in 1878 Romania received international recognition of her full independence, but despite Plevna, was obliged to yield southern Bessarabia to Russia. In March 1881 Romania's politicians declared the country a kingdom, its Prince a King. Carol I celebrated his coronation with a ceremony in which he placed on his own head the steel crown forged from metal from one of the cannon at the field of Plevna.

Established by referendum, invested by a Turkish sultan, crowned by administrative decree, Carol brought a new element to the somewhat exotic image of Romania's fledgling monarchy by his marriage to the colourful Elizabeth von Wied, well known to Europe's fashionable reading public for her books and poems under the name of Carmen Sylva. Her only child, a daughter, died in infancy and King Carol decided to adopt as heir his nephew Ferdinand. The young man dutifully abandoned Roman Catholicism for Orthodoxy, thus outraging his family, mastered the rudiments of the Romanian language and was bundled off to Berlin via the courts of Holland and Belgium to find a suitably royal mate. His choice, made at the Kaiser's court, fell on Marie, the daughter of Alfred Duke of Edinburgh and of Saxe-Coburg-Gotha, one of the sons of Queen Victoria. He was also a sovereign in his own right, since Saxe-Coburg-Gotha remained one of the independent territories in the German imperial federation created by Bismarck who spared this particular toy-town duchy dissolution on the grounds that it was 'Europe's royal stud farm'. Through her mother Marie of Russia, the Princess, who had been brought up to expect a crown, was also descended from the tsars. She was, then, undoubtedly royal, but whether she was a suitable in-law for the imperious King Carol I of Romania was another question. From the day of her marriage, this tall blue-eyed blonde of regal bearing effortlessly overshadowed her gauche spouse and proved far less biddable to Uncle Carol's whims. Nor did she see eye to eye with the Queen who prided herself that, thanks to her, Bucharest was known as Little Paris and who found her literary standing at court now had a rival – for Marie too wrote poetry.

In 1893 Marie gave birth to a son (the future Carol II). In 1914, only weeks after the outbreak of the Great War, Carol I died, Marie's husband succeeded as Ferdinand I, and she became Queen. Overriding Ferdinand's pro-German sentiments, she and the government persuaded him to enter the war on the side of the western Allies. The result was a military disaster and a forced armistice. However, in the last days of the war Romania was able to re-join the winning Allied cause and 'retake' sizeable territories from her neighbours. At the subsequent peace treaties these successes, notably Bessarabia, were confirmed. The Queen of Romania, with her twenty-room suite at the Paris Ritz and what one might call her 'diplomatic wardrobe' of sixty gowns, with hats and furs in proportion, became one of the celebrities of the peace conference and boosted Romania's international image in the style-conscious 1920s. Whether thanks to the Queen's couturiers or to the less flamboyant skills of her diplomatic corps and the intervention even of the King, Romania emerged from the peace settlement with the greatest territorial extent in its history. The prospects for post-war Romania looked bright, but within the palace a maelstrom was stirring. The heir to the throne had presumed to choose his own wife.

Passionately in love with Giovanna, 'Zizi' Lambrino, the daughter of a prosperous upper-class family, Prince Carol deserted his regiment and secretly married her. He issued a statement to the

The wedding of the Hapsburg Archduke Karl of Austria, for monarchist devotees His Imperial and Royal Highness, heir to the thrones of Austria and Hungary, and Francesca Thyssen–Bornemisza in 1993.

The service preceding the solemn interment of the remains of Tsar Nicholas II and members of the Russian Imperial family, St Petersburg 17 July 1998.

The former Greek king, Constantin II, with Queen Elizabeth II and Princess Margaret, among the spectators at an English country event.

The wedding of Prince Pavlos of Greece, for monarchists Duke of Sparta and heir to the Greek throne, with American born Marie Chantal Miller, London July 1995.

The christening of Prince Konstantinos Alexios of Greece, son of Crown Prince and Princess Pavlos, in London's Greek Orthodox Cathedral, April 1988.

The remains of King Nicholas I and Queen Milena who died in exile in Italy are re-interred at the Cipur Monastery in Montenegro 1 October 1989 in the presence of Crown Prince Nikola.

Simeon II of Bulgaria in 1945 at the Rila Monastery with his mother
Queen Ioanna and his sister Princess Marie-Louise, they are escorted by the abbot.

Boris III of Bulgaria on a motoring tour in Spring 1943 with his children,
Princess Marie-Louise and Prince Simeon.

King Simeon and Princess Marie-Louise of Bulgaria photographed here with the choir of a Sofia church during a visit in 1999.

Crown Prince Alexander and Princess Catarina of Yugoslavia arrive as guests for the wedding of Princess Alexia of Greece to the Spanish architect Carlos Morales Quintana, July 1999.

political parties of Romania that he wished to renounce the throne. On his father's orders the Prince was placed under what amounted to house arrest. The world press revelled in the story. Meanwhile Madame Lambrino was delivered of a son, Mircea-Gregory (recognized by his father but not by the palace) and left for Paris with the promise of a respectable annual pension. In the view of the palace, the marriage had no dynastic validity. Members of the royal family required the permission of the King before they could marry, and King Ferdinand had not given his permission. Prince Carol was obliged to agree to an annulment. In 1921 he married Princess Helena of Greece, his sister-in-law (Crown Prince George of the Hellenes having married Carol's sister Elizabeth): on 25 November the same year a son was born to the princely couple. He was named Michael (Romanian, Mihaï) after the archangel, champion of good against evil and in tribute to Prince Michael the Brave.

Even while his Queen was pregnant with their child, Prince Carol had gone missing once more from court, this time with a bewitching redhead Iliena, known as 'Magda', Lupescu, whose presence was to haunt the rest of the reign. In 1925, Carol would be forced to renounce his rights to the succession. Meanwhile letters arrived from the volunteer exile, sometimes incoherent, sometimes announcing his intention of disappearing off the face of the earth, or at least of living the rest of his life incognito. Carol seems never to have concerned himself with the impact on his family of his flamboyant infidelity, which lasted the rest of his life. The wounds inflicted on his son never healed. In 1992, talking to his French biographer Philippe Viguié Desplaces for his book *Le règne inachevé* ('The unfinished reign') to which this chapter is greatly indebted, the seventy-year-old monarch opened his sad heart: 'Even today I cannot explain ... my father's behaviour. He claimed, particularly in public that he "loved me", that he "would take care of me", that he "missed me a lot". But if that was true, why had my mother and I been abandoned?'[10]

The secret police tracked down the Crown Prince and Lupescu first to Paris, then to Milan. Probably her greatest offence was to be a Jew, though it was rumoured that senior government politicians had paid Lupescu to keep the Crown Prince out of Bucharest. Carol himself wrote to his mother, Queen Marie, from Milan renouncing his claim to the crown in favour of marriage to his mistress. With King Ferdinand's health failing, arrangements were made for a council of regency and the five-year-old Prince Michael was declared heir apparent. Carol and Lupescu divided their time between Paris and the casinos of the French Riviera – a suite was permanently reserved for them at the Hotel Negresco in Nice. In Paris they maintained a luxury apartment on the boulevard Bineau at Neuilly, where Magda cooked some Romanian speciality for the midday meal fearing, reasonably enough, that the servants were probably in the pay of the Romanian secret police.

When King Ferdinand finally died on 20 July 1927 he was succeeded by his six-year-old grandson Michael. Sad and serious, the boy, advised by a regency council controlled by the prime minister, could only sit and hope, as he would later recall, that some miracle might deliver him from the intrigues of the palace to let him begin his boyhood.

But there were intrigues going on abroad too. On the death of his father Carol had published an announcement in the French newspaper *Le Matin* describing himself as a patriot wishing to be of use to his country and to answer its call. In 1928, impatient for the call, Carol fell in with a plot for a coup d'état. This involved flying from an aerodrome in England to Alba Julia, the town where his parents had been crowned. Once there, he and thousands of supporters were to march on Bucharest while airforce planes scattered leaflets carrying the royal manifesto. Unfortunately Carol was arrested by Scotland Yard officers as he entered the airfield.

Then in 1930 the Peasant Party came to power and invited Carol II to return on condition that he broke with Lupescu and agreed to live with Queen Helena. On 5 June 1930 Carol left their home in Normandy at the wheel of a powerful limousine, destination Munich. There he boarded a little open-cockpit plane to head for Romania. As it climbed to clear the final hurdle of the wooded slopes of the Carpathian mountains on the border of Romania, the engine backfired and then cut out. Somehow the pilot managed an emergency landing in a clearing on the Romanian side of the mountains. In due course Carol arrived in Bucharest. Three days later the national assembly, against the opposition of the liberals, formally deprived the nine-year-old Michael of the crown and invested his father with it. After two years, ten months and nineteen days the first, albeit titular, reign of King Michael I of Romania had come to an end. According to the deal done with his father, the family should now have been reunited. But Queen Helena refused to go back on her divorce from Carol of 1928, took no part in the coronation and, worse still for Michael, lost custody of her son. Within days of these traumatic events the boy learnt, with the whole of Bucharest, that his father's mistress was back in the capital installed in her own residence.

There she became the centre of an unofficial court of bankers, industrialists and courtiers of the King. Carol, hoping to drive the Queen into exile, openly encouraged the court to treat her with slights and insolence. He tyrannized his family, refusing his brother Nicholas permission to marry because his fiancée was a divorcee, and promoted sycophants and favourites. As he entered his teens Michael, the former king, often to be seen in public wearing a beret like the Straja Tsarei, the youth movement founded by his father, had to watch helpless these humiliations of his mother and his uncle. Meanwhile the red-headed *maîtresse en titre* queened it over her coterie, dispensing patronage to her family and extorting money from Carol's cronies at poker parties where the stakes were astronomical and any serious thoughts of winning were, in career terms, suicidal.

As the banks failed and government salaries diminished, some minor officials ceased to be paid altogether – as did the lower ranks of the army. But the army faced other problems too. One colonel was not too worried about the troops – they could live off the country; nor about the officers – they were doing nicely enough seducing rich women; the real question was: how to feed the horses?

Behind such bizarreries stalked realities which were terrible enough. While King Carol's secret police, worthy ancestors of Ceausescu's *Securitate*, terrorized in private, the green-shirted Iron Guards of Cornelius Codreanu's anti-Semitic, fascist Legion of the Archangel Michael, flaunted their power on the streets of the capital with impunity.

For a time, Michael escaped the hectic world of Bucharest for the more peaceful pace of London when he attended the coronation of George VI. He had a room in Buckingham Palace for a week, but he decided to prolong his stay and took rooms in a central London hotel. This, like any deviation from the prearranged programme, was reported back to his father by his equerries, who spied on him as a matter of course. Carol, who even fretted when the boy went into long trousers, was always aware of his son as a rival – after all he had, so to speak, usurped the crown from him.

In 1938 Queen Marie died, despairing at the condition of her country. In November that year Michael returned to London with his father on a state visit. Riding through the streets in the state landau they made an odd couple, this king and ex king, the boy's beret perched somewhat incongruously above a dress tunic studded with medals and stars while his father played the role of monarch in his German-style plumed cavalry helmet. Lupescu did not go with them, to her great chagrin. The Romanian government was utterly opposed and the idea of an official royal mistress receiving, so to speak, diplomatic recognition in post-Edward VIII London was out of the question.

But she joined them on their return, in Paris. Here Carol took a suite for the three of them in the Hotel Meurice. Michael later recalled that he contrived to have virtually nothing to do with her. Father and son were taken hunting by President Lebrun at Rambouillet where Michael, an increasingly capable marksman, found the game was not so splendid as in Transylvania. After Paris they travelled to Berchtesgarten in Bavaria, where they were received by Hitler.

From the railhead it was a pretty long journey by car up into the mountains to the Eagle's Nest. The German Chancellor was awaiting his guests at the base of the monumental staircase that swept up to the house. There they entered the grand salon with a picture window extending the length of an entire wall, giving a magnificent panorama. Almost immediately Carol and Hitler withdrew into the Führer's study. The German officials took Michael up to the very summit in Hitler's famous Mercedes, and then in a lift which ascended inside the rock.

During the meeting Hitler apparently proposed to finance Carol if he would get rid of Lupescu and release the imprisoned Codreanu. The Romanian refused. In fact, soon after his return to Bucharest Codreanu and his lieutenants were shot by a police escort 'while trying to escape'. It was assumed in Germany that the police had been acting on the orders of King Carol. In any case, Hitler took it as a personal affront. Ten months later came the assassination of the Romanian prime minister, Armand Calinescu.

The news broke in dramatic fashion over the radio at lunchtime. Carol and Michael, like thousands of other Romanians, heard the regular programme interrupted by shouting in the background and then nothing. 'I remember it as if it were yesterday,' recalled the King when describing the event to Vignie Desplaces decades later. A distraught courtier burst into the dining room with the words: '*Armand est mort.*'[11] Having killed their man, the assassins had dashed to the radio station to announce the coup, but the alert official broadcast monitor had cut the transmission. The killers were overpowered and summarily executed with a bullet in the back of the neck. That night, before going to bed, in a rare moment of intimacy with his son, Carol warned the boy to be prepared for the death of his father since he and Lupescu were probably next on the hit list. The following year, 1938, King Carol established the Front for the Rebirth of the Nation with its blue tunics and fascist salute. Intended as a counterweight to the Iron Guard, it was in fact seen as an arm of a burgeoning royal dictatorship.

But Carol seemed more interested in his mistress and fanciful new uniforms for his army than in up-dating his military hardware. Between the German hammer and the Russian anvil, Romania's position would be precarious indeed if it should come to war; the Ribbentrop-Molotov Pact of August 1939 between Germany and Russia in fact made matters worse. Free of the threat of Russian intervention, Hitler invaded Poland. In June Russia ordered Romania out of Bessarabia and then, by the Diktat of Vienna, Hitler made over northern Transylvania to Hungary. Without a shot being fired the Greater Romania of 1919 was deprived of a vast tranche of territory. Carol felt powerless to react. In fact, he sided with Germany.

On 2 September 1940 there was a massive demonstration outside the royal palace, organized by the Iron Guard and partisans of General Ion Antonescu, a former war minister. The King had lost the confidence of the army and within the week Antonescu was able to force him to withdraw in favour of his son. Decades later in his book, *Le règne inachevé*, King Michael recalled how, in the morning of 7 September, after a sleepless night, he was roused by a telephone call to present himself at the palace to take the oath to the constitution. Half asleep he found himself confronting Antonescu flanked by a crowd of dignitaries, among them the minister of the army and the Patriarch. He duly swore his dedication to his country and his people, an oath which he was always to consider binding. Dazed by exhaustion and the speed of events he also set his signature to a document which purported to confirm ex-King Carol's concession of full powers to the General. Two days later Carol left the country for Franco's Spain. Millions of dollars worth of treasure the fallen monarch had plundered from his country was never recovered.

Public opinion welcomed the return of the young King and with him the Queen Mother. Escorted by cavalry troopers they rode in the state coach to the palace through crowded streets, the windows crammed with spectators. After a brief rest they went out into the streets of the capital, occasionally turning into the stores and shops to shake people's hands. An early royal walkabout, in fact. But in reality little was changed. Where the boy King had been mascot to the ship of state, the nineteen-year-old was merely the figurehead. Antonescu was in control.

Michael withdrew to the palace of Sinaia. He liked to tour the countryside at the wheel of his car, stopping off here and there to chat to the locals and visiting Bucharest only when 'summoned' (his word) by Antonescu who was now governing by decree. When his country declared war on the Soviet Union in 1941, following the German example, the King first heard the news on the BBC World Service.

Now in his twenties, he still had his movements watched by aides appointed by his chief minister, just as his father had monitored his every move during his boyhood. But Antonescu also kept a close eye on the King's private accounts – understandably so, perhaps, in view of his father's peculation with the national funds, though a complete misreading of Michael's character which was always devoted to his royal duty. The minister's attitude to the Queen appears to have been a mixture of uneasy respect and suspicion. He mistrusted her confirmed anglophilia, mother and son spoke English habitually, even in his presence, but he always treated her with the utmost correctness.

There was, of course, little that mother and son could do to affect government policy. But in one vital area, it seems they did have an effect. In his autobiography the King proudly describes how he refused to countenance legislation requiring Jews to wear the yellow star, and claims that to the best of his knowledge not a single Jew was surrendered to the Germans by Romanian authorities.

Despite the close surveillance of his activities, Michael was determined to subvert his government's pro-Axis policies. In 1943 he sent secret emissaries to investigate the possibility of a separate peace treaty between Romania and the Allies. In addition they made practical proposals to inform on German troop dispositions if the West planned paratroop landings. There was no response. In fact, Churchill had probably already decided on trading Romania as a Soviet 'sphere of influence' after the war, in exchange for

Greece as a British sphere. The fact that these tentative approaches failed is perhaps less remarkable than the fact that this inexperienced young man, continually spied upon, was able to go so far. Antonescu simply underrated him, reassuring the Gestapo, who *were* suspicious, that the King was 'just a kid'. The royal 'kid' and his co-conspirators, who were collected in an unmarked car and delivered to a hidden entrance behind the palace, were soon meeting twice a month in the royal apartments. They even had secret radio facilities. The King's secretary, one of the few reliable members of his staff, had a reliable contact in the foreign office cipher department responsible for decoding all messages. Those for Antonescu went to Antonescu, those for the King went to the King!

In 1944, astonishingly, he was able to carry out a coup d'état against his collaborationist regime. On 23 August Antonescu received an invitation for an audience of the King at about four in the afternoon. A group of junior officers had been stationed in an inner room with orders to rush out on a pre-arranged signal. With the King was a general who was in the plot. When Antonescu arrived ('late as usual', the King wryly recalled) he was asked to break with Germany and to make a separate armistice with Russia. He refused. The general mildly observed that they would have to find another government. Furious, Antonescu demanded to know whether they aimed to leave the fate of the country in the hands of a child. Now the King raising his voice, gave the cue for the officers in the inner room. They burst in and snapped to attention in front of the King, before the captain took Antonescu by the shoulder. 'What does this mean? Get your hands off me!' he ordered. The captain hesitated. But a royal aide-de-camp shouted out contemptuously: 'It means your execution.' The spell was broken. The fallen dictator marched off to one of the securest rooms in the palace – the strongroom which had until recently housed King Carol's stamp collection.

Michael now moved fast ordering the arrest of the other ministers, setting up a communications centre in the palace, and appointing a new administration. At half past eight the German ambassador arrived at the palace with his deputy. Both were tight-lipped.

The King, speaking through an interpreter, told them that Antonescu had resigned and recommended they listen to the radio at ten o'clock that evening. In the broadcast Michael announced that Romania was no longer at war with Russia and that liberty and democracy had been restored to the country. Within minutes there was a huge crowd outside the palace chanting 'Long Live the King!' The BBC World Service broadcast the news and then played the Romanian national anthem. But the King's advisers, apprehensive as to German reactions, urged him to leave Bucharest. At about 2.30 in the morning of the 24th the royal party left the city in a convoy of four cars, the King at the wheel of one of them. Although coming under fire they reached a country house which a friend had made available. Later that same day German forces bombarded the palace and the royal enclosure containing the house where the King had lived.

Over the next two weeks the Romanian army rounded up German troops still on Romanian soil. Far from 'liberating' Romania, the Russians pressing on into Hungary in pursuit of the German army arrested tens of thousands of Romanian soldiers who were waiting to welcome them with grounded arms. They pillaged and terrorized the civilian population and left behind them 'representatives of the people' – communist agents charged with setting up a party organization. They were helped in their work by turncoat bully-boys from the Iron Guard. Early in September the King and the Queen Mother returned to the capital, secure in the knowledge that he had ousted the Gestapo.

Michael of Romania and his advisers had achieved a classic demonstration of the latent possibilities of monarchy. By all the rules of conventional wisdom the palace was virtually bereft of political power. In the event it had transmuted the often derided and sometimes perverted attitudes of ancient royal Europe – fealty, loyalty and a sense of honour – into mighty weapons with which they had reversed the policy of a seemingly irresistible occupying power and overthrown its government of collaborators. During the Cold War years the magnitude of the achievement was never recognized by official opinion in the West; and yet for the King what hurt most, even in his old age, was that he never received a word of approval from his father. For monarchs, more than for other people perhaps, the values of the family remain paramount.

For a short time King Michael I of Romania continued to run the affairs of his country. The aim was to return as soon as possible to normal pre-war conditions. He restored the democratic constitution of 1923. Until parliament could be reconvened government was through royal decrees discussed and agreed in cabinet. To judge the mood of the country and to signal the return to normality, Michael made frequent forays from Bucharest at the wheel of his unmarked car. The palace began to resume the rhythms of court life established by Carol I but the King still preferred to live in a private residence. In place of the one destroyed in the German bombardment he and his mother moved into a comparatively modest house in a residential area of Bucharest in which just three rooms were exclusive to the King.

In Moscow, in September 1944, Michael signed the armistice with the Allies. The Romanians had effectively liberated themselves and the country's armies were now part of the Allied war effort. The Russians rewarded them by exacting the harshest possible reparations and by annexing Bessarabia and Bukovina. King Michael had to accept a Russian army of occupation and was ordered to change his prime minister. Obstinately, he appointed a notoriously anti-communist general. Under orders from Moscow, Romania's communists began systematic subversion of the Romanian political structure in the country at large – where their numbers had mushroomed to close on a million thanks to Red Army protection and a terror campaign against other political parties – and in government where their leader promised a cabinet crisis once a fortnight until the King capitulated. Having destabilized the country, the Russians cynically used this 'instability' as a pretext for insisting that Michael 'appoint' Stalin's nominee.

At first it suited the Western Allies to accept the pretence that it was the King's own choice. But then, in August 1945, President

Truman announced that the US would not sign an armistice with Romania until it had established a democratic regime. Michael recalled that he seized the opportunity to insist on the dismissal of the Russian appointee as prime minister and sent a letter giving his reasons to the British and American governments. He then summoned the senior Russian general in Romania and handed him his copy in person, explaining that the western Allies already had theirs. According to the King's account, this senior soldier literally staggered with surprise before registering his formal protest. Moscow instructed the general to tell the King to punish the person who had sent the copies of the West. Michael told him, 'I did it myself'. In a strangled voice the Russian protested against what he termed an act of hostility. Observing that he was terribly sorry, the King terminated this second interview.

That evening he withdrew to the summer palace at Sinaia and from that time on refused to sign any decree submitted by the government in Bucharest. The 'royal strike' continued until December 1945 when the Romanian Question was put at the head of the agenda of the meeting of the Three Great Powers. It seemed that the young monarch had won. But Michael found himself once more in conference, this time facing the Soviet minister for foreign affairs and the American and British ambassadors in Moscow. Together they presented the King with a compromise intended to meet his objections to this imposed government, in effect it was an ultimatum. To the exclusively Communist cabinet were to be added two new ministers, one from the National Peasant Party, the other from the Liberals; but both would be minsters without portfolio, and neither would have any say in government.

At a private meeting with the British and American diplomats, King Michael and the Queen Mother learnt that these proposals, coupled with elections at some future date, would satisfy the American demand for a democratic regime in Bucharest. Stupefied, they begged that at least the elections be called as soon as possible to forestall communist manipulation of the electoral system for a prepared result. When these 'free' elections were eventually held late in 1946, they returned an 80 per cent vote in favour of the communists. In the months which followed, thousands died in pro-communist purges – all army officers faithful to the crown had already been sacked. It was now, with Romania completely at his disposal, that Stalin, with a characteristic gesture of gallows humour, awarded King Michael the Soviet Order of Victory for his part in the events of August 1944. The Soviet dictator made the award in person at an immense, boozy banquet. As was customary at such events, the military drank themselves senseless with vodka. Acting on advice from his American doctor, the King aimed to mitigate the damage by consuming quantities of butter. It appears to have been the only practical aid he received from the democratic West.

In November 1947 there was a break from the gloom of events in his own country when Michael, with the permission of his communist prime minister, attended the wedding of Princess Elizabeth of Great Britain and Prince Philip of Greece. At one of the receptions attendant on the London celebrations, held by Luxembourg's Crown Prince, the King met and fell in love with Princess Anne of Bourbon-Parma. In 1948 they married and forty-nine years later they were once more guests of Elizabeth and Philip, this time for their golden wedding anniversary. King Michael, who had never relinquished his title, was the only person present to have attended both ceremonies as a monarch.

The return of the popular monarch to his capital in 1947 had been greeted with glacial hostility by his communist ministers who had hoped he would take advantage of the London trip to abandon his throne. Indeed, it emerged later that while his appeals for help for Romania met with what he was to call 'a deafening silence', he had been offered asylum in Britain, but returned home determined to remain with his people if at all possible.

If the King's return troubled his government, his plans to marry depressed them still further. A royal wedding was certain to provide immense public enthusiasm for a head of state whom it was their fixed purpose to remove. But the lady had consented and, being descended from both Christian IX of Denmark and Charles X of France, fulfilled the constitutional requirement that she be of royal ancestry. Only the government sanction was now required by Romanian law. On 29 December 1947 the King was summoned to return to Bucharest for a meeting about 'a family matter' – he assumed his marriage was meant. The next morning he and his mother found themselves facing senior government ministers who said they wished to discuss terms for an amicable divorce. It was a malicious joke: the divorce was to be between the King and his country and he was presented with a document for instant signature – a deed of abdication. The question of his marriage was not even mentioned. Michael protested that such an act was unconstitutional. In response, he was told that unless he signed forthwith, one thousand students already selected for the privilege would be shot as subversives.

The terms for his departure were oppressive in the extreme. He and his mother were to leave the country within the week. They would not be permitted to remove a thing from the palaces, all royal property would be confiscated, even their personal luggage would be searched for anything of value. There was talk of substantial compensatory payments – none was ever made. Even so, something would be rescued of the family's assets. Thanks to the loyalty and daring of a royal pilot, the King's private plane was flown out of Romania under the noses of the authorities. One of Michael's first acts as an exile would be to sell it to raise funds.

On the night of 3 January 1948, he drove with his mother under armed guard to the deserted railway station which served the palace of Sinaia. On the platform they passed by a sort of guard of dishonour leading to the doors of their coach – two lines of officers facing outwards. Just as the King prepared to mount the steps, one of the young officers turned his head for a last look at his monarch. His face was streaming with tears.

The curtains on the carriage windows were drawn. The route to exile lay through the American zone of Austria to Switzerland, where Michael was able to revive his morale with a few days of skiing with his bride-to-be. Then they travelled to London where, in a brief press statement, he disclaimed his abdication as having been extorted under duress. In return, Bucharest stripped him and his family of their Romanian citizenship. In June 1948, thanks to the friendship of King Paul of Greece, and much to the anger of the Bucharest regime, the Romanian royals were able to celebrate the wedding in the royal palace at Athens with all the pomp due to a head of state; the entire Greek cabinet was present, as were the hierarchy of the Greek Orthodox Church.

Realizing the futility of attempting to establish a government in exile, King Michael set up a Romanian National Committee with the brief to monitor events in the home country and maintain contact with expatriates. Resident for some years in the early 1950s in England, the King for a time ran a small farm and market garden, and afterwards had a number of jobs both in the United States and in Switzerland where he eventually settled. The death of his father in 1953 was followed by the revelation that the huge fortune Carol had magicked out of Romania had evaporated. The death of his mother in 1982 was inevitably a cause of special sadness.

In 1990, in the wake of the revolution which had overthrown the dictator Ceausescu, Michael decided to visit Romania to test public reactions. The account which follows is based on the King's own recollections in his book *Le règne inachevé*. Easter, the great festival of the Orthodox religious year, seemed the natural time for a monarch as committed to his religious faith as he was to his country. It was also the period scheduled for the country's first democratic elections in some fifty years. He made approaches to Bucharest through the Romanian ambassador in Paris, who was known to be sympathetic to the royalist cause. Procedures were initiated to provide him with valid travel documents. But when the day came, as he prepared to board a scheduled flight to Bucharest, he was advised that the Romanian authorities had cancelled his visa, his visit being judged inopportune during the period of the elections.

The royal family seem to have rethought their strategy. In December his eldest daughter Princess Margarita was in Bucharest on a humanitarian mission. She asked for an interview with the new prime minister. He too regretted that the right moment had still not arrived. Did that mean, the Princess mused, that the country would always debar its king from entry? The wording of the question clearly implied an assumption of legitimacy. To this the prime minister did not demur; he merely replied, rather uncomfortably, 'But of course not'. When the Princess phoned her father and reported the conversation, Michael judged that since the prime minister had not formally debarred him from entering Romania, he could go ahead. On his instructions the Princess wrote to the prime minister's office informing him of the King's intention to make a visit to pay his respects at the tombs of his ancestors at the royal mausoleum some 120 kilometres from Bucharest.

It was to prove an escapade worthy of his ancestor Carol I's incognito venture down the Danube, through the unfriendly territory of Austria-Hungary, or his own father's buccaneering flight from Munich in 1930. Michael travelled without a visa but with a Danish diplomatic passport. This time he avoided the regular scheduled flights and commissioned a private plane from Geneva, with the help of a press photographer in quest of a story. In the afternoon of Christmas Day 1990, the machine took off for Bucharest. On board were King Michael and Queen Anne, their daughter Princess Sophie, the King's secretary, an English bodyguard, and the press photographer. The mood was sombre and for the King, returning home after forty-three years of exile, deeply emotional. Unaware of the royal cargo aboard this charter flight from Geneva, the control tower at Bucharest airport gave them routine clearance for landing, and minutes later the shuttle bus was rolling out across the tarmac to ferry them back to the terminal building.

Michael refrained from kissing the tarmac – 'a little too theatrical for my taste'.[12] Nevertheless the identity of the tall distinguished passenger just arrived in the little charter plane was known within minutes. The royal party were received by the airport manager who immediately conducted them to the VIP lounge, had their passports stamped and returned to them in a matter of minutes, and assured them that their baggage would not be searched. A couple of soldiers came to attention with a smart military salute and groups of relaxed and friendly bystanders cheered. As the King prepared to get into the hire car waiting for them outside the terminal, a plainclothes official asked for their passports for further formalities. The royal party continued on to the reception which had been prepared for them by a friend. The foreign press corps was there in strength, among them a French TV crew. But the high spirits were somewhat dampened by a phone call from the ministry informing them that their passports would have to be held a little longer. On a flying visit of just twenty-four hours, King Michael decided to press on.

He and Queen Anne with Princess Sophie between them settled into the back seat of their limousine. Some thirty kilometres short of their destination, the road was blocked by a 'traffic accident' and the royal cars were surrounded by armed police. The arrival of the foreign press corps and the TV crew rather cramped their action. Evening was drawing in. In the glare of the police car searchlights they argued with a stony-faced colonel who had orders to escort them back to the airport where they were to collect their passports. As midnight approached Michael conceded defeat. The return journey began, the press contingent keeping up as best it could. After only a few minutes the police escort turned off down a nar-row country road. There was menace in the air. Michael ordered the driver to stop and make a U-turn. But the road was blocked by police vehicles. At four in the morning an officer from the visa sec-tion of the notorious Securitate state secret police arrived to demand an interview with 'Mr Michael'. The King agreed to talk – but only at the airport, not in the open fields. The man from the Securitate disappeared, to be replaced by a senior airforce officer who author-ized the return to the airport.

Within view of the airport buildings they were ordered to re-main in their car and told that a plane of the Romanian airforce would fly them back to Switzerland. They were told that the pilot of their charter plane had been found drunk (he was, in fact, being held under guard). This potentially dangerous fiasco had its compensations. Romanian TV viewers were able to see the humiliating expulsion of the royals at the airport, even if the commentary had a hostile spin, and many Romanians were shocked at the treatment handed out to the King.

One of the royal family's main concerns was the restoration of the Romanian national heritage plundered and desecrated by the Ceausescus (in Bucharest alone twenty churches of the seventeenth and eighteenth centuries had been demolished). The Princesses took a lead here, contacting leading international architects for their advice. But Princess Margarita was also active on behalf of Romania's orphaned and brutalized children, and the charity she established became an established feature of the Romanian and international scene. The charity's gala for the winter of 1998, with King Michael and Queen Anne as guests of honour, was held at Namur in Belgium. Given the troubled state of the Balkans in 1999, and given the fact that with only daughters to succeed Michael in a country whose monarchical constitution banned women from the succession, it would be hard to predict a hopeful future for the Romanian crown. And yet in 1991, after decades during which the achievements, almost the very existence, of its kings had been expunged from Romania's records and school history books, reliable polls showed percentages in the mid seventies in favour of some form of restoration.

Possibly a more severe, certainly a more hurtful blow for the King in his declining years was the judgment of a Paris court relating to the family of his half-brother. The King had never recognized the legitimacy of Mircea-Gregory Lambrino (who adopted the name of 'Carol') and never made contact with the Lambrinos during his exile because, among other things, he considered they had acted in bad faith. After his father's death they had claimed, before a French tribunal, the right to bear the family name – a right which the court had granted them. It was Michael's view that no foreign court could make such a grant. As far as the King was concerned the son of 'Carol' Lambrino, Paul of Hohenzollern-Romania was merely Monsieur Lambrino.

In 1998 King Michael and Queen Anne made a triumphant return to Romania on what, according to the protocol, was a five-day private visit. The welcome by a cohort of government dignitaries at Bucharest airport, broadcast live on national television, was little less than a love feast; he was presented with what for him was the most precious of all gifts – a Romanian passport. In the capital's main square, the royal couple were received by a crowd thousands strong, many wearing the King's photograph and all of them roaring loyal greetings. Moving into the throng they shook hundreds of people by the hand. Michael Binyon's report in *The Times* carried the news – one can imagine the King thinking back to that day years before when he and his mother went walkabout down the Calea Victoriei.

For all that it was a private visit, King Michael and his wife were received by Romania's president and prime minister, for there was more than affection and nostalgia at play. Only weeks later the ageing King, in characteristic and tireless service to his country, was touring the capital cities of Europe's Nato countries, pressing the case for Romania's membership. In London, where he was entertained at Buckingham Palace by the Queen, he spoke emotionally of his love for England (but also recalled the blank response his appeals for support against the communists had received in the dark days of the 1940s). For Michael the case for Romania's membership was not a question of condescending charity from Nato but rather a case of transparent self-interest. If Poland was to be admitted, then his country, second only to her in size in central Europe, could hardly be excluded; and if Hungary were to be considered, how could a government in Bucharest, manfully confronting the problems of a Hungarian minority population, hope to contain resentment from the majority Romanian community, should their claim be rejected? Above all, he saw a rebuff as an affront to the pride of a country struggling to regain membership of the democratic family – an affront which might unsettle a newly emerging constitutional balance and thus produce a destabilizing element on Nato's southern frontier. The King's standing as a goodwill ambassador was confirmed by the fact that the Romanian Embassy in London held a reception hosted by King Michael himself.

At the end of 1999 King Michael and Queen Anne, accompanied by Princess Margarita and her husband Radu Dudu, Prince of Hohenzollern Veringen, attended a solemn *Te Deum* in Bucharest's metropolitan cathedral to celebrate the tenth anniversary of the overthrow of the Ceausescu tyrrany. There were surely those in the congregation who, looking back over their country's tragic history during its communist years, must have wondered how much better things might have been had the good king not been driven from his kingdom back in 1947. For if Juan Carlos of Spain could be called the most important European monarch of the twentieth century, Michael of Romania must surely be one of those who most fully embodied all the values of nobility, honour and service to one's people with which the word monarchy is most properly associated.

8

FRANCE: A HOUSE DIVIDED
AGAINST ITSELF

———•◦•———

On 21 January 2000, the two groups of French monarchists loyal
to the ancient royal house of Bourbon commemorated the death of
King Louis XVI, called the 'martyr king', who was executed on
that day in the year 1793. Those loyal to the Orléanist branch of
the family, which traces its descent from Philip d'Orléans, younger
brother of Louis XIV, congregated to hear mass at the church of St
Germain l'Auxerrois on the Place du Louvre, once the parish
church of the French kings. For them, the king in waiting, 'Henry
VII', was Henri, Comte de Paris. Those who support what they
call the 'legitimist' branch of the family descended from Louis XIV
himself, assembled in the basilica of St Denis, the mausoleum of
the kings, outside the northern ring of the city's boundaries,
marked by Péripherique ring road. For them the true king was
'Louis XX', Louis Alphonse de Bourbon, Duc d'Anjou.

Throughout the twentieth century, so far as the French media
and most French people who at all interested themselves in the
question were concerned, it was the Orléanists, honoured by their
supporters as the Maison de France, who maintained the monarchist option in politics. There was, to be sure, talk of family feuding
and gossip of serious scandal surrounding the figure of the old
Comte de Paris who, for fifty years dominated the world of monarchist society and politics. He died aged ninety in April 1999 and
when his will was published, it was discovered that the once huge
family fortune had dwindled almost to nothing. In October that

year, Prince Jacques Duc d'Orléans, one of the old count's younger sons published what amounted to a character assassination of their father. In *Les affaires tenebreuses du comte de Paris* ('The Murky Business of the Count of Paris') the Prince charged that their father had alienated and dissipated the assets he had inherited from his father – assets once estimated, in 1999 values, at two billion francs – precisely to ensure that his descendants should not have the wherewithal to continue with the prosecution of the family claim. The rival legitimist seized the opportunity for what the right wing newspaper *Le Figaro* called, 'a crusade for the throne of France'.

In January 2000, Louis of Anjou, 'Louis XX', after a lapse of more than a decade and to the resounding plaudits of 'Vive le roi' from his supporters participated in the commemorations for Louis XVI. Afterwards, he hosted a luncheon for more than 200 guests, giving an address which from the lips of a common or garden politician would have been considered rank electioneering. Placing the institution of monarchy firmly in the context of contemporary events, he urged his followers to look to Europe as an environment in which the institution had not only been recently revived (an obvious allusion to Spain where he was brought up) but in which it was functioning effectively in numerous of its member states. He expressed satisfaction that even in the present age, the French were often happy to associate past greatness of the country with the traditions of the monarchy and he pledged himself to remain loyal to the oaths of service to the county made by each of his forebears. The same week, he made a practical gesture of inspired P.R. by accepting the patronage of an international appeal for the replacement of the thousands of trees destroyed in the park at Versailles by the storms which had swept France in the last week of 1999. Together with the oil spillage from the tanker *Erika* which had polluted much of the country's Atlantic coast in the same month the storm was considered a national catastrophe and covered as such for weeks in the media. By associating himself with this vastly emotional ecological appeal and particularly with the damage to the former royal parklands 'bequeathed to the nation by the kings' he linked the traditions and concerns of the monarchy with the concerns close to contemporary national sentiment. As the year 2000 dawned, it seemed that Anjou and not Orléans became the focus of interest in any royalist future for France.

But these were not the only pretenders to the throne and some would say not even the best qualified. Before turning to their story I propose to review others who do or who could advance pretensions to the monarchy inaugurated in the year 987 by the election of the French nobleman Hugh Capet, son of the then Count of Paris. In a book on the pretenders to the throne of France, published in 1990, Raoul de Warren and Aymon de Lestrange, for the sake of completeness, argued the case of a person who has never advanced the claim and whose ancestor abandoned it some two hundred years earlier but one who, in international law, had a remarkably strong one – the case of Her Gracious Majesty Queen Elizabeth II of England.

Following his astonishing victory at Agincourt in 1415 and the subsequent occupation of much of France, Henry V of England had been able to enforce a settlement of his questionable pretensions to the French crown, inherited from his ancestor Edward III, grandson of a French king, in legally binding form. By the Treaty of Troyes the English king was nominated regent for the mad Charles VI of France; Charles's supposed heir, the Dauphin, was declared a bastard – on the testimony of the Queen of France herself – and it was provided that on his death the failing King Charles should be succeeded by Henry, many years his junior. In June 1420 Henry was married to Princess Catherine of France, Charles's daughter and in December the Treaty which had been signed by the French Queen as acting regent for her husband, was approved by the Estates General of France. In January 1421 the Parlement of Paris and then the University of Paris both ratified the Treaty. It is doubtful whether any pretender's claims have been more comprehensively or more conclusively legitimated.

Henry, in fact, died in August 1422 and his father-in-law, Charles of France in October: so the English king's baby son,

Henry VI of England, was proclaimed as King of France, being crowned in the cathedral of Notre Dame in Paris in 1431. His widowed mother Queen Catherine would take as her second husband the Welsh esquire Owen Tudor whose grandson Henry Tudor, proclaimed King of France, became king of England by right of battle on the field of Bosworth in 1485. All subsequent English sovereigns inherited and maintained their rights to the French crown until the early nineteenth century when the lilies of France were removed from the royal arms and the claim formally renounced by King George III. But as any legitimist knows, rights do not die with the renunciation of a claim.

Although the Windsors technically may be said to have a claim, they do not for one moment advance it. According to Waren and Lestrange, others in this outer circle of probability, not so reticent, included the family of a M. Balthazar Napoléon de Bourbon, a barrister from Bhopal in India and also a French family which claims descent back to the Merovingian royal family who ruled the Franks long before the 'kingdom of France' as such existed. Ignoring such excursions and accepting conventional history that the last royal dynasty to occupy the throne of France in one or other line was indeed that founded by Henri de Bourbon who, as Henry IV, ascended the French throne in 1589 and whose descendant Louis XVI was guillotined in 1793 we are liable, nevertheless, to find ourselves beckoned down some intriguing genealogical byways by legitimists of different persuasions.

There was for example, the family of Anthony Freeman, born in 1983, who claim descent through unbroken male succession from King Charles X (deposed in 1830), the last Bourbon of the senior line to rule in France. The Bourbons spent many years in exile in England during the French Revolutionary and Napoleonic regimes. During this time the future king's son, Charles Duc de Berry, was said to have secretly married his mistress Amy Brown. They certainly had children and one of these, John Freeman, fathered a line which, if the secret marriage could be proved, would, one might suppose, be the senior Bourbon claimants.

But Louis XVI and Marie Antoinette had two children, Princess Marie Thérèse and the eight-year-old Prince Dauphin, Louis-Charles, who shared their parents' imprisonment in the sinister medieval Temple Tower, on the site where the town hall of Paris's 3rd Arondissement now stands. The King was guillotined in January 1793 and within the month royalist emigrés had proclaimed his son King as 'Louis XVII'. On 8 June 1795, some two months after his tenth birthday, broken in health by the dank and hostile conditions of his confinement, the boy died. Royalists now accepted his uncle, Louis Comte de Provence, as Louis XVIII. But there had been mysterious comings and goings in the Temple before the boy king's death and it would be claimed that the dead child had in fact been a changeling, 'Louis XVII' having been spirited away to safety. However, a certain Dr Pelletan, one of the surgeons at the official autopsy, 'abstracted' the heart from the infant cadaver and preserved it in alcohol in a crystal specimen jar. After Louis XVIII's restoration in 1814–15, the doctor attempted to restore the grisly little relic (since 1975, following a saga of adventures, housed in the crypt of the basilica of St Denis just outside Paris) to the royal family. Marie Thérèse, now Duchesse d'Angoulême, granted Pelletan an interview but despite his proofs and testimonies refused to accept the organ as a genuine relic of her dead brother. In fact, there was at this time, a pretender, a German of obscure origins called Karl Wilhelm Naundorff, claiming to be the fugitive Louis XVII. The Duchesse d'Angoulême's action titillated the gossips – perhaps the Bourbons had reason to believe in the substitution theory. Descendants of the Naundorff claim continued to find adherents down to the late twentieth century. Then, in 1998, DNA tests comparing tissue samples from Naundorff's skeleton with hair from Queen Marie Antoinette and her sisters as well as tissue samples from living descendants in the female line of the Habsburg imperial family showed no biological correspondences. However, Naundorff had not been the only 'false dauphin' and over two centuries more than 800 books were published on the mystery. It seemed that only DNA tests on the supposed heart of the boy king, could determine the issue once and for all. Accordingly, in 1999 the Duc de Bauffremont, President of the Memorial de France, guardian of the relic, agreed to tests. These, which followed the procedures used in the Romanov tests (see page 46), were conducted by scientists in Belgium and Germany acting independently. Their joint report described the results as offering very forcible support to the official version that it was Louis XVII and not a substitute who died in the Temple in June 1795. Prince Louis de Bourbon, Duc d'Anjou and for his supporters King in waiting as 'Louis XX' of France announced the outcome in a televised press conference in April 2000. Some days later Henri Comte de Paris, for his supporters 'Henry VII' of France, issued a communiqué describing the boy king's 'assassination' as a deplorable act against the royal family of France, the principle of which he embodied. No doubt, the wording of the scientists' report which, with its 'very forcible support', stops short of unequivocal affirmation and reports from England later that year questioning the validity of certain procedures in some forensic DNA tests lent comfort to die-hard Naundorffists. As always in the world of the pretenders the debate over legitimacy is never settled.

In fact, there are some devotees who would argue that even the first of the Bourbon kings was a usurper. For them, the true line of the French monarchy today is represented by the distinguished de Bourbon-Busset family who can trace their descent to a Pierre seignieur de Busset, the son of a liaison between a fifteenth-century Bourbon (the older brother of the ancestor of Henry IV) and a lady whom he almost certainly never married. Advocates of this claim, who do not include members of the Bourbon Busset themselves, assert that there was in fact a legitimate marriage so that Pierre's descendant should have been preferred to Henry IV. Even when we discount such speculation we are still left with the entirely different matter of the Napoleonic claimant before we turn to the claims of the Spanish Borbóns. To both these we will return later after looking at the House of Bourbon Orléans and the Counts of Paris.

In 1997, the northern French towns of Eu and Aumale celebrated the millennium year of their foundations with a seeming paradox. The municipalities wanted, they said, to reunite themselves with the tradition and heritage of France and with that purpose in mind petitioned the Count of Paris, who alone had the power to grant titles to members of the family, to confer on his grandson Prince Foulques d'Orléans, son of the Duc d' Orléans, the historic titles of Duc d' Aumale and Comte d'Eu. The Château d'Eu, now the town hall and a museum, is the ancestral home of the House of Orléans, and the Countess of Paris, who was born there in 1911 and owned woods on the estate and had a residence there in the Pavillion de la Grande Mademoiselle, expressed her delight and the Count expressed his confidence that the young Duke-Count would be worthy of his predecessors. To the surprise of an English observer, the *maires* of both towns were in attendance, neither sporting his Republican tricolour sash of office.

But it is not only in England that 'everyone loves a lord' and with 3000 noble families still bearing their titles and 20,000 would-be aristocrats buying theirs from a network of flourishing agencies, the cause of *la noblesse* is not necessarily a lost one in the republic. Where there is a nobility there must be the possibility of a king. In fact, the French took a very long time indeed to shake free of their monarchy. Monarchist parties continued to play a role in national politics during the twentieth century and in 1987 the Republic celebrated the millennium of the inauguration of the royal dynasty, founded by Hugh Capet in 987. A public opinion poll conducted by the magazine *Le Point* during the millennium year found that a surprising 17 per cent of French voters would favour some form of monarchical government, perhaps on the democratic Spanish model. Left unanswered was the question of who might take the crown. The French Bourbon claimant, the Comte de Paris and Duc de Clermont descends from the last Bourbon ever to rule in France, Louis Philippe, King of the French who seized the throne in 1830 and ruled until 1848 when he was displaced by revolution. But as we have noted he was contested on dynastic grounds by a member of the Spanish Borbón family, 'Louis XX' with the French title, Duc d'Anjou. The origins of the dispute lie in the seventeenth century.

In 1643 King Louis XIII, son of Henry IV, founder of the Bourbon royal line, died. He left two sons. The older boy succeeded him as Louis XIV and was the ancestor of the kings of France down to Charles X. The younger son, Philippe, who was to adopt the title Duc d'Orléans, sired a dynasty that was to intervene in the history of France on a number of occasions. Descended as they were from Louis XIV's younger brother, the Orléans were of course the junior branch of the Bourbon dynasty but achieved the throne in 1830 when Louis Philippe set aside Charles X's grandson, the ten-year-old Count of Chambord (hence the charge of usurpation). However, when the childless Chambord died in 1883, the senior line of the French Bourbons died out with him and the Orléans assumed the headship of the House of France.

Their opponents, however, claimed that the succession should lie with members of the Spanish Borbón family, itself descended from Louis XIV and not, like the Orléans, from his younger brother. For Louis XIV, had two grandsons. From the older descended the kings of France down to Charles X and from the younger a line which in 1700 ascended the throne of Spain. The other great powers of Europe, notably England and Austria, dismayed at the prospect of union between France and Spain, had gone to war. At the Treaty of Utrecht in 1713 the ageing Louis XIV was forced to agree that his grandson, Philip V of Spain, should renounce in perpetuity for himself and his heirs all rights in the succession to the kingdom of France. Thus in 1883 when the senior branch of the French Bourbons died out, the succession to the title depended on the validity of the terms of the Treaty of Utrecht as it related to the French succession. If these held good, then there was no question of any Spanish interest in the French crown and the Orléanist claim was incontestable. But if the relevant clauses of Utrecht could be invalidated, then a Spanish Borbón claimant was the legitimate one. According to French dynastic lawyers, Philip V's renunciation had violated fundamental French laws of inheritance and thus was null and void.

Such considerations had not, of course, troubled Napoleon I, for having no hereditary rights at all he had simply founded a new dynasty by having himself proclaimed Emperor, rather than King, of the French and by crowning himself. Following the overthrow and exile of Napoleon the Bourbons were restored in the person of Louis XVIII, brother of the guillotined Louis XVI and uncle of the boy king Louis XVII. Louis XVIII was succeeded by his brother Charles X, and when Charles was forced to abdicate in the Revolution of 1830 the royal line of Louis XIV was effectively terminated.

The collapse of Charles X's regime was partly connected with the religious conflict, but more so with this king's incompetence and remoteness from post-Napoleonic political realities. The French were still wedded to the idea of monarchy but a burgeoning middle class also wanted a more accessible, a more constitutional monarchy, and many thought the Bourbon most likely to deliver was Louis Philippe. King Charles, who seemed capable only of obstinacy, manoeuvred himself into abdication. From 28 to 30 July, three glorious days of rioting and street fighting in Paris (*les trois glorieuses*, as the French call them) were enough to force the King to vacate the throne. But before going into exile in England, he did his ineffectual best to secure the continuance of the dynasty. First he surrendered the throne in favour of his fifty-five-year-old son, who was already preparing for exile. He was technically 'King' as Louis XIX for a matter of minutes on 2 August 1830 (legally his was probably the shortest reign on record, but its notional existence explains why at the end of the twentieth century the Borbón pretender styles himself Louis XX). King Charles then nominated his ten-year-old grandson, Henri Comte de Chambord (child of the dead Duc de Berry) as his successor, and named his distant cousin Louis Philippe, Duc d'Orléans, the boy's guardian and regent of the realm. In fact after a 'reign', never publicly proclaimed, of just eight days 'Henry V' was set aside by the regent who, with the sanction of the National Assembly, took the throne with the title 'King of the French'.

In French constitutional history this 'July Monarchy' represented a new style of Revolutionary legitimacy – the King accepted the tricolour as the national emblem and even spoke of the values of the Republic – but it was and remains for legitimists a simple case of betrayal and usurpation. However, it did not greatly surprise them. In 1793 Louis Philippe's father, who first associated the Orléans name with liberal ideas in politics and was known to his contemporaries as Philippe Égalité, had startled even the Revolutionaries, just as he disgusted royalists by voting in favour of the execution of his distant cousin King Louis XVI. Many believed he did so in the hope of being offered the throne as a constitutional monarch but it did him no good, he was himself guillotined later the same year.

In 1831 the July Monarchy faced a feeble, almost farcical challenge on behalf of the ten-year-old 'Henry V' led by his mother, the Duchesse de Berry. Landing in Marseille in disguise she had travelled across France, winning promises of support but nothing more, to the Vendée region, staunchly royalist even during the Revolution. There a small group of insurgents rose in her support but were easily dispersed, and later that year the Duchess herself was caught and was found once again to be pregnant. Had the baby been a love child, monarchists might have forgiven the indiscretion but the dreadful truth was that she had acquired a new husband, not of royal blood but from among the Italian lesser nobility. She was ostracized by the royal family and politically was a spent force. The name of Chambord now disappeared from the scene of French politics for the next forty years, the young pretender biding his time with the blind confidence of his dynasty and establishing himself at Schloss Frohsdorf in Austria.

In France, meanwhile, Louis Philippe spoke the language of liberal constitutionalists but his regime became oppressive, and in 1848, Europe's Year of Revolutions, he like his predecessor was overthrown and in his turn took the French exiles' ferry for England

– to make room for a provisional government followed by a constituent assembly and then elections for the president of a Second
Republic. The main republican bloc led by Adolphe Thiers chose
as their candidate Prince Louis-Napoleon Bonaparte, nephew of
the great Napoleon. He seemed ideal; boasting the famous name,
he was also, according to Thiers, 'a cretin whom we shall easily
manage'.[13] But someone has lost the script. The cretin was indeed
elected as President of the Second Republic but some four years
later, having outmanoeuvred his manipulators, he had himself proclaimed Emperor as Napoleon III on 2 December 1852. The next
eighteen years of French history belonged to the Bonapartists. But
then, in September 1870, his army having been crushed by German
forces at the Battle of Sédan, Napoleon's Second Empire collapsed
and he too had to cross the Channel.

France's Third Republic was proclaimed in Paris by a provisional
Government of National Defence. Late in September the German
forces began their siege of Paris. On 28 January 1871, the provisional government agreed an armistice. By its terms there was to be
a three-week cessation of hostilities which would allow for the election of a national assembly that could make peace. German troops
had occupied forty of France's ninety departments and the capital
was still ringed by the besieging force. The elections were held on
8 February. Of some 630 deputies by far the largest number were
monarchists supporting one or other of two Bourbon claimants
(Chambord had 182 supporters, Orléans 214). Unsurprisingly,
Bonapartism was humiliated, but the 230 seats won by assorted
republican parties hardly seemed a ringing endorsement for the
legacy of 1789. In fact, at this time, France had experienced only
sixteen years of republican rule since the deposition of Louis XVI
in September 1792. In the hour of the nation's trial the electorate
seemed to have opted for the old and trusted traditions of the
throne room. The prospects seemed bright for yet another Bourbon
restoration.

However, constitutional issues had to be put on hold. The capital
was in the hands of the Left which considered the new Assembly

members were provincials, elected under pressure from clerical and reactionary elements in the regions. (In Paris, even more than in London, there is nothing more 'mere' than a provincial.) However, the Assembly leaders, establishment politicians such as Adolphe Thiers, called on the Paris National Guard to disarm, and when it refused Thiers had the Assembly withdraw to Versailles and prepared to bring the mutinous Parisians to heel. There followed the days of the Paris Commune. The German army round the capital stood by, while the forces of the Assembly at Versailles destroyed all resistance. Several thousand deaths later, Paris had been reduced by French forces, in the traditional Revolutionary manner, and thoughts could turn to forming a new, permanent government and constitution.

With an overwhelmingly monarchist Assembly, the moment of destiny beckoned for Chambord. But while the fifty-three-year-old exile was able to recognize that the substance of power had fallen from the old monarchy, he could not accept the tricolour, emblem of revolution and also now the irrevocable emblem of France. The more pragmatic Louis Philippe II of the House of Orléans, grandson of King Louis Philippe I who had endowed him with the historic title Comte de Paris, was flexible in his approach, modern in his outlook, had studied trade unionism in England and had some of the intuitions of a democratic politician. It was proposed that Chambord should have the crown for life and the succession be assigned to the Count of Paris and his descendants. However, in July 1871 'Henry V' let it be known that he would never abandon the white flag of the Bourbons and the fleur de lys, 'the standard of Joan of Arc'. It was true that the new republican regime did not have a constitution and the majority of the deputies were monarchist, but, for Chambord, pristine legitimism was the one overriding consideration for the government of France. The Orléanists' ideals of a modern liberal monarchy were an affront to everything he stood for. He remained immovable in his refusal to accept the tricolour, and the monarchist majority in the Assembly chamber was never called upon to exercise its apparently irresistible voting power.

[146]

Without the support of the legitimist deputies, there was no prospect of that majority in fact being effectively mobilized. Without 'Henry V' that support would never be forthcoming; without the flag of the Bourbons fluttering in the Place de la Concorde – formerly the Place Louis XV and site of the Paris guillotine where Louis XVI had been taken to his death – Chambord would not return to Versailles. It has been said of the Bourbons that they forgot nothing and they forgave nothing, and yet Henry IV, founder of the dynasty, had been a political realist. A Protestant who escaped with his life from the butchery of the massacre of St Bartholomew's night in which some 3,000 Protestants were slaughtered in Paris alone, to win the throne he had turned Catholic, prepared to surrender not just a flag but his religion, with the cynical quip that Paris was 'worth a mass'. But for Chambord it was not worth even a tricolour. Even the Pope was dismayed. Pius IX, who proclaimed the doctrine of papal infallibility and whose reign of thirty years was the longest in the history of the office, had always considered Catholic interests in France to be bound up with Bourbon legitimacy and had refused to crown the Bonapartist Napoleon III. He was bemused by Chambord's devotion to the Bourbon flag. 'To surrender all that for a napkin!'[14] was his comment on hearing the terms of the Bourbon's ultimatum.

When the obdurate Chambord died at Schloss Frohsdorf on 24 August 1883, the way should have been open to a restoration of the monarchy under the more liberal minded Orléanists. But France now had a socialist president – the monarchist moment had passed. Not all recognised the fact. In his telegram addressed to crowned heads of Europe in which he notified them of Chambord's death, Louis Philippe II of Orléans formally took up the succession.

Brief and dignified, it was signed not Louis-Philippe but Philippe Comte de Paris. To the cognoscenti it was apparent that, while intending no disrespect to the memory of his grandfather Louis Philippe I of the house of Bourbon-Orléans, the Count of Paris was now asserting himself as the head of the House of France.

[147]

Should he ever succeed to the crown he would be known, not as Louis Philippe II, 'King of the French', but as 'Philip VII King of France'.

The monarchists now found themselves embroiled in a new conflict of legitimacy. Whatever agreement the Comte de Chambord might have come to with the Orléanists, his Countess and many ultra legitimists considered that the true succession lay with the Spanish Borbóns. But which Spanish Borbóns? Having no sons, the nineteenth-century Spanish King Ferdinand VII (d. 1833) had unilaterally abrogated the rule which said that females could not succeed so that his daughter Isabella might do so. His brother Carlos naturally contested this and he and his descendants provided pretexts for the Carlist wars which troubled Spain for decades. Being fully occupied with their own concerns they had little interest when French monarchical purists proposed they lay claim to the French throne. The last Carlist died in 1936. But supporters of the Spanish Borbón claim, to the French throne in the twentieth century, basing their arguments on the fact that Queen Isabella's husband, Francis d'Asis, Duke of Cadiz, was a cousin descended in the male line from Louis XIV, pointed to his descendant, Luis Alfonso de Borbón, in French Louis Alphonse, Duc d'Anjou, as the rightful 'King Louis XX' of France.

As the Comte de Chambord carried the title of *Henri V roi de France* into history, it might have been supposed that with it he carried the royalist cause into oblivion. The great and the good of the Third Republic were not so sure. Proclaimed in September 1870 and superseded only in July 1940 by the German occupation, the Third Republic would prove to be the longest-lived French constitutional regime since the execution of Louis XVI (and, incidentally, also the only one not to have had a written constitution). But its founding fathers seem to have been by no means confident of its longevity. They looked for some pretext to justify a law which should deprive a certain group of French citizens, namely those with monarchical pretensions, of their most important right of citizenship – the right to live in their country. Three years after

Chambord's funeral, the Republican deputies supported by the left-wing press, reckoned they had the occasion.

This was the marriage of Marie Amélie, the eldest daughter of the Count of Paris, to Charles Duke of Braganza, of the royal house of Portugal. The reception was held in what is now the Hôtel Matignon, residence of France's prime ministers. Dukes and counts, seigneurs and highnesses emerged by the score from a river of dazzling carriages, their orders and stars, tiaras and diamonds like precious flotsam on the flood. The following day the right-wing newspaper *Le Figaro* hugged itself: 'All the personalities of the future monarchy passed in review last night.' Within weeks, the Chamber of Deputies passed a law proscribing the heads of former ruling houses and their heirs from the soil of France immediately and without appeal and banning all the princes of these families from entering the army or exercising public functions. The law was rapidly ratified by the Senate. On 24 June 1886 the Comte de Paris and his eldest son, Philippe Duc d'Orléans, then aged seventeen, embarked at Dieppe for England to shouts of 'Vive le roi' to which he responded with 'Vive la France'.

With the death of the Count of Paris in 1894 his son, the twenty-five-year-old Duke, found himself head of the house of Orléans and – should he wish to press the matter – head of the House of France with the notional title of Philip VIII. Tall and regal in his bearing he was a handsome figure of a man and, with his marriage in 1898 to a Habsburg Archduchess, of considerable standing in the ranks of Europe's royals. But in France the Third Republic had long been rooting itself firmly in the banking sector and industry, the bourgeoisie and even the nobility. Asked by the Comtesse de Paris for his recommendations as to what sort of steps might bring her and her husband to the throne of France, a pragmatic marquis serving as a general in the Republic's army had replied, 'Ah, Madame, for you I can see only one possibility. Your Highness should first separate from Monseigneur le Comte and then marry Monsieur le President.'[15]

By contrast, her son, viewing the French scene from his exile in England, still regarded the cause as practical politics. He did not even exclude the possibility of a coup and told a confidant that he would board the London-Paris express the day he was shown plans which offered a serious prospect of success. Until that time, regarding himself as the guardian of the destiny of the House of France, it was for him to take an historical perspective, which might mean protecting the royalist cause from its own more strident supporters. During the Dreyfus affair he made no attempt to conceal his anti-Semitism and attracted support from the ragidly anti-Semitic and anti-republican journal *Action française*. Unfortunately, he seems to have been more angered by the journal's spoiling tactics than by its anti-Semitism. Anything that might cause trouble for the Republican authorities was grist to its mill and, in 1908, it sided with the railway unions against the government's strike-breaking measures which the official royalist organ *Correspondance nationale* praised as commendably 'energetic'.

At the same time the Duke's distant royal cousin Ferdinand of Bulgaria was soliciting Paris for financial support so that the Duke's standing among his own royal circle was jeopardised. His personal advisers urged public censure of *Action française* lest he appear to compromise the very idea of monarchy by association with the politics of public disorder and mob rule. From his exile in England he condemned the article as an act of rebellion. This merely attracted criticism of his advisers by the recalcitrant journal. Content to overlook his unlovely supporter's racism, the Duke could not stomach its attacks on his friends. But *Action* had much support among monarchists and when at the end of 1908 Orléans formally renounced it, he had to face turmoil among his local party chairmen. The Duke's careful policy had never been approved by monarchist militants and the circulation of *Action française* rose by some 15 per cent almost overnight, while a large proportion of the party chairmen withdrew from the movement. Now he had alienated his most active supporters. People spoke of a king without royalists and royalists without a king. The gesture did not last long. In April the following year, he was reconciled to the editorial board of *Action française* and even ordered the closure of the official royalist organ, the *Correspondance nationale*. To many it seemed that French monarchism had taken a dangerous lurch further to the right.

With the outbreak of the Great War in 1914, 'Philip VIII' had one overriding priority – to be involved in the war itself – but the efforts of this notional commander-in-chief to join the colours were turned down by the authorities. After the war, he established himself near the French frontier at the Manor Anjou in Belgium. There he devoted himself to his museum of hunting memorabilia destined one day to be bequeathed to France. He kept by him at all times a little silver box containing a handful of French soil and over the door displayed the crossed flags of the tricolour and the white of the house of Bourbon. He died on 28 March 1926, at his bedside the faithful sister whose brilliant wedding all those years ago had provided the pretext for the law of exile.

Childless, he was followed in his claim by his cousin Jean, Duc de Guise ('John III' of France), father of three daughters and a son Henri Comte de Paris. 'John III' marked his accession to the title with a statement which was framed in the style of a royal address to the nation but could also be construed as a rallying call by monarchists and their well-wishers. It was dignified and adroit and was carried by all France's main news agencies. In the view of many political analysts it raised French monarchism to a higher level in public esteem than it had ever enjoyed under his predecessor.

During the 1930s right-wing attitudes and authoritarian regimes gained ground throughout Europe. More active in politics than his father, the young Count of Paris watched events in France from the family's exile in Belgium. The decade had opened for him with his marriage to Isabelle d'Orléans-Bragance in Palermo in April 1931. As the couple emerged from the church the Count saluted the crowd, many French among them, with cries of 'Vive la France!' and they responded with 'Vive le roi!'

In January 1934, the Count headed a conference involving leaders of the *Action française* and other right-wingers convened in his father's name at the Manor Anjou to discuss the general political

[151]

situation and the prospects, however long-term, of France's returning to a monarchical system of government. The programme, such as it was, spoke of political renovation, moral and intellectual honesty (code for the abolition of corruption in political life) and, of course, the greatness of France. He wanted the support of the veteran Charles Maurras of *Action française* but was determined to retain his own independence of action. Plans were agreed for the launch of a new, specifically royalist monthly *Le Courier royal*. The accord was superficial. But the Count's mother, who longed for a full reconciliation, was received like a queen by the *AF* whenever she came to Paris. The movement's right-wing leader prompted the polemicist to publish a eulogy of the young heir to the claim. Next he chartered a cruise liner, the *Campana*, on which hundreds of monarchists made the voyage to Genoa where they were joined by the Count who came on board for a state reception.

But the mood of bonhommie was as short-lived as it was contrived. The Right embarked on a campaign of extreme violence against republican policies. Suspicions of corruption and malpractice were levelled against the *AF* and its friends. The Count of Paris saw that monarchism could only suffer from association with such a movement and, at a conference in Lausanne organized by monarchists opposed to it, he formally repudiated all association between the House of France and the *AF* and denounced its principles as entirely incompatible with the traditions of the French monarchy. He was moreover convinced that extreme nationalism led to fascism and so became a threat to individual liberties. For all that, the popular association of monarchism with extreme right-wing politics was not and never would be entirely dissipated.

With the death of 'John III' in August 1940 his son became, to Orléanist devotees, 'Henry VI of France'. With the outbreak of war the previous year he had enlisted with the French forces in Africa under the name of Henri Orliac, a fairly evident portmanteau combination of 'Orléans' and 'Armagnac', the nickname for Orléanists at the time of Joan of Arc. With the capitulation of France in June 1940, the Count returned to France; the law of exile was still in force but the Republic which had passed it no longer was. As head of the State of France Marshal Pétain welcomed the head of the House of France and, it is said, offered him the Ministry of Supply in the Vichy government. The Count declined it and crossed over to join French forces in North Africa. With the British and American landings in Algeria, his thoughts turned to an imperial council, with himself at the head, as a way to moderate the rivalries between the army's Pétainist commander-in-chief and Charles de Gaulle, the increasingly important leader of the Free French. It was surely unrealistic. Such over-ambitious ideas and other tentative initiatives behind the scenes had brought him no nearer to real influence in the conduct of the war. Then, in November 1942, Admiral Darlan, the Vichy leader in Algiers who had gone over to the Allies, was assassinated. A monarchist plot was rumoured. The Count left Algiers for Morocco, sidelined from all participation in events.

These murky and peripheral events have their place in the history of monarchism in France. The extent and intimacy of the Count's dealings with General de Gaulle are, perhaps, open to question but the Count always claimed that they were close and his *Dialogue sur la France: correspondance avec General de Gaulle*, published in 1994, depicted a debate upon the destiny of France conducted with mutual respect between equals. Whatever may have been the case after the war, in the early 1940s the Pretender's views were irrelevant to the decision-makers, a fact of considerable relevance to the standing of monarchism. The Count always considered it his family's duty to hold themselves 'in reserve for France in case any catastrophe should befall the Republic'. No greater catastrophe could befall the Republic than the capitulation of June 1940 and its aftermath of national division. To the historian Alfred Cobban it seemed obvious that if even in this crisis the Count 'was to be pushed aside and ignored [then] ... for all the sound and fury of the monarchists, their cause was dead.'[16]

In fact, after the war, the cause continued in diverse, sometimes strange directions. In 1946, monarchist journalists launched something called the Socialist Monarchist Movement, with its own journal *The Red Fleur de Lys*. The following year the Count relaunched the *Courrier royal*, renamed *Ici France* ('France Calling') and with a more democratic agenda. Neither caught the public mood. With the accession of General de Gaulle to power in 1958 and the establishment of the Fifth Republic with its autocratic presidential constitution, it would appear to some that France had restored the monarchy in all but name. Certainly, French commentators themselves have spoken of an elective monarchy, and the General wielded powers which Louis XVI himself might have envied. Some have speculated that he toyed with the idea of grooming the Comte de Paris as his successor. If so, nothing came of this improbable idea and over the next twenty years monarchism faded from practical relevance in French politics. In 1974, the leader of a 'New Royalist Action' party stood in the presidential elections and received just 42,722 votes (0.17 per cent of the votes cast).

The repeal of the 1886 exile prohibition in 1950 enabled the Count to return to France. The numerous properties of the family were restored to him. His subsequent decision to sell parts of this real estate, as well as the house in Portugal, and to auction furniture and jewellery from the family collections was rumoured to have caused much dissent among other members of the family. But it seems that the Count himself was convinced that the family assets should not be dispersed piecemeal and that much of the proceeds of these sales went into the foundation he set up with the express purpose of consolidating and securing the resources of the dynasty. In any case, as he was wont to remark, 'The next generation should expect to work.' His eldest son Henri, who succeeded as Comte de Paris, followed the injunction by exploiting his name and titles in various business ventures such as the luxury scent market, targeting in particular the Arab countries and the US with fragrances with names such as 'Most Royal' and stoppers in the shape of the fleur-de-lis. However, Henri divorced his wife and married by civil ceremony a commoner who was also a divorcee. Incensed, the Comte de Paris required that his eldest son, the Dauphin, make a public disclaimer of his rights in the succession and when he refused to do this issued a pronouncement stripping him of his titles. He spoke about princes who abnegated their responsibilities and the need for respect for the traditions of the dynasty. However such dictats by the old Comte de Paris acquired for some a hollow resonance when, after his death, the dynastic legacy he himself had bequeathed was revealed.

The rift in the family was at its worst in 1987, the year in which the whole of France was celebrating the millennium of the Capetian dynasty, the ancestral 'House of France'. Indeed, the very title Comte de Paris was chosen by Louis Philippe in the nineteenth century for his heir, to underline the descent of the Orléans branch from the parent Capetian stock. The millennium year was something of an *annus horribilis* for the Orléans.

In 1987 Republican France was brazenly celebrating the millennium of the election of Hugh Capet, ancestor of France's royal dynasties – Capetian, Valois and Bourbon. Naturally the Orléans were invited to numerous functions as guests of honour. But so too, in many cases, was Alfonso Duke of Anjou and of Cadiz, son of the Duke of Sesoná and grandson of King Alfonso XIII of Spain and regarded by the 'White' Bourbon legitimists as the true successor. Those functions with which he graced his presence had to resign themselves to the absence of the Orléans. Not only was his claim to the crown unacceptable to them; his assumption of the title Duke of Anjou was entirely outrageous. The Orléans determined on legal action. It was an unusual state of affairs, to say the least: a claimant to a defunct monarchy seeking the arbitration of a republic court against a rival. The accusation was that the Spanish rival had no right to bear the title Duke of Anjou, as this had formerly been an honour in the house of Orléans, and no right to bear the royal coat of arms. The tribunal, refusing to concern itself with questions of defunct royal law and basing its judgment on civil law governing relations between citizens of the republic, ruled: with regard to the question of the title, that the only person who could contest the usurpation of a title was the bearer of the title said to have been usurped – the last member of the house of Orléans to carry the title duke of Anjou had been Philippe, the brother of Louis XIV, who, in 1662, had exchanged 'Anjou' for 'Orléans'; and, with respect to the coat of arms, that the full arms belonged to the senior line of a family and that by the terms of ordinary civil law the Spanish was undoubtedly the senior branch of the Bourbon line. Just one month after receiving news of the judgment in his favour, the Spaniard met a terrible death on the ski slopes of Colorado. Nevertheless the Comte de Paris appealed against the judgment in the court of Paris, citing the new Duc d'Anjou and Duc de Cadiz, then a fatherless fourteen-year-old, to his French supporters Louis Alphonse Prince de Bourbon 'King Louis XX' in waiting. The court confirmed the earlier ruling.

In December 1998, there was a seemingly happy tailpiece to these stories of family feuds and dynastic infighting, with the announcement of the engagement of Eudes Duc d'Angoulême, grandson of the old Comte de Paris, to Marie-Liesse, grand daughter of the leading aristocrat among French supporters of the Spanish Borbón claims. At the time, it was hoped by some Orléanist supporters that, in the future, this 'Romeo and Juliet' romance would heal the dynastic rift. Even so, there were opponents to Orléanist pretentions to the title Maison de France, who held that this dynastic title was exclusively the prerogative of a reigning royal family. The death of the old Comte de Paris in 1999, meant the 'succession' of his son, the putative 'Henry VII' and with the dawn of the year 2000, the decision of the now twenty-five-year-old Duc d'Anjou, the Spanish-born 'Louis XX', to assert himself on the French monarchist scene, gave his cause a new prominence.

It goes of course without saying that royalists of both camps discount the Napoleonic claim. For them, the first and second empires are no more legitimate than the five republics to have followed the execution of Louis XVI in 1793. The distinguished but austere Louis Prince Napoleon, who descended from the great Emperor's brother Jerome, and who died in 1996, held himself aloof from monarchist activities but was thought not to rule out entirely the possibility of putting himself at the service of France, should a national referendum on the question declare in his favour. It is true that in 1804 the first Napoleon, having instructed a sub-servient Senate and Tribunate to declare him emperor ordered a national plebiscite which indeed returned a gratifyingly complete majority to give a populist veneer to the fait accompli. However, the possibility of such a combination of circumstances repeating themselves in any foreseeable future is, one feels, remote and Prince Napoleon lacked the dictatorial proclivities of his great predecessor. In fact, 1990s Bonapartists tended to content them-selves with honouring the memory of the great emperor and cel-ebrating the high anniversaires of the First Empire. Chief among them were members of the imperial family, members of the imperial nobility – still proud to bear their privileged honorifics in republi-can France – and descendants of Napoleon I's companions in his captivity in exile on St Helena. The same was no doubt true of his son Charles and his grandson Jean Napoléon, born in 1986.

In fact, in September 2000, Prince Charles Napoléon, an im-pressive figure at more than two meters in height, ventured into electoral politics in the municipal elections in Ajaccio, Corsica. An economist by training he was campaigning against incompetent city management and in a large field of candidates achieved about 7 per cent of the vote. Hardly a huge success but an innovative de-parture for a Napoleon! The same month witnessed a remarkable ceremony in monarchist circles, at the Château of Amboise, for-merly a home of the late 'Henry VII' the old Comte de Paris, head of the Orléanist House of France, which he had given to the Foun-dation Saint Louis of which he was President. On Saturday 16 Sep-tember Louis Alphonse, Duc d'Anjou of the Spanish Borbón family, the putative 'King Louis XX' was formally received with full republican honours by the town's dignitaries. In his speech of wel-come the *maire*, spoke with pride of the town's royalist as well as republican past. But the highlight of the proceedings came when the young pretender to the throne of France, a successful Madrid based banker, was permitted to view the religious relic (housed in the church of St Ours in the nearby town of Loches) believed to be the Girdle of the Blessed Virgin Mary – a privilege traditionally reserved exclusively to the kings of France.

9

THE HEIRS

So far, we have looked at the careers ambitions and convictions of the men who would be kings; some with more reason to hope than others, in one or two cases they have been people of talent and devotion who could surely serve their countries in difficult times. Now we turn to the men and one woman who, given the normal run of events, may reasonably expect to become their countries' sovereigns. At the turn of the century just four of them were married or had families, they were to give them their principal titles – Charles Prince of Wales and Prince of Great Britain and Northern Ireland; Philippe, Duke of Brabant, Prince of Belgium; Alois, Crown Prince of Liechtenstein, Count Rietberg; and Henri, Hereditary Grand Duke of Luxembourg, Hereditary Prince of Nassau. With the announcement in January 2000 that his father Grand Duke Jean was to abdicate in September, Henri's son Guillaume (born 11 November 1981) was deemed the new Hereditary Grand Duke.

To marry, the heirs to Europe's thrones require the permission of the sovereign and in some cases of their country's legislature as well. Take for example the case of HRH Willem-Alexander, Prince of Orange, Crown Prince of the Netherlands (aged thirty-three in the year 2000). His choice of wife must be cleared by his mother Queen Beatrix but also authorized by a law debated and passed by the two houses of the Dutch Parliament in joint session. Should he marry without submitting his choice of partner to this procedure he would lose all rights in the succession to the crown for himself or his children. This is precisely what his aunt Princess Irene did so that she could marry the Catholic Prince Carlos Hugo Prince of Bourbon-Parma. Converting to Roman Catholicism in January 1964, she married the Prince later that same year having neither sought nor received the permission of her mother Queen Juliana nor of the Parliament. Sadly, the marriage ended in divorce seventeen years later, but both the Princess and her four children were excluded in perpetuity from the succession to the throne.

The Prince of Orange faces the most complicated process of permission but Felipe, Prince of the Asturias, heir to the crown of Spain (whose name was for a time linked with that of Princess Tatiana of Liechstenstein) loses his rights in the succession if he proceeds with a marriage against the express prohibition of the King and Parliament. For Crown Prince Frederik, Prince Royal of Denmark (born in January 1972) the position is slightly different. He requires the permission of his mother, Queen Margrethe, formally given in the Council of Ministers. His neighbour and junior by one year, Crown Prince Haakon of Norway, requires only the permission of his father King Harald V (whose father Olav V for some years withheld permission for his marriage to Sonja Haraldsen now Queen Sonja). In Sweden, Crown Princess Victoria, Duchess of Västergötland (twenty-three at the turn of the century), would require the consent of the government given at the request of the King.

Princess Victoria, alone among the heirs to the reigning monarchs of continental Europe, is excluded from participation in the councils of the realm. Belgium's Crown Prince has a seat in the country's senate, while his counterparts in Denmark, Norway and the Netherlands can sit in on meetings of the councils of ministers. The same is true of the Hereditary Grand Duke of Luxembourg and also of the forty-two-year-old Crown Prince Albert of Monaco, Marquis des Baux, though neither of these can reasonably be classed as modern democratic monarchies. In addition to suffering restrictions on their marriages and enjoying privileged access to their countries' governments, these royals are liable to discrimination as to religion, whether constitutional or implicit, and sex.

In the question of female succession, the case of the Swedish Crown Princess is of particular interest. Should she in due course succeed to the throne, she would not be Sweden's first female monarch – her seventeenth-century predecessor Queen Christina is one of the most dramatic figures of European history – but she would be the first queen regnant of the House of Bernadotte, founded by Jean Baptiste Bernadotte, Marshal of France. Bernadotte, that most unusual phenomenon in the annals of monarchy, an adopted heir, was the son of a provincial French lawyer. He was forty-seven with a brilliant career as a soldier behind him and the Napoleonic title of Prince of Ponte Corvo when the ageing King Karl XIII, acting on a vote in the Swedish parliament, adopted him as his heir, Bernadotte having taken up the Lutheran confession.

The choice of a French commoner as Sweden's king with the title Karl XIV Johan, requires some explanation, especially as there was a prince of the blood royal alive at the time. This was the son not of Karl XIII, who was childless, but of his predecessor Gustav IV Adolf who had led the country into unsuccessful wars against France and Russia and had been deposed and sent into exile for his pains, and his heir barred from the succession. The Swedish establishment hoped that their new French prince – one of Napoleon's most brilliant lieutenants, minister of war for a time, and in 1807 appointed governor in the French-occupied territories of the north German Hanse cities of Hamburg, Bremen and Lübeck – would keep their country in favour with the Emperor. After all, Bernadotte's wife and Sweden's queen-to-be, the Marseille-born beauty Desirée Clary, had been for a time Napoleon's fiancée and the two men were believed to have been friends. In fact, as Crown Prince and commander-in-chief of Sweden's army, Bernadotte participated in the defeat of Napoleon's forces at the Battle of Leipzig, and, thanks largely to his intervention, Sweden emerged from the post-Napoleonic settlement of Europe in 1815 with Denmark's former dependent kingdom of Norway now added in personal union with her crown.

However, Bernadotte was not French for nothing, and a new law of succession passed in September 1810, the month after the Parliament had elected him as successor and two months before he was formally inaugurated as Crown Prince, established the succession in the House of Bernadotte by primogeniture in the male line. The rule held good until 1 January 1980, when a new law came into force whereby the succession to Sweden's throne lay by simple primogeniture, irrespective of sex. Because the effects of this new law were retrospective, it displaced Carl Philip, born on 13 May 1979, Duke of Värmland, as Crown Prince by his elder sister Victoria, born on 14 July 1977, as Crown Princess.

The new Swedish succession law perhaps seemed a little unfair to the prince. In Norway, women were given equal rights in the succession by an amendment to the constitution introducing simple primogeniture made in May 1990. At this time HRH Prince Haakon, the Prince Royal of Norway, was seventeen and had been generally accepted as heir to the crown, while his sister HRH Princess Märtha, Princess of Norway, although two years older, had been excluded by the Salic law provisions of the 1814 constitution. Since the 1990 amendment was not made retrospective, the position of the two young royals was not altered with respect to the succession.

By the turn of the century, all but one of the continental monarchies admitted women, though not necessarily on equal terms with men. The most exclusive regulation for female succession is in Luxembourg, where the crown descends in the direct line by male primogeniture and a woman becomes eligible to succeed only when there is no male heir either in the direct or in collateral lines of the House of Nassau. There are four countries – Belgium, the Netherlands, Norway and Sweden – where women are admitted on fully equal terms with men, but the rest follow some variant of the British succession in which women are admitted but the male line has precedence. Thus the Princess Royal at the opening of the millennium

[162]

came eighth in the line of succession, after her younger brothers Andrew Duke of York and his children, and Edward Earl of Wessex (a title which harks back to the name of England's Anglo-Saxon royal house). In Spain Crown Prince Felipe is five years younger than his sister, the Infanta Elena. A similar rule applies to the House of Grimaldi of Monaco where Crown Prince Albert, Marquis des Baux, takes precedence over his sister Princess Caroline of Monaco, even though he is fourteen months her junior. It is open to a crown prince of Monaco, subject to the approval of the reigning prince, to adopt an heir and confer on him all the rights of the crown. But it is also open to a princess of Monaco to succeed in the absence of a male heir – though if she does so, her husband and children must take the name of Grimaldi.

Alone among Europe's reigning dynasties, the family of Liechtenstein excludes succession by women. Perhaps the point is, after all, somewhat academic since Hereditory Prince Alois, Count Rietberg has not only two sons and two brothers but also cohorts of male cousins of various degrees. Born in June 1968, and brought up with his brothers and their younger sister Princess Tatiana in the family castle of Vaduz, he went to Sandhurst, Britain's military academy, before serving for a time in the Coldstream Guards and then going on to a degree course at the University of Salzburg. Following the death of his grandfather, the eighty-three-year-old Prince Francis Joseph I, in 1989 and the accession of his father as Sovereign Prince Hans Adam II, the Crown Prince took the oath to the constitution at the same time as his father in August 1990. During the mid 1990s, he and his wife HRH the Princess Royal Sophie, Duchess in Bavaria, were based in London, where the Crown Prince had a job with a leading firm of accountants. Following family tradition, they lived a modest and unostentatious life for a couple of their standing and wealth and attracted little media attention. Returning to Liechtenstein, Prince Alois, a skiing and tennis enthusiast, devoted most of his professional time to the family's business interests. A happy family, the young Liechtensteins had of course required the permission of his father the sovereign Prince for their marriage, solemnized in Vaduz in July 1993. This standard requirement for all with serious royal prospects has the added provision in Liechtenstein that any member of the princely family is free to make written representations to the Sovereign Prince if they have objections to a proposed dynastic marriage. It is hard to imagine that the charming and intelligent Bavarian princess would have presented any such problems. Descended from one of Europe's former royal families, she is of impeccable standing and, being a Roman Catholic, of the right religion (Catholicism is Liechtenstein's state religion and its rulers must be members of the faith.)

Most monarchies have strict stipulations relating to religion though there is one, somewhat surprising, exception. The modern Spanish monarchy, successor to the Catholic Kings Ferdinand of Aragon and Isabella of Castile, whose union inaugurated the Spanish state, has no constitutional provision as to the religion of the sovereign. Modern Spain is a secular state in which such a provision would be out of place – though it is worth noting that the constitution does require the heir to the throne to go through a religious ceremony of marriage, and, as noted above, the Prince of the Asturias cannot marry without the approval of the sovereign. Elsewhere on the monarchical map, religion is of fundamental constitutional importance. The Danish, Norwegian and Swedish constitutions stipulate that the sovereign must be of the Lutheran confession; the British require he or she be Anglican; while every Dutch monarch has been a member of the Dutch Reformed Church, and since the marriage of the heir to the throne requires the approval of not only the sovereign but also of Parliament, a breach in that tradition would presumably provoke heated debate. In Monaco, as in Liechtenstein, the constitution requires the monarch to be Roman Catholic, while entrenched tradition dictates the same for the sovereigns of Luxembourg.

But if in religion – an issue of general public concern – monarchies by and large cleave to traditional prescriptions and proscriptions, in matters of exclusive concern to their unique caste they have proved much more adaptable. While as the third millennium opened Charles Prince of Wales would not be permitted to marry a Roman Catholic as his second wife and retain his rights in the succession, nor would Prince Henri of Luxembourg have been expected to marry a Protestant, in neither case have there been any objections to marriage with someone not of sovereign status – in the one case Lady Diana Spencer, descended from the Earls Spencer, in the other Señorita Maria Teresa Mestr y Batista.

Britain, of course, has always been much freer in this matter. Edward IV, Richard III and Henry VII all married into the English nobility rather than into foreign royalty. Even Henry VIII, that royal devotee of marriage, divided his attentions pretty equitably between two sovereign ladies, Aragon and Cleves, two noble women, Howard and Seymour; and two commoners, Boleyn and Parr. His cousin, Mary Queen of Scots, an almost equally dangerous spouse, had one royal husband Henry II, King of France, and two aristocratic ones – Darnley, in whose murder she was probably implicated, and Bothwell. By 2000 the monarchies of continental Europe had adopted British practice; indeed had, in some cases, gone beyond it. Where the Hohenzollern and Habsburg families still required those in the dynastic succession to marry into sovereign families, or such as were so technically designated, the monarchies still actually on their thrones could even countenance the marriage of a reigning monarch with a commoner, as when in Stockholm on 19 June 1976 King Carl XVI Gustaf married Fräulein Silvia Sommerlath. There are those, it must be said, for whom the sovereigns of modern Sweden are barely monarchs in any real sense. For the Swedes themselves the king is the symbol and embodiment of national unity. A head of state who can truly fill that character is a valuable asset to his or her country. The Swedes will surely think twice before dispensing with the radiant and dedicated Crown Princess Victoria in favour of a presidential system.

10

MONARCHS OF THE NORTH

———•◦•———

The British often seem to imagine that the cult of monarchy is confined to their shores and that elsewhere, in the 'more democratic' lands of Scandinavia or the Benelux countries the royal families are tolerated as necessary adjuncts to the constitutional process but attract little interest for their own sakes. This is not really true. The Dutch are on occasion uneasy about the extent of the influence Queen Beatrix exercises behind the scenes, during the weeks or months it can take to select a Dutch government from among the patchwork of parties produced by their complicated system of proportional representation. The Swedes are generally proud of their figurehead of a king and his beautiful queen and looked with increasing fascination on the career of his heir, Crown Princess Victoria while the Luxembourg press no doubt thinks twice before risking serious criticism of their rather powerful Grand Duke.

The Scandinavian monarchies are rarely subject to the withering fire which periodically enfilades the castle of Windsor from the massed batteries of the British media. In all these countries there is general and sympathetic interest in the ruling families. Even when in the summer of 2000 the Norwegians learnt that Crown Prince Haakon was going to remain true to the love of his life, an unmarried mother, a poll showed more than half of those questioned in favour of the prince's decision. Monarchy did not seem under serious threat in the rest of northern Europe at the opening of the new millennium. The 1990s saw at least ten books on Norway's royal family; nine on Swedish royalty and ten on Danish. This list excludes books on palaces and royal collections, like the Norwegian king's series of historic postcards, and it also excludes the annual royal year books. In addition there were two general books on the Scandinavian monarchies and even a historical account of a short-lived monarchical venture in Finland in the 1910s.

For much of its history Finland was subject to the Swedish crown until in 1809, under the terms of an agreement between Napoleon and Tsar Nicholas I, it became a Grand Duchy of the Russian Empire. After the collapse of that empire patriots, taking advantage of the turmoil in the fledgling Bolshevik Soviet state, declared the country's independence in December 1917. Following the example of recently independent Norway, the first plans were for a monarchy. In October 1918 after months of preparation the election was proclaimed of Friedrich Elector of Hesse. Brother-in-law of the German Emperor, he in fact withdrew his candidature a month later, and for the next eight months Finland enjoyed the unusual constitutional status of a kingdom ruled by regents in search of a king. In July 1919 the Finnish Republic was inaugurated under President Dr Kaarlo Stahlberg.

For a time in the 1960s, it seemed to many international observers and to the Swedes themselves that the country might go the republican way. At the opening of the twenty-first century, most people would say that Crown Princess Victoria of Sweden has little need for apprehension about her future. She did, it must be said, start life with something of a problem. Her parents' first born, she was not qualified to succeed by virtue of her sex, for while the conventions of the monarchy had recently been changed to allow her father to marry the woman of his choice, although she was not of royal or aristocratic birth, the succession still lay with male children, following the general Continental tradition. Born in July 1977, Victoria was followed on 13 May 1979 by her brother Karl Philip, who was proclaimed Crown Prince and Duke of Värmland. It was an honour he was to enjoy for somewhat less than nine months. A new law of succession was already in preparation and on

1 January 1980 this duly came into force. On that day Sweden found itself with its first Crown Princess and a week later she was invested with the honour and title of Duchess of Västergötland.

Such resounding titles are about the only concession to the past still allowed to Sweden's royals. It is, indeed, hard to see how the country could improve the security of its democratic institutions by becoming a republic with an elected head of state, for no republican president has less power than her father, King Carl VI Gustaf (his preferred spelling of his name) and few have as little. The triumphant success of his marriage to a commoner wife demolished one of the traditional constraints on members of the royal family, while other changes have led to a detached role for the monarch in the country's constitutional arrangements which must surely be a liberating factor for anyone called upon to play it. It is true that the Princess is not free in the matter of religion and, should she ever transfer her allegiance from the Lutheran Church of Sweden to, for example, the Roman Catholic faith, she, like her famous predecessor Queen Christina, would have to abandon her rights to the throne. As she is patron of Sweden's Luther Association, any such conversion is hypothetical in the extreme and, apart from the standard requirement that she receive official permission to marry, in all other respects she enjoys the same freedoms as a commoner.

Born in 1977 in Stockholm's Karolinska Hospital – rather unnervingly, perhaps, for the heir to a throne, on Bastille Day, 14 July – Crown Princess Victoria celebrates her birthday afternoon with open house at the royal summer residence, Castle Solliden standing in extensive parkland on the Isle of Öland, dressed in folk costume to receive the bouquets and congratulations of tourists and local residents. Such a gesture fits the democratic style of the royal house. When Victoria was five, the King made the charming palace of Drottingholm in the countryside outside the capital the family's principal residence and the Princess was enrolled in the local nursery school, completing the other stages of her primary education in the public sector. From there she went to Stockholm's

[169]

elite high school, the Enskilde Gymnasiet taking her baccalaureat in 1996. This was followed by university at Yale and, as part of her vocational training for the monarchy, attendance at sessions of the UN as an observer, sitting in with the Swedish delegation under the tutelage of Ambassador Henrik Salander. In 1998, in the company of her mother Queen Sylvia she got the chance to meet Secretary General Kofi Annan at the unveiling of the statute to commemorate the fiftieth anniversary of the death of Count Folke Bernadotte, Sweden's roving ambassador for peace.

The decision to send Victoria to Yale, as opposed to Uppsala near Stockholm, for five generations the university for Sweden's royals, may have been in part affected by the fact that in her late teens she was subject to bouts of anorexia and it was felt that a complete change of scene might break the cycle. Other reports claimed that it had been her own choice, to avoid intrusive press attention. One Swedish paper had, apparently, published a diagram purporting to be the floor plan of the apartment she had been pro-posing to take at Uppsala. In America, she lost all traces of the anorexia and spent much of her time in company with her high-school friend of long standing, Swedish millionaire's son Daniel Perrson Collert who within weeks of Victoria's departure for the States had himself crossed the Atlantic and enrolled in a course at New York's Juillard School. At weekends Victoria turned from the Connecticut campus to an elegant Manhattan apartment, and the two became a familiar sight, hand in hand in jeans and trainers on the side walks of New York's smart Upper East Side, or strolling in Central Park plastic cupped cola drinks in hand, or clubbing in Greenwich Village or kissing over drinks in fashionable restaurants.

With her parents consent, Victoria continued her American idyll, with interruptions for official engagements, for some years and during a Swedish radio interview in November 1999 said she hoped to complete her course at Yale, interrupted many times with special dispensation from the university authorities. Throughout that time, it seems, that the friendship with Daniel Collert held good. There were those, perhaps, among Sweden's dwindling class of diehard traditionalists who frowned at such familiarities between the heir to the crown and a commoner. It is said that Daniel himself, from a high-profile family in Sweden's public life, objected to press intrusions into their private life and tried to break the friendship. But, both at Drottingholm and on the royal jet set circuit he remained her preferred companion. A marriage would require authorization from King Carl XVI Gustaf and the assent of the council of ministers, but after years of parental indulgence it seems the Crown Princess would have no cause to doubt her father's consent. Some Swedes no doubt recalled the debt the country and the monarchy owed to that other commoner Silvia Renate Sommerlath, daughter of German businessman Walther Sommerlath and Alicia Suares de Toledo when she married King Carl XVI Gustaf in June 1976.

He was the first king of Sweden since the time of Bernadotte to marry a commoner, but it was in the spirit of the innovative measures introduced by the constitution of 1975. It was by its terms that the monarch's role was reduced to an exclusively representative one. The royal family were given the right to vote in parliamentary elections, though by convention it is a right they do not exercise. The most egalitarian aspect of the document is surely to be found in the words defining the age at which the monarch attains his or her majority. According to this, the only people eligible for the position of head of state must be over twenty-five.

But while there was no constitutional problem over his wife, there could have been debate as to his regnal numbering. The fact is that the origins of the Swedish monarchy are lost in the mists of the ninth century. *The Pocket Encyclopaedia to the Kings and Rulers of Sweden* published in 1995 lists as its *first* entry 'Eric VI' while the first King Carl is numbered 'VII'. The confusion would appear to be the result of a certain amount of medieval chauvinistic antiquarianism, but that, as they say, is all in the past and no one was about to propose that the new king adjusted his numeration to 'X'. In fact, thanks to the Union of Kalmar engineered by Margaret of Denmark in the 1380s and incorporating the three Scandinavian kingdoms under one crown, Sweden's monarchs lost their sovereignty for more than a century. It was Gustav I Vasa who in 1521 restored the country's independence; a leading noble, he was elected king by his peers in 1523, it was also he who established the state religion as the Reformed Lutheran Evangelical faith, and it is from this period that the history of modern Sweden may be said to date.

In the seventeenth and eighteenth centuries Sweden was one of the great powers of Europe. It ruled a Baltic empire which comprised Finland, parts of Estonia and Latvia, Ingermanland, Karelia, parts of Pomerania and for a time the Archbishopric of Bremen. The country can boast a dazzling trio in the annals of monarchy. Two great kings and one great queen: Gustav II (d. 1632), the Protestant champion in Europe's Thirty Years' War; Karl, or Charles, XII (d. 1718) who earned an admiring biography from Voltaire; and Queen Christina (abdicated 1654), who engaged the French philosopher Descartes as her personal tutor and left Sweden for Rome (dressed as a man) because she would rather abandon her kingdom than her Catholic religion.

During the eighteenth century the glory perhaps begins to dwindle. Like England, the Swedes were given to ministries of silly names, the pro-Russian 'Caps' and the pro-French 'Hats' sounding every bit as eccentric as 'Whigs' and 'Tories', and to foreign dynasties, most notably that of Napoleon's marshal Count Jean Baptiste Bernadotte, founder of the present ruling house. Adopted as his heir by the childless King Karl XIII, he succeeded to the crown in February 1818 as Karl XIV Johan. Like a good Frenchman he never bothered to learn Swedish (French was then in any case the European language of diplomacy); like a good Swede he acquired Norway in personal union to the Swedish crown.

Quite unlike England, however, was the number of intellectual, not to say intelligent and gifted, royal heads that occupied the space between the crown of Sweden and the shoulders of its monarchs. Gustav III (1746–92) was not only sufficiently Machiavellian to organize two *coups d'états* (the second in the year of the French Revolution) to regain the absolutist prerogatives lost by his predecessors; he was also a dramatist and poet of some talent and, incidentally, founded the Swedish Academy. His nineteenth-century successors included Oscar I, author of a formative book on the reform of criminal law and the need for prison reform, and Oscar II who, if reactionary in his politics, was a talented musician and author of the best biography of Karl XII since Voltaire's.

The tradition of Sweden's learned royals was broken by the bespectacled, elegantly bearded and moustachioed Gustav V who acceded in 1907 at the age of 49. As well as his passion for Sèvres porcelain (he had the world's largest collection), Gustav was a keen sportsman devoted to elk-hunting but also to tennis, playing regularly on Stockholm's indoor courts and still capable of a tolerable game in his late seventies. This royal example did a lot to promote the popularity of the game in Sweden and may be a factor in the country's great tradition of top international players. An early devotee of hormone treatment and the longest-lived of Sweden's kings (he was ninety-two when he died in 1950), he was also fully aware of the importance of the royal office. On at least two occasions Gustav V exerted real influence in policy matters.

Early in 1914, when there was much national debate over the left-wing government's defence policy, the King received a multi-thousand demonstration, organized by the Peasants' Party, in the great courtyard of the royal palace. A petition with some 60,000 signatures had been prepared, asking the King to authorize defence expenditures sufficient to ensure foreign respect for Sweden's neutrality in case of war. In response, the King dissociated himself from his government's policy, thanked the demonstrators for their patriotism, and spoke of working together with them. This was followed by huge cheers from the crowd and a mass rendition of the national anthem. This was certainly not constitutional monarchy, and the entire cabinet resigned. The King appointed his own prime minister and for three years may be said to have ruled as well as reigned. 'In 1917,' to quote Lagerqvist and Åberg's *Kings and Rulers of Sweden*, 'Gustav accepted the parliamentary system.'

Nevertheless, the King's hand is almost certainly to be seen behind the government's decision to accommodate Nazi Germany's demands for troop transit facilities along Sweden's rail system between Norway and Finland during the Second World War. Haakon VII of Norway, for one, had no doubt that 'the old scoundrel' was behind it. There were even those who thought that Gustav would have favoured displacing Haakon (in wartime exile in England) as king, in favour of his grandson the baby Harald (now King as Harald V). The Swedish monarch certainly did contact King George VI of England to offer himself as a mediator between Britain and Hitler, but George wanted nothing to do with the proposal.

Gustav's marriage to Victoria of Baden, by whom he had three children, was a loveless affair. She spent much of her time in the south of Europe for health reasons and also because, some said, she could not accept her husband's bisexual orientation. Accompanied by the fashionable society doctor Axel Münthe, author of *The Story of San Michele* which described his fight to save Europe's migrating songbirds from the murderous fusillades of southern Europe's hunting fraternity, for a time she lived the simple life on the island of Capri. The ecologically advanced Münthe, who was frequently engaged as court physician and dined from time to time with the King, was, if gossip is to be believed, either his illegitimate brother or his illegitimate cousin.

Gustav V died in 1950 aged ninety-two. He was succeeded by his eldest son, Gustav VI Adolf, then in his late sixties, who would match his father's longevity, dying at the age of ninety-one. He continued the royal family's intellectual distinction. In a long career as a renowned archaeologist he carried out important digs not only in Sweden but also in Greece and China (he had a worldwide reputation for his knowledge of Chinese antiquities). By his marriages the King had double links with the British royal family; his first wife, Princess Margaret of Great Britain and Ireland, was the niece of King Edward VII and the young couple were married in June 1905 in the chapel at Windsor Castle. Winsome and warm-hearted, she was also frail in health and died, to national mourning, in 1920 while expecting her sixth child. Their heir died in an air crash in 1947 leaving a baby, Carl Gustav, while their daughter Ingrid was to marry King Frederick IX of Denmark. In 1923, just three years after Margaret's death, her widowed husband married the lady who was to become his queen, Lady Louise Mountbatten. Apparently on hearing news of the engagement, Sweden's masters of protocol were uneasy about the lady's standing: was she or was she not of the blood royal? If not, as things stood at that time, the Crown Prince would lose his rights in the succession to the crown by marriage to a commoner. It was once, perhaps unkindly, said that the origins of the Mountbattens are lost in the mists of the nineteenth century (unlike Sweden's monarchy); however that may be, London was able to provide Stockholm with satisfactory assurances and the marriage went ahead. As the years went by Gustav Adolf, with his love for his wife and her country, was a frequent visitor to the Mountbattens' house, Broadlands in Hampshire, and became a close friend of her brother Lord Louis Mountbatten Earl Mountbatten of Burma.

Gustav VI Adolf, like his father, had a great liking for tennis and was active on the court well into old age. There seemed little likelihood that, although he came to the job some five years after the normal age of retirement in other professions, he would resign, so to speak, in favour of his grandson, Prince Carl Gustav. Like politicians, monarchs are free to continue in post for as long as they will or for as long as they can persuade the populace to accept them. As the reign progressed, this second possibility seemed likely to become a talking point, not with relation to the King himself but rather to his heir. In 1960s Sweden republicanism was very much on the political agenda – the Crown Prince confided in a British friend that most of his acquaintances had republican sympathies. A few political pundits and others too doubted whether the monarchy would survive into the next generation. In fact on 19 September

1973, four days after his grandfather's death, the twenty-nine-year-old Carl XVI Gustaf took the royal oath according to Sweden's 1809 constitution.

As Crown Prince he was said to have indulged in a pre-marital lifestyle considered somewhat permissive even by the conventions historically conceded to princes of the blood. At a time when some people wondered whether the monarchy would survive in Sweden, the country's parliament, the Storting, removed even notional authority from the job description and arranged things so that the country had a head of state who embodied its historical traditions, who provided a natural focus for the nation's sense of identity and who, when in due course the grim reaper should call him to his final game of chess, could be replaced without the cost and tedious politicking attendant on the election of a president. In fact, posed in an immaculate suit and tie and against an immaculate garden setting for the cover picture of the authorized pictorial biography published for his fiftieth birthday, the monarch seemed quite staid. He had been brought back to the straight and narrow, it was said, by his marriage to a woman who, for all her lack of royal ancestors, was not only of great beauty and style but also had a truly regal bearing.

At the banquet following the 1998 Nobel ceremony to honour among others John Hume and David Trimble, the peace prize winners from Northern Ireland, at which more than 1,200 distinguished guests sat down to table, Queen Sylvia, radiant in pearls and a golden tiara mounted in French empire style with antique cameos, was able, thanks to her Brazilian background, to discuss the works of the Portuguese writer Jose Saramago, that year's Nobel laureate for literature, with the author in his own language. In the tradition of the monarchy she married into, Queen Silvia demonstrated herself to be a woman of cosmopolitan interests and wide culture.

She is also, with her husband, the fortunate inheritor of Europe's finest private collection of jewels, limited as their constitutional powers may be. The collection includes a diamond encrusted diadem made by a London jeweller for Margaret of Great Britain, from whom it descended to her grand-daughter Queen Victoria of Sweden together with a parure in diamonds and massive rose topazes of ear-rings and necklace with pendants. Many of the Swedish royals' jewels were created in Paris in the early 1800s for Karl XIV Johann, founder of the House of Bernadotte, his French wife Desirée (Queen of Sweden as Desideria) or for Napoleon's Empress Josephine who bequeathed them to her grand-daughter Josephine, the wife of Bernadotte's heir King Oscar I and Queen as Josefina. Among these are a matching diadem and necklace in diamonds and amethysts, the diadem can be worn as a necklace while the necklace is designed also to be worn as two bracelets. Some of the royal jewels belong to the Bernadotte Foundation, but many are the personal property of the Queen and the royal family, indeed some of the Bernadotte jewels passed to Norwegian and Danish royals thanks to the marriages of Swedish princesses into these families.

If Sweden flirted for a time with republicanism in the 1960s, it would be a rash prophet who predicted such developments in Denmark much before the 2060s. Ruled by kings for the best part of 1100 years, its court protocol was until the mid 1900s among the most rigid and austere in Europe. In the latter half of the twentieth century the public image changed to one of democratic accessibility. In the 1990s opinion polls showed Queen Margrethe II, who came to the throne in 1972, had an approval rating of as high as 90 per cent. Her ministers were said to pay serious attention to her opinions. While the twice-monthly public audiences in the royal palace maintained a style of openness and transparency, it seemed to some royalty watchers that Margrethe of Denmark, rejected the role of tailor's dummy. In any case, according to clause 23 of Denmark's Constitution, she already had the right, in an emergency to issue provisional laws.

The Queen, her husband Prince Henrik and their family attend the opening of the Danish Folketing, the Parliament, but as observers only, seated in a balcony above the floor of the deputies.

The aim is to emphasize the sovereign's impartiality above the world of party politics and the independence of the parliamentary body. Yet appearances are deceptive. The monarch is not merely a decorative head of state. 'The Queen plays an important role during the formation of a government' says the official Danish information service. 'It is her duty to nominate as prime minister that party leader able to form a majority government.'[17] Since there may be as many as ten parties contesting a Danish general election under a system of proportional representation, the job is not necessarily straightforward and must allow the monarch a degree of judgement and, with that, power to influence the course of events. Like all heads of state, Queen Margrethe authenticates the acts of the legislature. The terms are explicit and businesslike: 'We Margrethe II, by the Grace of God Queen of Denmark, let it be known: the Folketing adopts and We approve and sanction the following law... .' It is presumably conceivable that Queen Elizabeth II might refuse her assent to some measure, just as it is conceivable that the sun might not rise tomorrow. That Margrethe II might exercise a royal veto over some legislation is also difficult to imagine, but this possibility is in the written constitution which governs the state of Denmark. In fact the Queen of Denmark claims and is allowed independence of action in activities which in England are rigorously monitored by the Queen's ministers. She writes her own speeches when she addressed the United Nations and her own Christmas TV messages to the Danish people. In Britain the monarch's Christmas radio and TV broadcasts were systematically diminished both in length and scheduling by the political and media establishment. The parallel institution in Denmark, the Queen's New Year message, of much more recent vintage, was from 1980 written as well as delivered by the Queen and broadcast at peak viewing time. It goes without saying, Denmark being a Continental culture, that, in addition to the content, the language itself is accepted as important: 'The mode of expression must reflect the Queen's own manner of speech, in an unfailingly aristocratic tone while using a modern vocabulary.'[18]

Margrethe had a comprehensive and cosmopolitan education. A year at the University of Copenhagen was followed by a year studying archaeology at Cambridge. From Britain, she returned for further studies in Denmark at Aarhus University, thence to the Sorbonne in Paris and finally back to England and the London School of Economics. It was in London that she met her future husband, Henri de Laborde de Monpezat who was Secretary at the French Embassy there. A woman of talent and various interests, Queen Margrethe made her mark as a designer, and was asked to devise sets and costumes for a production by the national ballet company. She did designs for a set of Christmas postage stamps and also for the official royal monogram. An amateur artist who has exhibited with success, the Queen sat for Andy Warhol though was, reportedly, not over pleased with the result. For a time, the image graced the spinaker of her husband's yacht. The Prince Consort, it would seem, while loyal and supportive quietly remains his own man. 'I do not often complain,' he told the French magazine *Point de Vue*, in an interview in June 1999, 'but people have come to think of a prince like a puppy – content to trot along behind and be fed the occasional sugar lump.'[19]

She came to the throne when she did because a change in the constitution had displaced one of the most venerable traditions of monarchy in favour of a more liberal, more modern law of succession. The death of her father Frederick IX of Denmark in January 1972 marked a double break in the history of the monarchy. For 400 years, by the convention of the dynasty, a Christian had succeeded a Frederick, a Frederick a Christian, and of course, since in Denmark as in most other European monarchies primogeniture in the male line was the rule, man had followed man, even when in the notorious case of Christian VII that man had been clinically mad. But in January 1972 King Frederick was followed not by the next male in succession, his seventy-year-old brother Prince Knud (in English Canute), but by his chain-smoking thirty-two-year-old daughter, bearer of a name for Danes as resonant of past glories as Canute. At the celebrated Union of Kalmar of 1397, Margaret I, who had won power as queen regent for her son Olaf, presided over the union of the Swedish and Norwegian crowns with that of Denmark. It was a remarkable achievement (the Norwegian association lasted the best part of 400 years) which owed much to Margaret's ability and determination. Even after the death of her son aged seventeen, she retained power as co-ruler. As we have noted, her twentieth-century namesake ascended the throne in her own right.

In the early 1950s the question of the succession was causing a lot of concern in the Danish establishment. The King and Queen and their five daughters were a model royal family but, as the King had no son, his heir was his brother Crown Prince Knud. The Prince was extremely unpopular and, people said, of limited intelligence. Neither quality, it must be said, had been a bar to the succession in the past but in the democratic atmosphere of the time it seemed quite possible that the monarchy itself might come into question. Margrethe, the eldest daughter, was a twelve-year-old school girl and seemed likely to make a popular and capable successor when the time came, moreover, if centuries of tradition could be overthrown to permit the succession of women that would be more in tune with contemporary egalitarian ideas. In February 1952, Britain's King George VI died. He too had no son so was, of course, succeeded by his daughter the twenty-five-year-old Elizabeth II. The British example was no doubt a factor in prompting the Danes to up date their own system. At all events, Prince Knud agreed with great reluctance that the question could be put to a referendum. The government prepared a draft bill to effect the change and when, in May 1953, this was put to the vote a majority of more than three to one was returned in favour of the change. Parliament duly approved the necessary legislation and in June King Frederick signed his royal assent at a meeting of the Council of State. In 1958, Crown Princess Margrethe (the title was hitherto unknown in Denmark) herself attended the Council of State for the first time.

Queen Margrethe has something of a reputation as an intellectual. With her second son Prince Joachim and his wife, the immensely popular Princess Alexandra, gracing the family image of Danish monarchy and Crown Prince Frederik pursuing a career in the Danish diplomatic service, the Queen seemed to be shaping a new style of democratic monarchy – a combination of popular symbolism and hands-on professionalism in its dealings with the business of government which suggested that, in Denmark at least, the institution could look forward in hope to a future of developing commitments and perhaps even responsibilities.

Within two years of the death of Diana, Princess of Wales, the European fashion and gossip magazines reckoned they had a replacement in Alexandra of Denmark, 'the Diana of the North'. Her beauty, spontaneity and charm matched the model, while from the moment she was introduced on to the royal circuit in the spring of 1995 she demonstrated a confidence and sureness of touch which would have been remarkable in a princess of the blood royal. But the Hong Kong-born Alexandra Christina Manly, child of an Anglo-Chinese father and an Austrian mother, was a qualified economist and a marketing executive for a major investment company at the time of her meeting with Prince Joachim. Born in June 1964 in the Chinese year of the dragon, baptized in the name of one of Denmark's best known and most beautiful princesses (the consort of King Edward VII of England) and, unexpectedly perhaps, a member of her school ice-hockey team, she seemed well omened for a destiny as princess of the northern kingdom, heir to the tradition of the Viking drakar ships. The Prince, it is said, went on his knees to propose. She repaid the compliment by devoting herself to becoming a true Dane. The difficult language of her husband-to-be presented few problems for a polyglot with some Chinese and Japanese, and fluency in English, French and German. The sacrifice of her career no doubt presented greater difficulty – she even changed her hairstyle from the trim cut of the business woman to a more flowing look. Married from Copenhagen's delightful Frederiksborg Palace in November 1995, Alexandra commented that to marry a prince is to marry his country. The Queen was to assure her that she could look upon the whole country as her in-laws. She and Prince Joachim introduced, so to speak, the ideal family note to the palaces of the Amalienborg. Crown Prince Frederik, who had yet to marry, by no means begrudged them their popularity, though he had not found the same idyll.

At the turn of the century, when for their contemporaries marriage is a debatable option, Europe's crown princes find themselves faced with old-fashioned pressures and constraints not placed on their compatriots. Young professionals, men and women, commonly delay the start of a family into their late thirties or early forties, deciding to marry or not on grounds of tax advantage as much as romantic commitment, and on the assumption that if the partnership does not work out, then divorce and remarriage are the normal options and carry absolutely no stigma. Thanks to what might be called pioneering work by the Windsors, some such social norms should apply more or less to royalty. And yet they do not really do so. Just thirty years old when he was appointed to a junior post at Denmark's Paris embassy, Crown Prince Frederik was the target of speculation as to 'who' and 'when' and sometimes, it seemed, 'whether' he would marry. For his part, when asked about his matrimonial plans, Prince Frederik was wont to point out that the woman he chose as wife would in all probability become his people's queen. It was also true that any choice he might make, should he wish to retain his rights in the succession to the crown, would have to be approved by his mother and by the Danish government. According to Denmark's official Information Service publication, *Le prince héritier* (1996): 'Those are the rules of the game and the Crown Prince has accepted them.'

Born in May 1968, star sign Gemini, the Prince, created Prince Royal in 1972, has had the pick of most options for a full and interesting life. His obligatory stint in the armed services included training as a frogman and getting in his hours in free-fall formation parachute-jumping. Public appearances with celebrities included sharing a bottle of wine in a Parisian café with a veteran Danish artist of the 1950s. Co-hosting a pop music show on the radio and giving the slip to his security guard on the way to the opera offered lively variants on the culture photo opportunity, while student years spent taking degree courses in political science at Aarhus in Denmark and Harvard in the US were enriched by involvement in Denmark's delegation at the UN. Moreover, Denmark's Crown Prince seemed to have no doubt about the future of the monarchy in this country's system of government.

Denmark's royal family was a notable factor in Europe's inter-dynastic relationships with the progeny of that veritable patriarch, King Christian IX, who died in 1906 aged eighty-eight after a reign of forty-three years. Grandfather of the Russian Tsar Nicholas II and of the Norwegian King Haakon VII, father of George I of the Hellenes and through him the Greek dynasty, he was also, through his daughter Alexandra, father-in-law of King Edward VII and grandfather of the future King George V. Theirs was a generation doomed to see the cataclysm of the First World War, and many a royal house was to sink in the rubble of its aftermath.

News of Great Britain's declaration of war on Germany on 4 August 1914 was greeted by the majority of the population with rapturous enthusiasm. In Buckingham Palace George V was alarmed to find his mother attached to the lapels of his coat and shaking vigorously. 'I told you so,' wailed the exasperated Queen Alexandra, 'I told you that Willie was the very devil.'[20] By this the King understood her to mean that his cousin Wilhelm II, Emperor of Germany, was a slippery customer and his country an untrustworthy and unscrupulous player in the great game of European diplomacy. The seventy-year-old Queen Mother had been nursing a deep-seated grudge against the Germans ever since 1866, when the Prussian army had deprived her native Denmark of the Duchies of Schleswig and Holstein – a third of the country's territory. Her English family had expressed very proper outrage on her behalf, but their government had done nothing and the young Princess of Wales had been left, like some Victorian

Cassandra, to utter periodic protests and prophecies of doom. Now, as she saw matters, the womb of time had brought forth the predicted disaster.

The historical connections between the English and Danish royal families had witnessed a number of more or less sad episodes – few more so than the tragic life of King George III's daughter at the court of the mad King Christian VII. Sexually profligate if not over-virile, Christian early on contracted syphilis. He was a masochist before the term was coined and found sexual gratification in being beaten by his groom of the bedchamber. He was also considered mentally unstable to a clinical degree and was duly certified insane in 1784, aged 35. Christian's childhood had been a catalogue of horrors, from a dipsomaniac father in the grip of delirium tremens who died of alcohol poisoning at the age of forty-three, to a tutor who regularly thrashed the young prince into insensibility.

His unfortunate wife was Caroline Matilda, sister of King Goerge III of Great Britain. Somewhat above middle height with startling blond hair and her complexion 'the finest imaginable', she had been packed off to Copenhagen in the cause of dynastic politics at the age of fifteen. In the next few years she grew up into a strikingly beautiful woman who, after the English fashion which shocked the staid Danish court, displayed her bosom more than strict modesty could approve. Even so, she had to vie for the King's favours not only with the flagellant favourite Count Holck but also with a string of common prostitutes to whom it was Christian's engaging practice to detail his wife's performance in the royal marriage bed.

Despite these distractions, Christian managed to give his wife not only syphilis but also a son. He celebrated the event with a riotous progress through Europe accompanied not by the Queen but by Count Holck and by his court physician Frederik Struensee. Tall, black haired and handsome, the thirty-year-old doctor displaced the ruling favourite and, on the court's return to Denmark, was put in charge of the Queen's health. He cleared her of syphilis and soon became her constant companion, having been ennobled by a compliant monarch. Christian next appointed him chief minister and, while he himself was held under house arrest in his own palace, his court physician ruled the country by day and the Queen by night. It could not last. Struensee made important and radical reforms which, among other things, lifted the immunity from imprisonment for debt enjoyed by the aristocracy. He consequently made powerful enemies. In the small hours of 17 January 1772 he was surprised in the Queen's bed and hauled off to prison. On 28 April after months of incarceration and torture, he was publicly dismembered before being beheaded.

There were many who thought that his paramour should have accompanied him to the scaffold. But her powerful brother George of England intervened on Queen Caroline's behalf and, after being divorced from her lunatic husband, she was sent into exile where she died three years later. Her son Frederick VI backed the wrong side in the European wars unleashed by Napoleon. As a result, Norway, a Danish dependency since the time of Kalmar, was assigned to the Swedish crown in the Treaty of Kiel (1814). However, by a diplomatic oversight, the treaty failed to assign also Norway's dependency, the vast, but remote territory of Greenland. Accordingly it remained with Denmark, so that when in 1975 the Kingdom joined the European Community, the land surface of members under the rule of monarchies became much larger than that of those under republics.

King Christian X, like the other Scandinavian monarchs, succeeded in guarding his country's neutrality throughout the First World War, and Denmark in fact gained something from the conflict, being awarded northern Schleswig. But the outbreak of the Second World War presented the country with new, yet more worrying problems.

Given the supremacy of German airpower in the region and the requirements of her submarine strategy, the occupation of Denmark was only a question of time. When the inevitable ultimatum came in April 1940, Christian followed the advice of his ministers and capitulated. But Danish subjection did not lead to whole-hearted collaboration. The Danish Resistance began to sabotage munitions factories, railways and port installations, and Resistance pipelines were used to smuggle the bulk of Denmark's Jewish population to safety in Sweden. The spirit of resistance seemed to be embodied by the King, who followed his peacetime routine of a morning horse ride, unaccompanied and unprotected, through the streets of Copenhagen, until in October 1942 his horse shied and threw him, and he was severely injured. He withstood all German demands for anti-Jewish legislation and while, as head of state, he could hardly refuse to appeal against the perpetration of sabotage, he did refuse to hand over Danes charged with sabotage to justice in German courts and refused also to proclaim martial law. The army of occupation was eventually forced to install its own government of occupation. After three years, during which the Germans had flattered themselves that their occupation had a cloak of legalism, they had to admit reality. The charade was over. The emperor was suddenly seen to have no clothes.

The quiet heroism and regal determination of Christian X had brought the monarchy close in spirit to the people, though the etiquette of court life retained its austere traditions. With Christian's death the way was open for a new, more democratic regime of royalty, and the opportunity was recognized and exploited by the 48-year-old heir, Frederick IX. Under him the celebration of the monarch's birthday was institutionalized. On that day, 11 March, the actual birthdate not an officially designated day in the court calendar, the citizens of Copenhagen gathered in the courtyard of the Amalienborg palace to give their King the day's greetings. Frederick also granted public audiences on a routine basis which were open to any subject with a reasonable petition or grievance to discuss. Moreover, thanks to their increasingly frequent foreign tours and royal visits, he and his Swedish-born Queen Ingrid promoted the image of Denmark's new 'democratic monarchy' abroad. The admission of women to the succession marked a further, if belated step in that democratization.

[186]

Christian of Denmark very definitely had a good war by staying at his post. But on the news of the German invasion of his country, Haakon VII of Norway and members of his government decided to set up a regime in exile. The decision was to have valuable consequences for Britain's war effort. The royal party left Oslo by train heading north on 9 April, but after only a few kilometres the train came to a halt because of German air raids. A railway regulation prohibited all movement during enemy action and the driver refused to move on before he got authorization from the chairman of the railways board. It was surely a fitting start of a manhunt for a constitutional monarch.

Regarded as their figurehead by the Norwegian Resistance, King Haakon became public enemy number one for the German authorities when he broadcast an appeal to all Norwegians to resist the Nazi aggressors. Hounded by German forces with standing orders to take the King 'dead or alive', the fugitives dodged across the border into Sweden to evade German fighter planes observing that country's neutrality. Haakon's objective was still embarkation for England from a Norwegian port. However, Swedish authorities officially refused a telephoned request for a guaranteed safe passage back into Norway, and it was only thanks to the connivance of a friendly frontier officer that the party were able to continue their escape. The chase continued over precipitous mountain roads, with the cars slithering on melting snow as they jolted on between cliff and precipice. They changed transport to avoid detection, on one occasion riding in the mail van of a local stopping train. But their pursuers were disturbingly well informed, and even Norwegians who helped them were relieved to see them on their way once more. They made it to the coast where a British battle cruiser, its hold freighted with the gold reserves of the Bank of Norway, took the royal party aboard. They reached Scotland on 10 June 1940 and a few days later the BBC World Service broadcast to the world the news that the King of Norway had arrived in London. He was given a welcome at Buckingham Palace where, like his royal hosts King George and

Queen Elizabeth, he lived on the far from regal rations imposed by wartime exigences.

During the war years the septuagenarian king regally discharged the role of national hero. He was, however, also able to pay his own way and make a vital contribution to Britain's war effort. Thanks to the £36 million in gold (1940 values) he had brought with him, the Norwegian government in exile was not in need of handouts. Still more valuable, by refusing to cooperate with the Nazi-controlled regime in Norway, Haakon ensured the allegiance of the vast Norwegian-registered merchant fleet not in home ports at the time of the invasion to the Battle of the Atlantic. What has been estimated at close on a thousand ships was administered from the Norwegian shipping and trade mission in London. During the Battle of the Atlantic, when Britain's survival depended on supplies convoyed from the United States, a British cabinet minister stated that two-fifths of the country's petrol requirements were being carried in Norwegian tankers. As a contribution to the war effort he ranked it with the performance of the Spitfires during the Battle of Britain and mused on what would have happened if Norway's royal government, like some stronger nations, had not resisted the German occupation authorities. Few people then or later realized the practical value of Norway's intervention. Soon after Haakon arrived in Britain, a BBC receptionist, putting through a call for the King in Broadcasting House, turned to the tall grizzled figure with the question: 'Where was it you said you were king of?'

From his home near Windsor, King Haakon travelled regularly up to London; a typical day's business would include some personal shopping, a meeting in the Norwegian embassy with his ministers in exile, lunch at the Norwegian Club mingling with civilian exiles, or at the Senior Services Club meeting officers in the Norwegian armed forces in the Allied war effort. Sometimes he made the long journey up to the Norwegian army's training camp in Scotland. By the end of the war he was well known in many parts of Britain, and his return to Norway on 7 June 1945 – five years to the day since he had sailed into exile – meant breaking many wartime friendships. When he died, in September 1957, he was mourned by many in Britain as well as by the whole of Norway.

Haakon had come to the Norwegian throne in 1905, the first king of a fully independent Norway in some 400 years. His four-teenth-century predecessor Haakon VI had married the Danish princess (later regent) Margaret of Denmark and thus set in motion the sequence of events which brought the country into its dependent client status to the Danish crown. When, as punishment for the alliance with Napoleon, Denmark was deprived of its vast province by the Treaty of Kiel, hopes of Norwegian patriots were dashed as they saw their country awarded to Sweden with the status of an independent government under the Swedish king. Whatever the constitutional niceties (Norway was awarded its own constitution and a separate parliament), the vast majority of Swedes and many Norwegians too considered the country as little better than a province with the token autonomy of a home-rule govern-ment. Then, in 1885, the Stockholm parliament deprived King Oscar II of his voice in Swedish foreign affairs (henceforward to be directed by a council of state) while continuing to recognize his personal direction of Norwegian foreign affairs. Norwegian public opinion was indignant. Even so, nationalist agitation confined itself modestly enough to demands for separate Norwegian consuls to represent Norwegian government interests abroad. But the Swed-ish royal authorities refused even this. In 1905 the Norwegian gov-ernment resigned and it was obvious that King Oscar II of Sweden and Norway would find no Norwegian politician prepared to form a new administration. The Storting (parliament) formally resolved that since there was no royal government, the constitutional royal power was in abeyance. It empowered the resigning administration to 'exercise the power granted to the King ... subject to the changes made necessary by the fact that the union between the crowns of Sweden and Norway under the said King is dissolved.'.[21] Its business concluded for the time being, the assembly dispersed. Among the journalists watching as the serious-minded top-hatted deputies streamed out of the Storting building was *The Times* correspondent who observed to a Danish colleague that it seemed to be a rather 'gentlemanly revolution'. But it was a revolution nonetheless.

Rumour hinted darkly, and absurdly, at impending war between Norway and Sweden. Politicians sat down to discuss possible forms of constitution. It was a blank page in a new chapter in the country's history. Republicanism was a possibility, but was it practical? Apart from Switzerland and France, Europe was solidly monarchical, and while Switzerland could look back more than 500 years of continuity, in France the Third Republic was only thirty-five years old, had no written constitution and was the sixth regime in France in the 112 years since the overthrow of Louis XVI in 1792 – a period which had seen two kingdoms and two empires as well as two republics. In fact monarchy, the system under which Britain had led the world's industrial revolution and under which Germany was already overtaking her, might seem the preferred European way. It was, at all events, the system Norway opted for.

Following a referendum in which the country approved the institution of a monarchy, the Storting elected the thirty-three-year-old Prince Charles of Denmark, an officer in the Danish navy, married and with a baby son, Olaf, who would presumably grow up into a good Norwegian. The Prince accepted the crown on condition that the offer was confirmed by a plebiscite. Although, as was to be expected of a prince, he had no fewer than six first names, not one of them had been borne by Norway's medieval kings. In fact, since it was the marriage of Haakon VI to Princess Margaret of Denmark which had preluded the loss of Norwegian autonomy back in the 1300s, he was proclaimed as Haakon VII at his accession on 18 November 1905. The coronration was set for 22 June the following year. It was to be the last such ceremony in the annals of the Norwegian monarchy.

A suitably imposing ceremony had been devised in which the prime minister shared the handling of the crown with the Bishop of Bergen, while the sceptre, orb and sword of state were handed to the King by other ministers. A large body of Norwegian opinion, however, found even this excessive. Two years later, almost as if regretful of their decision against the republican form of government, the Storting abolished the symbolic act of coronation. Future Norwegian kings were to be inaugurated with a simple oath-taking ceremony. They have never been allowed, even if they wished, to entertain notions above their station as democratic heads of state. At the venerable age of eighty-two Haakon faced the dilemma of constitutional propriety confronting royal prerogative in a peculiarly irritating context. Drenched to the skin while conducting an open-air review at Stavanger, he, along with the other members of the little royal party, adjourned to the royal hotel where it was agreed that a stiff tot of brandy might be a wise as well as a pleasant precaution. Unfortunately, Norway's strict licensing laws forbade the consumption of alcohol on the premises. Heir to a Viking tradition, the King boldly stretched the rules. He suggested that the Mayor of Stavanger might open the bottle, the sheriff could fill the glasses and if the Minister of Justice would hand them round then they might consider it permissible to drink the brandy for medicinal purposes.

But pomp and formality are observed in the sovereign's dealings with his government. Each year parliament is opened with the speech from the throne, delivered by the King in ceremonial uniform wearing decorations and the chain of the order of St Olav, and flanked by the Queen and the Crown Prince also in dress uniform. The speech is, of course, written by his ministers and handed to him on the step of the throne by the prime minister in person, his head bowed. In England this function has traditionally been performed by the Lord Chancellor.

When Haakon died, after a lifetime of service and a distinguished record during the Second World War (the royal monogram 'H7' was adopted as the symbol of the resistance) most Norwegians accepted the institution of monarchy with enthusiasm. The new king, Olav V did not have a coronation, but was nevertheless honoured with a church service of dedication and blessing. The fact that many parliamentary deputies from the governing Labour party

[191]

attended this service despite a cabinet prohibition indicated just how far public opinion had consolidated behind the monarchy. Olav, often known as the people's king, died in January 1991 at the age of eighty-seven and after thirty-four years as head of state of what for years had been a fervently socialist country: it was an occasion for universal and genuine mourning.

Olav's parents had been married at the private chapel in Buckingham Palace. His mother, Princess Maud of Wales, was devoted to Appleton House on the Sandringham estate, a wedding present from her father King Edward VII (then Prince of Wales), and it was there that Olav was born and there that he spent many visits in later life and even part of his honeymoon. English was literally his mother tongue and he completed his education at Balliol College, Oxford in the 1920s. The best man at his wedding to Princess Martha of Sweden in Oslo in 1929 was the Duke of York (later King George VI). Years later when King George and Olav's Queen Martha were dead, the gossipmongers on both sides of the North Sea whispered that the widowed Norwegian King had gone courting the Scottish-born Queen Elizabeth the Queen Mother. In 1962 Olav became the first foreign monarch to make a state visit to Edinburgh and in 1983 the Queen Mother was an honoured guest at the King's eightieth birthday celebrations. He was an honorary colonel of the Green Howards, one of the crack regiments in the British Army. All his life he was a redoubtable sportsman. In his twenties he made a reputation for himself in international sport as a skier but above all as a yachtsman, taking a gold medal in the six-metre class in the 1928 Olympics. Thirty years later he was elected as president of the International Yacht Racing Union. At the age of seventy-five he skippered his team to take second place in a major world championship and was still skiing and sailing into his eighties.

His son Harald, who became King as Harald V, succeeded also to his father's prowess in the cockpit; he also began to share in the duties of the monarchy at a comparatively early age. If Norway's enemies had had their way, his accession would have taken place decades earlier. When his father, then Crown Prince Olav, followed King Haakon into exile in England during the Second World War, his mother went with her children to her native Stockholm. From there she telegraphed to England with the disturbing news that there was talk of her returning to Oslo where the three-year-old Harald should be proclaimed King and his father regent. Some commentators subsequently claimed that King Gustav V of Sweden was involved in these machinations but the evidence is lacking. Shortly after this Princess Märtha and her children sailed safely to the US at the invitation of President Roosevelt.

Relations between father and son were on the best of terms until Harald disclosed his marriage plans. His choice, clearly deeply felt, had fallen on Sonja Haraldsen, the daughter of an Oslo business-man. No doubt to the Prince's surprise, his father refused his per-mission and maintained his objection for some years. It seemed that the 'people's king' was stepping out of character in objecting to his son marrying a commoner. Perhaps he remembered his father's apprehension back in 1953 when his sister Princess Ragnhild wanted to marry a prosperous shipowner. King Olav con-sulted his prime minister as to whether the marriage of the princess to a commoner might harm the standing of the dynasty, even in democratic, socialist Norway. On the prime minister's advice that public reaction would probably not be negative, the marriage went ahead and was perfectly well received by public opinion. The children of the union have no place in the succession to the Norwegian throne, unlike the children of Princess Anne and her first, com-moner, husband Captain Mark Phillips in the succession to the British crown. The fact that Olav held out for so long against the wishes of his son, despite the fact that his sister's marriage in fact caused no political problems for the dynasty, might prompt the question whether these considerations were his primary concern. At all events, when the King finally gave his consent, the young couple left Oslo cathedral after their August 1968 wedding for their honeymoon, knowing that they were to return to the country house of Skaugum in its spacious grounds, just outside Oslo where

Olav and Martha had passed some of their happiest times, and where Harald had been born, and which the King had given them as a wedding present.

In the late 1990s the royal couple were to attract a good deal of criticism for what was seen as their, and particularly the Queen's, extravagant lifestyle, though there were also grumbles about the King's passion for shooting parties as the guest of rich friends in which hundreds of pheasant were dispatched. Early in 1999, after a year in which the royal couple had been subject to hostile comment of a kind more familiar to the House of Windsor, a public opinion poll showed a popularity rating for the Queen barely in double figures. Restoration work to the royal palace provided a last straw to break the public patience. Rather like Britain's New Labour Lord Chancellor who fitted out his apartments at huge public expense in pursuit of 'authentic' luxury, the Norwegian royal couple attracted much criticism for the expenditure they authorized on royal properties. Public discontent was further embittered by the fact that Norway's taxpayers were footing the bill, and the King, with a tax-free allowance of some nineteen million Kroner, did not seem to be among their number.

With the collapse of the Soviet Union the Scandinavian countries began to reopen their historic links with the Baltic states. As to Norway, her Baltic neighbours must have been pleased by the friendly compliment implied when King Harald and Queen Sonja made an official visit to Latvia, Lithuania and Estonia in the guise of a trip to celebrate their pearl wedding anniversary. Norwegian critics of the monarchy took a more jaundiced view. Some time before, Princess Martha-Luise had received the gift of a horse from a Norwegian retail chain millionaire so that she could continue to compete in the national show-jumping team. King Harald's decision to open the group's new store in Riga, Latvia, it was charged, smacked of a quid pro quo. At Vilonius Lithuania's President Valdus Adamkus honoured the King by investing him with the Order of Gediminnas named after the fourteenth-century Grand

Duke of Lithuania whose campaigns against neighbouring Russian principalities inaugurated his country's golden age. By the end of the century, the Lithuanian state comprised Belarus, much of Ukraine and parts of Russia, and its grand duke was also king of Poland – fitting memories of a royal past for a republic when honoring a visiting monarch in the twentieth century.

11

ROYAL BENELUX

—•—

His Royal Highness Willem-Alexander Prince of Orange (he acceded to the title when his mother Queen Beatrix ascended the throne), flyer and yachtsman by inclination, Crown Prince of the Netherlands by destiny, is one of the figures in public life whose constant PR smile seems the expression of genuine ebullience and good-humoured *joie de vivre*. Boyhood holidays on the Austrian ski slopes or at the family villa in Tuscany enlivened his schooling in Holland's public education system and he took his international baccalaureat at Atlantic College, the One World College in Wales, and graduated in history at the University of Leyden.

Following the military training which befits the heir to a crown, he has commissions in all three armed services and pilot licences in air transport, jet-engined aircraft, as well as a private licence, and is aide-de-camp on special assignment to the Queen. Entitled to sit on the council of state since his majority, the Crown Prince (Holland's first in more than a century of female rule) has represented his mother on major international occasions, such as the swearing-in of Nelson Mandela as President of South Africa in 1994. In 1995 he set up his own establishment in The Hague and receives a civil list allowance for his office and living expenses. He is honorary member or patron of his country's leading flying and sailing clubs, while his interests in fast cars and pretty women are more or less par for the course in the world of a modern prince. It is true that, unlike his grandfather HRH Prince

Bernhard of the Netherlands, he is excluded from that truly select circle of drivers who have sat behind the wheel of their own spanking new Cord 812, but against this, Prince Willem can boast another treasure – a baby photo he need not blench to show his friends. At Porto Ercole in 1968, when he was just one year old, he was snapped being cradled in the arms of Charlie Chaplin.

This favoured child of fortune belongs to a family which, according to *Forbes* the US business magazine, is among the world's richest. As always with the excessively wealthy, nothing approaching an exact estimate of Queen Beatrix's fortune is possible – the Dutch say it is the nation's best kept secret – but experienced financial journalists have estimated it at £2.5 billion. They have no doubt that she is much wealthier than Queen Elizabeth II of Great Britain and Northern Ireland. While many of the choice gems available to the Windsors belong to the Crown, the finest diadems, jewels and parures worn by the royal ladies of the House of Orange Nassau are the personal property of the family and are valued at some £10 million. What some consider the finest item, the 40 carat Indian diamond, the 'Holland' came as a bequest from Mary II of Great Britain and Ireland to her beloved husband William of Orange, King William III. Since the inventory of Queen Beatrix's art collection, of her important collection of modern sculpture and of her objets d'art is unknown so, necessarily, is their undoubtedly considerable value. But the bulk of the Queen's assets is said to be found in a portfolio of global investments, which include between three and four per cent in Royal Dutch Shell. In addition to this ill-defined personal fortune, Queen Beatrix and Prince Claus, in accordance with the terms of the Royal House Finances Act, share with Crown Prince Willem, Princess Juliana the queen mother and Prince Bernhard an untaxed royal allowance totalling (in 1999) nearly fourteen million guilders.

For centuries a republican oligarchy, the Netherlands became a monarchy just twenty years after the execution of King Louis XVI should have sounded the death knell of the institution. However, Dutch sovereigns are inaugurated not with a coronation but with an investiture. The traditional emblems of royal authority – crown, orb, sceptre and sword of state – along with a vellum-bound copy of the constitution are displayed at this ceremony, but these regalia of the kingdom are the property not of the nation but of the Regalia Foundation of the House of Orange-Nassau, of which Queen Beatrix is the president. Like Elizabeth II, Queen Beatrix rides to the state opening of her Parliament in an elaborately ornate gilded coach, escorted by flunkies and foot-men. Three palaces are at her disposal, owned and maintained by the state – Huis ten Bosch and the Noordeinde Palace, with its magnificently restored ball room, in The Hague, and the Royal Palace Amsterdam. The Soestdijk Palace near Utrecht is provided for the residence of the queen mother. All four buildings date from the sixteenth or seventeenth centuries.

The House of Orange-Nassau traces its descent to the fifteenth century Engelbert Count of Nassau (now in Germany). A six-teenth century descendant acquired by marriage the autonomous principality of Orange in the south of France and the family retained the title when the principality reverted to the French crown. William I (1533–1584) known as 'William the Silent' was appointed stadholder (viceroy) in the provinces then ruled by the Habsburg emperor Charles V and subsequently by his son King Philip II of Spain. William led the opposition of the Protestant United Provinces for liberation from Spain's oppressive Catholic regime. Spain finally recognized Dutch independence at the Treaty of Westphalia in 1648.

In 1998 Queen Beatrix and King Juan Carlos of Spain joined in ceremonies of reconciliation to bury the memories of old political rivalries and religious divisions. And yet those old memo-ries may have impacted on the Crown Prince's marriage plans. In September that year it emerged that his four-year engagement to an attractive young Dutch woman had been broken off. Europe's royalty watchers saw the hand of Queen Beatrix in the decision, she was said to have been opposed to the marriage from the start and to have finally brought her son round to her way of thinking. A few weeks later it was learnt that the young woman herself had broken off the relationship, exasperated by reports that the Prince had said that he did not plan to marry for at least ten years. Machiavellian observers wondered whether this assertion had been inspired by Queen Beatrix, for the bride-to-be was not only a commoner but also a Catholic. In any case, under the terms of the Dutch constitution, the Prince would have had to receive the consent of the Estates General to his marriage, if he wished to retain his right to the succession.

Historical memories linger on in this part of Europe. In Belgium, Flemish separatists look back to the Battle of Courtrai in 1302, when a force of Flemish weavers and townsmen routed the chivalry of France, as a golden moment of national identity and look forward to the dismantling of the Belgian state and Flemish independence before the 700th anniversary of the battle in July 2002. Such tenacity of tradition comes as something of a surprise in the region which, as names like Brussels, Maastricht and Amsterdam attest, is at the heart of the European Union. But then the region was also the cradle of the dynasty of Pepin of Héristal (Herstal, now a suburb of the Belgian town of Liège), ancestor of Charlemagne, patriarch of Europe. The present ruling families are newcomers in the annals of monarchy. The modern history of Luxembourg as a fully independent state dates only from 1890; the Kingdom of Belgium was inaugurated in July 1831; and the Kingdom of the Netherlands in March 1815. At that time the Netherlands alone, thanks to the provisions of the Congress of Vienna, comprised virtually the whole territory now divided among the three monarchies.

For some 200 years the history of the United Provinces of the Netherlands was an uneasy contest between republican oligarchies and the stadholders, some of whom aspired to semi-monarchical status (one of them actually did become a king, as William III of England) but it was not until 1806 that the country received a king of its own. The benefactor was the French emperor Napoleon I. Only ten years earlier he had abolished the hereditary stadholder in favour of the puppet 'Batavian Republic'. Now, in 1806, the conquered territory was once again transformed, this time as the Kingdom of Holland with Louis Bonaparte on its throne. His queen, the renowned beauty Hortense de Beauharnais, was the Empress Josephine's daughter, and the royal couple had three sons, the youngest of whom, Louis-Napoleon, would in the course of time become Emperor of the French as Napoleon III. King Louis's own reign was brief. Ungratefully misinterpreting his duties, he endeavoured to rule his little country in the interests of its people, rather than as a province of the French empire in Europe. On 4 July 1810 Holland was overrun by his imperial brother's army. Forced to abdicate, King Louis named his eldest surviving son his successor. The futile gesture gave the six-year-old a reign of just five days before the territory was annexed outright to France.

In 1815, the son of the last of the stadholders returned from exile and was proclaimed King William I of the Netherlands under the terms of the Congress of Vienna. He became also Grand Duke of the newly reestablished Grand Duchy of Luxembourg. Moreover, the national territory was considerably enlarged by the acquisition of the recently formed United Belgian States. These territories, which had won independence from their Habsburg rulers in 1790 only to be annexed by France in 1795, were now assigned to the new Dutch crown. Dutch troops played their part in the final triumph over Napoleon at Waterloo, but unfortunately the new kingdom and its ruler did not distinguish themselves in the years of peace which followed.

William was fiercely conservative in politics, proudly Dutch nationalistic in sentiment, and unyieldingly Protestant in religion. The southern, largely Catholic and French Walloons were subject to harsh discrimination and in 1830 burst out in rebellion: the following year the newly independent Kingdom of Belgium joined the European family. In 1840 King William, known in

Dutch history as 'the merchant king', abdicated in favour of his forty-eight-year-old son William II, a charming and popular figure remembered as the man who gave the Netherlands its first modern democratic constitution. He was followed by his somewhat autocratic son, William III. He had three sons by a first marriage but tragically, all predeceased him so that when he died in November 1890 he left only one child, a daughter by his second marriage. The link with Luxembourg was broken. In Holland, William was succeeded by his daughter, the ten-year-old Wilhelmina. But the conventions then governing in the House of Luxembourg did not permit succession in the female line and so the Grand Duchy gained independence in fact as well as in name under the seventy-three-year-old Adolph I of the house of Nassau-Weilburg. Until Wilhelmina's coming of age in 1898, the royal functions of the Dutch monarchy were discharged on the advice of a regency council headed by Emma the German-born Queen Mother, who thus inaugurated more than a century of women rulers of the Netherlands and its overseas territories.

Wilhelmina's wedding photograph shows a sturdily built young woman wearing the modest domestic coif of the housewife and a bodiced jacket over a skirt of the same flowered pattern. A lace jabot up to the neck modestly conceals her cleavage, and, falling from the waist, is a rich lace apron with, on her hip, the purse and chatelaine of the mistress of a bourgeois household, and on her head a simple domestic lace cap. The dress was typical of a prosperous Dutch bourgeoise matron. Dutifully, her hand is tucked through the arm of a uniformed man about a head taller than she, well accoutred with decorations and epaulets and on his head the feathered cocked hat of high rank. Her husband was Prince Hendrik of Mecklenburg Schwerin, one of the score of petty states which made up the pre-1918 German empire. The wedding photograph depicts the domestic ideal of Holland's prosperous middle class – manly authority and wifely obedience. It no doubt flattered the Dutch sense of national identity that, while in public affairs their Queen was head of state, within the private world of the palace the supremacy of the pater familias appeared secure. But few who had dealings with Wilhelmina, Queen of the Netherlands, doubted her iron determination of will, her almost mystical reverence for the royal house of Orange-Nassau, or her deep sense of personal betrayal, as her husband fell victim to a severe drink problem.

The Queen needed all her will-power during the difficult years of Dutch neutrality in the First World War. Whereas Belgium, lying athwart the German lines of advance on France, was over-run and could not avoid the conflict, the Netherlands held aloof. At the end of the war as the German empire crumbled in socialist revolution, there were those who thought the House of Orange-Nassau might also be unseated by Dutch revolutionary social ele-ments. In fact there was controversy. It seemed that the Queen had been closely involved in the decision not to hand over the refugee Kaiser to the allies. His decision to seek refuge in November 1918 rather than take what she considered the honourable course – to stay with his armies in defeat – had shocked her. But once he was on the Dutch side of the frontier, neither she nor her ministers would surrender him for fear that to do so would endanger the Netherlands' standing as a country of refuge.

As the depression years of the 1930s advanced, Wilhelmina de-spaired of her inability to intervene in her government's peacetime policies. She more than once considered abdicating, only to be dissuaded after long discussions and some heated arguments with Princess Juliana and Prince Bernhard, the heiress to the crown and her consort.

Among European royal houses abdication does not have the negative resonances associated with it in the English tradition. Here it has been a ten-letter word of blackest omen ever since in 1399 Richard II made the 'voluntary gesture' of resignation to his cousin Henry IV and was never seen alive again. And, of course, just two years before Juliana dissuaded her mother from this course of action, Edward VIII had left the throne under circumstances which traumatized the British monarchy for two

[203]

generations. For Continental rulers, by contrast, the idea of royal retirement has an illustrious precedent. In 1555, at the age of fifty-five, the Holy Roman Emperor Charles V, King of Spain, lord of Spanish America and of an empire on which the sun never set, and also ruler in the Netherlands, had retired to a monastery and left his vast dominions to the charge of his sons. Wilhelmina's great grandfather William I had abdicated because the newly emergent state of Belgium marked the failure of his policies. For Wilhelmina, abdication seemed the only tolerable perhaps honourable solution to her frustrated desire to help her country. By dissuading her from her intention the family made possible the most glorious years of her reign.

With the onset of the war which the Queen had so long been dreading, the Netherlands hoped that she might once again weather the conflict as a neutral. But on 10 May 1940 the country was invaded. With the consent of the commander of the armed forces, Wilhelmina phoned the King of England and three days later made the crossing to Harwich on a British warship. In due course she found herself with her daughter Juliana and her family being welcomed at London's Liverpool Street Station by King George VI.

The royal refugees were given apartments in Buckingham Palace, but the news from home was grim. German terror-bombing of Rotterdam on 15 May had compelled the Dutch government to capitulate or see the demolition of their entire country. Even so, throughout the war Dutch forces fought alongside the allies. The bulk of the Dutch home fleet and airforce had escaped to fight with the British, while in due course warships of the Dutch fleet in the waters of the Netherlands East Indies (now Indonesia) continued the war in the western Pacific. Financed in large part from Dutch assets in the United States, the Dutch war effort was under the command of the government in exile in London. Constitutionally head of state, for some five years Wilhemina was also actively involved in the affairs of state, her forceful personality increasingly important in ministerial discussions. She had been unable to persuade her peacetime governments of the need to prepare for war; now, with armed forces actually involved in the conflict, her government headed by Prime Minister Gerbrandy was an honourable partner in a fighting alliance dedicated to the liberation of Europe.

Queen Wilhelmina's broadcasts from London bolstered morale in her occupied homeland; with her famous emblem of the little marguerite flower, she became the focus of national loyalty for hundreds of other Dutch exiles. In June 1942 she crossed the Atlantic to Canada, Britain's co-belligerent since the outbreak of hostilities, where Princess Juliana and her family had moved. Feted in Ottawa, she went on to Washington DC where she addressed a joint session of the Houses of Congress.

Wilhelmina made a triumphal return to the Netherlands in March 1945. But her war record could not change the underlying patterns of Dutch political life. Her wartime prime minister was forced from office in the June elections. Three years later in September 1948, the Queen, not content with the role of peacetime figurehead, at last abdicated. Her thirty-nine-year-old daughter Juliana, who now became Queen and who had been dreading the challenge of following so renowned and popular a figure, greeted the decision with resignation.

Yet by her obvious and close concern for all aspects of social welfare, Juliana soon won a place for herself in popular esteem. She and her German-born consort, Prince Bernhard of Lippe Biesterfeld, with their four daughters of whom Beatrix was the eldest, seemed a model royal family. Prince Bernhard, who had trained as a pilot, had acted as liaison officer between the Dutch and British airforces during the war and, with the coming of the peace, continued his association with aviation.

And yet there were ruffles on the placid waters of public approval. In 1966 Princess Beatrix married the German diplomat Niklaus von Amsberg. Although both her father and her grandfather were German, the choice revived bitter memories of the wartime years and provoked some violent demonstrations in which anti-monarchist sentiments could also be detected. His naturalization as a Dutch citizen (adopting the name 'Claus') at the insistence of Parliament, his good nature despite occasional depression, and his somewhat pawky sense of humour succeeded in reconciling the Dutch national sentiment.

Then, in the 1970s, rumour linked Prince Bernhard's name with dubious business methods practised in Europe by the Lockheed aircraft corporation, with which the Prince was associated, and in 1976 he resigned from most of his official appointments. It was a sad blow for Queen Juliana, then in her sixties, but in no way affected her personal popularity. Her abdication, on 30 April 1980, in favour of her daughter Beatrix, was accepted as routine in the Dutch tradition. In one respect, however, the new Queen's accession heralded a break with the tradition of a century. For the first time since 1884 the Netherlands had a crown prince. Prince Willem-Alexander (b. 1967) and his brothers, Princes Johan Friso (b. 1968) and Constantijn (b. 1969) suggested that the country would once more have a king. Whether this would mean sovereigns less involved in government remained however, to be seen.

Queen Beatrix may own a bicycle, the supposed badge of continental Europe's democratic monarchies (as a child she certainly flustered the respectable old ladies of Baarn as she rode down its quiet streets from the neighbouring Palace of Soestdijk, where she was born), but she can have very little time to use it. For she seems to be a monarch with a markedly hands-on approach. Because of a complex system of proportional representation, a Dutch election typically returns many political parties to the parliament and days of political horse trading may follow before a government coalition is formed. From a reading of the official government information service brochure, *The Royal House*, it appears that the Queen is kept informed and is consulted throughout the process. The author cites with approval the nineteenth-century English constitutional theorist Walter Bagehot's classic definition of the sovereign's rights – to be consulted, to

[206]

warn and to encourage – but one suspects that Queen Beatrix's intervention may on occasion have a somewhat Victorian ring of authority. It certainly seems a far cry from constitutional monarchy as understood in twentieth-century Britain where, for decades, experts in the constitution debated whether, in 1922, King George V did or did not seek proper advice in exercising the royal prerogative in appointing Stanley Baldwin as prime minister. Queen Beatrix gives her prime minister a weekly audience which, it appears, he regards as a two-way consultative process. She is President of the Council of State, which has the constitutional function of advising the government, and she is said to be in regular touch with members of parliament and with the burgo-masters (executive mayors) of major cities. To an outsider it all sounds like old-style monarchy in action. Given Dutch success in the modern world it also seems like an excellent testimonial for the institution of monarchy itself.

Like the Netherlands, the Grand Duchy of Luxembourg was ruled by women for many decades. Inaugurated in 1814 as a Grand Duchy ruled by the King of the Netherlands, modern Lux-embourg gained full effective independence only in 1890, when the personal tie with the Dutch ruling house was finally broken. The youngest of all the continental states of the European Union, diminutive Luxembourg owes its very existence to the centuries-old rivalries which that union was created to assuage. The early years of Luxembourg's history as a fully independent state seemed hardly eventful to the outside world. The London *Annual Register* of world political affairs noted in its entry for Luxem-bourg for the year 1910: 'Nothing worth registering happened in this happiest of all countries.' But it had not always been so.

On the fault line between the German Holy Roman Empire and the Kingdom of France, the medieval counts of Luxembourg reckoned themselves liegemen of the French king, but they also provided the imperial territory of Bohemia (today the Czech

Republic) with kings – Blind King John of Bohemia died fighting for France at the Battle of Crécy in 1346, leaving his crest of feathers and his motto '*Ich Dien*' to be taken as trophies of war by Edward the Black Prince, Prince of Wales. John's son Charles became Emperor Charles IV who presided over Prague's first golden age and founded its university. (The ancient Chech connections of the house of Luxembourg are recalled in the name of Prince Wencelas, a nephew of Grand Duke Henri). It was at this time (1354) that Luxembourg became a duchy. In the fifteenth century the territory passed to the French dukes of Burgundy, in the sixteenth century to the Spanish Habsburgs who lost it to Louis XIV of France in 1684, who had to yield it to the Spanish who in turn lost it to the Austrian Habsburgs. In 1795, French revolutionary armies overran the place and until 1814 it was the French 'Département des Forêts'.

Throughout this time, the medieval fortress on its great rock was always a major strategic factor. The Congress of Vienna created the territory an autonomous Grand Duchy, with King William I of the Netherlands as Grand Duke but with the fortress garrisoned by Prussian troops. In 1830, the Luxembourgers joined the Belgians in their rising against the Dutch crown, only for the newly independent Belgium to demand that the Grand Duchy be incorporated into its territory. At the 1839 London Conference, the claim was settled by the international community declaring more than half of it as the Belgian province of Luxembourg. The great fortress, with its Prussian garrison, remained in the Grand Duchy, which remained an autonomous possession of the Dutch kings. However, with the dissolution of the German Federation in 1866, the territory of some 2,600 square kilometers came once more into question and the King-Grand Duke was considering selling it to France. Dismayed by the possibility, Prussia intervened and at a conference in London the following year, Luxembourg was declared a neutral territory, its fortress to be dismantled and the Prussian garrison to be withdrawn.

Grand Duke William III died in 1890, leaving a daughter who succeeded him in the Netherlands as Queen Wilhelmina. In Luxembourg, however, the Salic law forbidding the succession of women to the crown was invoked. The Dutch connection was finally severed and the seventy-three-year-old German prince Adolph of Nassau-Weilburg, collateral with the House of Orange, was invited to succeed. Having lost his own micro-duchy as a result of allying with Austria in the war she lost to Prussia twenty-four years earlier, the redoubtable old gentleman was delighted at the prospect of ending his days once more a sovereign prince, and lived to the ripe age of eighty-eight, dying in 1905. His fifty-three-year-old son became Grand Duke as William IV but he and his wife Maria-Anna Braganza of the royal house of Portugal had only daughters. In April 1907 a ruling, based on provisions in the House of Nassau for a failure of the male line, established the right of succession in the female line.

In 1912 the Grand Duke's charming but delicate eighteen-year-old daughter Marie-Adelaide came to the throne. But political and social murmurings were beginning to be heard even in once placid Luxembourg, and the idyllic prospect darkened still further with the advent of the First World War. On 2 August 1914 German troops were to be seen marching in battle order on the country's neutral frontier. The Grand Duchess drove to the frontier post and swung her car across the road to bar the way. She radioed the German Emperor that to trample the Grand Duchy's neutrality would be to 'sacrifice the honour of Germany' and then reported her protest by telegraph to King George V of Great Britain. Her efforts were in vain and the Grand Duchy was occupied for the duration of the war. Indeed, for the first few weeks of the conflict the German emperor made Luxembourg his HQ and was received by Marie-Adelaide. This brought her much criticism after the war but in reality she had little option; and in fact she exploited the situation to oblige her imperial guest to commute death sentences imposed by the German forces of occupation on various dissident Luxembourger, Belgian and French elements.

[209]

Even so, many of her subjects thought Grand Duchess Marie Adelaide was too friendly with the Germans. In June 1917 she did indeed pay an official visit to the court of King Ludwig III of Bavaria whose son, Crown Prince Rupprecht, was commander of the German armies on the western front. Her intervention in Luxembourg's politics, termed by some the *coup d'état* of the Grand Duchess, made her enemies on the Left and, together with her friendship of the Bavarian royals, led the leader of her coalition government to hand in his resignation. With the coming of peace, she was criticized by the French foreign minister for having seriously compromised herself with the enemies of France. For a time, it seems, bitterness about her war record threatened to jeopardize her country's independent standing in the European family. Even in Luxembourg itself a majority of the population favoured closer association with either Belgium or France. In the event she entered an economic union with Belgium in 1922.

The ambivalent position of the Grand Duchess, in particular towards Germany, had encouraged republican agitation against the continuation of the monarchy. In January 1919 she abdicated in favour of her sister Charlotte. In a referendum that September, close on 80 per cent of the population rejected the republican option and voted to retain Grand Duchess Charlotte. The following year, Marie-Adelaide entered an Italian convent. But her failing health soon meant that she had to abandon the austerities of the life of religion, and she found refuge in the Bavarian home of her young sister Antoinette who in 1921 had married Crown Prince Rupørecht. She died in January 1924, not yet thirty.

Grand Duchess Charlotte and her consort Prince Felix of Bourbon-Parma were to find themselves also victims of German aggression. During the night of 9 May 1940, news reached the palace at Colmar Berg that German troops were crossing the frontier. It was decided that the nineteen-year-old Hereditary Grand Duke Jean should leave the country with his sisters by one road, while Prince Felix drove the Grand Duchess to France by another. It was a brave decision, aiming to double the chances of

King Michael of Romania acknowledges the cheers of the crowd on his visit to Budapest in February 1997, his wife Anne can be seen standing a little behind him.

Charles Prince of Wales and Felipe Prince of the Asturias, heir to the Spanish crown, during the latter's informal visit to Britain, February 2000.

King Harold V and Queen Sonja of Norway.

Queen Silvia of Sweden at the Nobel Prize Ceremony 1999. She is wearing jewels from the Bernadotte collection.

Crown Princess Victoria of Sweden attends birthday celebrations for Queen Margrethe of Denmark, at the Theatre Royal, Copenhagen, April 2000.

Queen Margrethe II of Denmark visiting Liverpool during her state visit to the United Kingdom, February 2000.

Part of the Amalienborg Palace, Copenhagen, Denmark.

Crown Prince Willem Alexander of The Netherlands (centre), he holds the military pilot's licence and in civilian matters is patron of the Global Water Partnership.

Queen Beatrix of The Netherlands arriving for the 1989 state opening of Parliament in the Golden Coach.

Crown Prince Philippe and Princess Mathilde of Belgium with the Prince of Wales at Hampton Court during their visit to Britain in early Spring 2000.

King Juan Carlos and Queen Sofia of Spain with their children (l–r Princess Cristina, Prince Felipe and Princess Elena) 1995.

Prince Albert of Monaco with supermodel Elle Macpherson 8 May 2000.

the continuance of the legitimate line rather than risk the whole family in one party, but it must surely have been a difficult one. The parents were able to make their way to safety unhindered, but the other car had to crash through a German patrol before it too could clear the frontier.

On 10 May a government in exile was set up at the Luxembourg legation in Paris. By then, however, France was on the verge of capitulation, and early in June the French government informed the Grand Duchess that it could not guarantee her safety. So the royal party, like thousands of other refugees, headed south. Driving down roads thronging with fugitives, they reached the French-Spanish frontier at Irun and motored on along the coast to San Sebastian, and thence south towards Lisbon. There they joined a growing contingent of refugee royals. Empress Zita of Austria with her son Otto von Habsburg, and the children of Leopold III of the Belgians – fourteen-year-old Princess Josephine Charlotte, ten-year-old Prince Baudouin and six-year-old Prince Albert – had arrived earlier that month. For Jean of Luxembourg it was surely a happy encounter, for he and Josephine Charlotte were to marry a few years later. Prince Felix took passage as soon as feasible for the USA while in August Charlotte sailed to London and from there, with her aged mother the Dowager Duchess Marie Anne, crossed the Atlantic to join him. In May 1941, they travelled north to francophone Montreal, in the province of Quebec.

Meantime Prince Jean, who had been educated at Ampleforth, England's leading Catholic public school, remained in England where he did his military training with the Royal Air Force under the name of Lieutenant Luxembourg. Two government ministers also remained in England, establishing close understandings with the Belgian and Netherlands governments in exile in London. It was there on 5 September 1944 that the Benelux Convention, basis for the post-war development of the three countries, was signed.

Four days later American soldiers crossed the Luxembourg

frontier. On the 23rd the government in exile returned and that same month Prince Felix and his son returned to the country. But the war was not over. In mid December Field Marshal von Rundstedt unleashed the German counter-offensive in the Ardennes which for a few heart-stopping days seemed as though it might reverse the inevitability of Allied victory. But the Germans could not maintain the momentum and in January 1945 were in full retreat. On 14 April Grand Duchess Charlotte made her ceremonial re-entry to her country amid jubilant celebrations. In the post-war years she promoted the standing of Luxembourg in the world community, receiving and returning state visits with world leaders such as President Kennedy and the Pope. In 1961 she withdrew from many of her official commitments, designating Prince Jean as Lieutenant-Representative. In November 1964 she abdicated in his favour and with Prince Felix retired to their residence, Château Fischbach, where at the age of eighty-nine she died honoured and deeply mourned in July 1985.

Of all Europe's royals the Grand Duke of Luxembourg has perhaps the most effective powers – indeed he is almost as powerful as the President of France. Georges Pompidou, French President from 1969 to 1974, apparently observed that if Europe were to decide on a hereditary president, it would be the Luxembourg Grand Duke. The constitution authorizes him to appoint the prime minister, whom he swears in in a simple, and private ceremony, as well as a number of members of the select Crown Council. He shares the executive power with the government and can take part in the judicial power and still has the right of veto, now rarely exercised, and the prerogative of mercy – he is also the only judge in cases involving the princes of his family. From January 2000 Grand Duke Jean having announced his intention to abdicate in September, Hereditary Grand Duke Henri became an increasingly effective partner in government.

Prince Henri was born, to a 101-gun salute, in 1955, he was educated in schools in Luxembourg and France, where he took his baccalaureat. He spent a year at Sandhurst, Britain's military academy (he is a colonel in Luxembourg's army). Fluent, of course, in German, French and Letzeburgesch he also has good Spanish and two years in the US helped him perfect his command of English. After Sandhurst he went to the University of Geneva to study economics – no doubt useful to a future sovereign of Luxembourg. Among his fellow students was the Havana-born Maria Teresa Mestre y Batista, and Prince Henri fell hopelessly in love. Her being a commoner provoked some opposition within the family. But the Prince held true to his love and the two were married on St Valentine's Day, 1981. From 1980 he had taken his place in the Council of State, learning the business of government and developing his participation in foreign trade missions.

In the mid 1980s the Hereditary Grand Ducal couple made their home at Château Fischbach. Set in some sixteen hectares of parkland with formal gardens and woods, walks and tracks for cycle rides, it is every family's dream of a private nature reserve. Like Château Betzdorf, where Prince Henri himself grew up, it is surrounded by the rich and diverse forest world of Luxembourg. For both of them, love of the natural world and rapport with it should be a basic in a modern education. This does not exclude a passion for hunting and in addition to being President of the Galapagos Darwin Trust, Luxembourg, the Prince is patron of the Grand Duchy's Saint Hubert Club. Maria Teresa, while fulfilling the traditional role of mother, is prominent on the international circuit, accredited as a goodwill ambassador with Luxembourg's UN delegation and with particular interest in projects orientated towards children and education.

At the outbreak of World War II, only Leopold III of the Belgians decided to stay with his people. His father, Albert, 'the Knight King', had fought in the First World War. But Leopold, all too conscious of the terrible price that would be paid, fruitlessly, by his vulnerable country, on 25 May 1940 took the fateful decision to surrender unconditionally after a matter of days. Explaining his decision he spoke of his duty to stay with his people. He also, tempting providence, spoke of the indissoluble ties which bound the dynasty to the state. After the war he was eventually forced to abdicate ignominiously, amid accusations of betraying his country. It was a tragic end to a reign which had opened with the happiest auguries.

It was also a setback for a dynasty with a somewhat chequered record. The nineteenth century founder, Leopold of Saxe-Coburg-Gotha, is known to British history as the sage, smug and, at first, much respected *éminence grise* of Queen Victoria. He married, as his second wife, Louiss Marie d'Orléans, the eldest daughter of Louis Philippe King of the French. She survived long enough to give him three children, during which time he seems to have lived a life of Victorian virtue. A noted patron of science and education and never happier than when advising other rulers on the conduct of their realms, he was considered by himself, and for a time even by some others, as the wise old man of Europe and model monarch. In his long widowerhood, however, his conduct became increasingly erratic. He took mistresses with an amiable contempt for public opinion and installed them in the royal palace where at least one is said to have lived *en famille* with her bastard children.

His reputation was such that, when three prostitutes were found drowned in a river near the royal property, they were rumoured to have been victims of royal contract killings. His son, the unlovely Leopold II, became very unpopular. Obliged to marry an archduchess, which he considered demeaning to his royal dignity, he could not stand his wife and for the later part of his long reign (1865–1909) they lived apart, leaving Leopold free to indulge himself, maintaining as his mistress a courtesan, whom he created a baronne. In so far as he was capable of love, he may have loved her; at all events she gave him two children and, shortly before his death, so people said, he abandoned the principles of a lifetime and contracted a morganatic marriage with her. This, if it happened at all, was certainly a private ceremony and was probably intended to make the King an honest man in the eyes of the church rather than the lady an honest woman in the eyes of society.

Leopold's oldest son, the handsome and reputedly virile Prince Baudouin, also attracted the attention of the gossips. His death aged twenty-one, reported by the palace to have been the result of a brain fever or pneumonia, was attributed by cynics, who claimed to be in the know, to a firearm deployed by an outraged husband who had found the heir to the throne in bed with his wife. Nevertheless, the populace at large had something of a weakness for the dashing young prince, so that when in 1909 his shy, apparently characterless brother Alfred succeeded their vastly unpopular father, people wondered whether he would be able to revive the flagging fortunes of the monarchy.

The history of Belgium as an independent country has its origins in the eighteenth century with a liberation struggle against the region's Habsburg ruler, the Holy Roman Emperor. In November 1788, the Estates of Brabant and Hainault voted to withhold their taxes. The Belgian patriots were headline news in Paris where the government of Louis XVI was also coming under mounting pressure. In April 1789 the State Council rejected a new constitution imposed by the Emperor. The Belgian revolt was ahead of events in France. The imperial army entered Brussels and dissolved the State Council in June 1789. But the garrison was expelled and in December that year an independent Union of Belgian States was proclaimed – almost three years before the end of the monarchy in France. In the opening year of the Revolution 'Paris did not lead Brussels', in the words of Norman Davies, the historian of Europe, 'Brussels led Paris'. The situation could not last. In 1797 the armies of Revolutionary France annexed the region. The Congress of Vienna of 1815 reassigned these provinces to the newly formed Kingdom of Holland. Discriminatory policies by the Dutch government provoked the Belgian revolution of 1830 and independence.

In 1865 the first Leopold was succeeded by his thirty-year-old son Leopold II, heartless and authoritarian and for years personal proprietor of the Congo Free State. Millions of square miles of equatorial Africa were terrorized in a regime of forced labour and ruthless exploitation to augment his personal fortune – an episode which was a disgrace even in the context of nineteenth-century imperialistic practice. The King sold the territory to the Belgian state. His autocratic temperament, cribbed within the confines of European constitutionalism at home, resented the curb on his activities in his African property. The humiliation rankled – the more so, perhaps, because his nephew Albert, destined to succeed him, was open and democratic by nature, and thus a constant reproach to the surly monarch. Even so, Belgium has good reason to look back on the reign of Leopold II on two counts. Thanks to his drive, and in part to his personal funding, various important public works and public buildings were erected, such as the Law Courts in Brussels and it was under him that the Act which established the parity of Dutch and French as Belgian national languages was passed.

Coming to the throne in 1909, Albert, unlike his father and grandfather, was a happily married man as well as a 'democrat'. His marriage to Elizabeth of Bavaria in 1900 had been a love match, and with two sons as well as a daughter they came to the throne with the succession assured, barring an act of God. The reign opened with a significant gesture of national solidarity when Albert became the first king to take the oath in Dutch as well as in French. Public opinion warmed to the family and later, when the Queen had recovered from a particularly virulent form of typhoid, crowds massed outside the palace to cheer the King. By 1912, despite the pessimists, the public esteem for the monarch had been restored.

Two years later Belgium was facing the threat of German invasion, but there was a tempting alternative. Hoping to avoid the opprobrium of invading neutral Belgium, the German Kaiser suggested that Albert and his German-born wife bring the country in on the German side. In reply, the King joined his army in the front line.

In fact, although both of German descent, Albert and Elizabeth had an exceptionally 'good' war. He ensured his popularity
as a war leader in personal command of the army; she confirmed
her place in public affection within days of Germany's invasion
with the ringing affirmation that thenceforth she considered herself divided from the country of her birth by 'an iron curtain'.
Nevertheless, the question of their eldest son Leopold's marriage
plans raised unease that he too might choose a German partner.
Accordingly when in September 1926 Albert and Elizabeth announced his betrothal to Princess Astrid of Sweden, the response
was generally favourable – the King emphasized, at the Queen's
prompting, that it was a love match and in no way arranged for
political reasons. The emphasis was worth making – first, because
their own marriage had been for love; secondly, because the two
previous reigns had involved notoriously unsuccessful arranged
marriages; and thirdly, because marriage to a non-German was, in
1920s Belgium, so very politically correct.

Of course there were objections and difficulties. For traditionalists there was the question of religion. The Swedish royal family
was necessarily Lutheran. But this was less of a problem than
might have been expected. On the condition that any children of
the marriage be brought up as Catholics, the Pope was prepared to
issue the dispensation necessary for Leopold to marry a princess
who would retain her Protestant allegiance even after their marriage. For some, more serious than the question of religion was
the fact that Astrid was used to plucking poultry, gutting fish and
even doing the dishes when occasion required. For French-speaking Wallonia, it was deplorable that not only could their future
queen not speak French but her native Swedish was Germanic
and therefore related to Dutch. But the historically minded
pointed out that there was even a precedent for this Scandinavian
union. Back in the fourteenth century the daughter of a Count of
Namur had married a Swedish king. And no one could deny that
Princess Astrid was very beautiful and had the most winsome personality. As to Prince Leopold, with a reputation to match his

good looks, he had fallen for her and, chaperoned by his mother, had made an incognito visit to the Swedish court under the title of the Count of Réthy.

There were two weddings – a Catholic ceremony in the cathedral of Brussels, celebrated without a Mass, had been preceded two days previously by a civil ceremony conducted by the Mayor of Stockholm, assisted by a Catholic bishop, in the throne room of the parliament building, Riksdaghuset, in Stockholm. From the moment the Belgians saw Astrid and Leopold together, it was obvious they were deeply in love with one another, and the nation for its part fell in love with the new princess of Belgium. The idyll only deepened when she gave the country a baby prince, Baudouin, Boudewign in Flemish and so assured the succession.

But this was surely of academic interest only. With his father still vigorous and immensely popular, Leopold himself seemed unlikely to come to the throne for many years. Accordingly, King Albert's death on 17 February 1934 in a rock-climbing disaster at the age of fifty-nine shocked the nation. The state funeral on the 22nd was followed the next day with the swearing-in of the new king. The ceremony was held in the Chamber of Deputies in the Palace of the Nation, Brussels, in the presence of Belgium's 212 deputies, some 180 senators, dignitaries and members of the diplomatic corps, and princes and princesses of Europe's royal houses. After the oath-taking King Leopold made a short speech of dedication ending emotionally: 'The Queen will assist me in the discharge of my duties with all her heart.' The words would surely have had a unique resonance for Edward Prince of Wales, representing the House of Windsor at the ceremony and already fatefully committed in his heart to Mrs Wallis Simpson.[22]

These were the years of world depression, and the royal couple worked as a team with genuine concern and with practical measures to ease the social need. The Queen's Appeal for social relief was opened in 1935 by Astrid herself with a personal contribution of 500,000 francs. Then, in the evening of 23 August 1935, news broke that Queen Astrid, the nation's darling, had been killed in a motoring accident near Küssnacht, in Switzerland's Rigi massif. The tragedy had a news impact hardly to be matched until the sensational death of Diana, Princess of Wales.

Holidaying incognito in one of Switzerland's more remote landscapes the royal couple, as Count and Countess de Réthy, had set off that morning, the chauffeur bodyguard in the back seat, the King having elected to drive, and the Queen, maps folded out across her knee, navigating at his side. Perhaps Leopold was taking the bends a little too quickly; at all events, when Astrid asked him to look over and give his opinion on the map bearing, he momentarily lost control of the line and the front wheel clipped the verge – enough to send the powerful sports car plunging down the slope. Today, when seat belts are standard, the Queen would have had a chance (just as Diana would have had had she been wearing one). As it was, she was thrown clear of the vehicle and was hurled against a tree. The King and the chauffeur were still in the car when it finally came to rest, and survived. One is left to imagine the remorse that etched the King's mind. Their love had been a byword. Two million people lined the streets of Brussels to mourn as their bandaged monarch, grey-faced and halting, followed on foot his wife's black-plumed hearse to the place of interment.

Remembered with affection still by the people of Belgium and by the royal family (King Albert II's and Queen Paola's second child is Princess Astrid), Belgium's Swedish Queen had been one of the beautiful people of the high society of the inter-war years. She belongs in that cavalcade of beautiful royal women, from Sissi of Austria to Princess Grace of Monaco and Diana, Princess of Wales who, already legends in their lifetime, seem certain of immortality in the popular annals of monarchy. In Astrid's case there was a commemorative postage stamp, but no official books of memoires, no anniversary rituals, no medal struck by the dynasty. But the cities and provinces of Belgium vied with each other with such medals and ceremonies and within a year more than fifty publications had appeared in French and Dutch, German and

Swedish, English and Italian. Astrid and her handsome, if serious, husband made a striking couple. There were those who said that her death was the disaster of his life in political as well as personal terms, and it is possible that, had she lived, her presence and advice might have saved him from decisions which led eventually to his abdication. Certainly her death was indeed a depressing start to a reign which was to have few relieving moments as the international scene darkened towards the Second World War.

Just two years before Belgium's second royal tragedy, the German President von Hindenburg had appointed Adolf Hitler Chancellor, reassured by his advisers that neither he nor his movement any longer posed a political threat. In 1934 Hindenburg died on the morning of 2 August; within the hour Chancellor Hitler was proclaimed also head of state and commander-in-chief of the country's armed forces. In 1936 Leopold's government abandoned its military alliance with France and reasserted Belgium's neutrality, and the next year Hitler solemnly pledged himself to respect it. The guarantee no doubt greatly reassured the King.

In the last days of 1938, there was talk in diplomatic circles about a secret plan by Leopold III and other sovereigns to avert the 'virtual certainty of war in Europe during the coming year'. It was, in fact, part of an initiative by the five monarchs of 'the Oslo conference' – Norway, Sweden, Denmark, Belgium and the Netherlands – in which joint letters were to be addressed to the four statesmen on whom at that time the issue of war and peace depended – Chamberlain for Great Britain, Daladier for France, Hitler for Germany and Mussolini for Italy – urging them to convene an international conference to debate all the points at issue. The plan leaked, the letters were never dispatched, and the conference of heads of state never held. Instead, opening a meeting of six foreign ministers convened at Brussels in August 1939, King Leopold made an appeal to the absent world leaders to submit their differences to negotiation so as to avoid what he called 'the catastrophe which is threatening humanity'. On the same day

Ribbentrop and Molotov, the foreign ministers of Germany and Russia, were signing the Nazi-Soviet non-aggression pact which freed Hitler's hands for the invasion of Poland on 3 September. In May 1940 the Wehrmacht invaded Belgium and its King was once more in the front line.

Born in 1901, Leopold belonged to that generation who had grown up during the First World War. It had been called the war to end war, and those who had lived through it fervently hoped that that was what it was – no people more so than the people of Belgium. When German armour once more rolled across the country's frontier, Leopold III, like his father before him, put himself at the head of the national resistance effort. But in the conditions of Blitzkrieg the chances of the Belgian armed forces inflicting serious damage on the Germans were slight. The lesson of Germany's terror bombing of Rotterdam could be read as well in Brussels as in the Hague. On 28 May, overriding his cabinet, King Leopold surrendered unconditionally. In a moving speech to the nation he pledged himself to remain with his people and his soldiers in their time of crisis. His country suffered occupation but it was spared annihilation.

Leopold's pledge came to be seen in a somewhat jaundiced light when, on 6 December 1941, it was announced that the King had contracted a second marriage, with Marie-Liliane Baels, the daughter of the former governor of West Flanders. The King himself, by notarial deed, confirmed that his new wife, having renounced all title and rank of queen, would henceforth be known by the title Princess de Réthy, and that any children of the marriage would have no hereditary claim on the crown. The secrecy surrounding the wedding ceremony and the dubious constitutionality of the proceedings raised suspicions in some minds, which seemed to be confirmed when a daughter was born in July 1942 and people did their sums. It was not the first time in the history of the world that a marriage had been followed by an apparently premature birth, but people did wonder whether the heroic commitment to share the tribulations of the occupation with his compatriots was making a virtue of necessity, and the more extravagant conspiracy theorists speculated on the possibility of the princess being a German spy. Certainly the country, including even the most devoted monarchists, were shocked and hurt by what they considered an affront to the love of his subjects and, above all, a betrayal of the memory of Queen Astrid. An adviser ruefully warned the King that by this marriage he had demolished the pedestal of respect upon which the monarchy rested. Few would have disagreed.

More serious to many of his subjects were Leopold's ambiguous dealings with the German occupying power. Whereas his government had set up in exile in London, and a secret army of resistance fighters and saboteurs was gearing up at home, in November 1940 the King went to Hitler's mountain retreat at Berchtesgad-en in Bavaria. Only much later did it emerge that his mission had been to petition for the continuance of an independent Belgium in any Nazi settlement for Europe and to negotiate for improved conditions for prisoners of war. All the Belgian people knew at the time was that their king had sought an interview with the hated Nazi leader. In any case, most of the French-speaking Walloon population considered that he was already guilty of treason by the act of surrender. After all, had not France's President of the Council, Paul Reynaud, with all the righteous indignation of a man whose country was to capitulate less than three weeks later, denounced Leopold as a criminal and traitor and issued a decree stripping him of his Légion d'Honneur Grand Croix? But, unlike Pétain in France, Leopold was not the puppet of the Germans, who showed their lack of confidence in him by holding him prisoner and taking him with them into Germany on their retreat in 1944. Freed by Allied troops in 1945, Leopold was to learn that Parliament had refused him permission to return. Accordingly, he went into exile in Switzerland while his brother Prince Charles assumed the royal functions as regent.

One more humiliation awaited the forty-four-year-old monarch. In the sixth year of his exile, a referendum on the question of his return showed a small majority of Belgians in his favour. But the King's return to the country was beset by opposition and demonstrations in Brussels which ended in rioting: for a time civil war seemed not impossible. First he handed over his powers to the twenty-year-old Crown Prince Baudouin and then, in July 1951, formally abdicated. He retired from public life, travelled widely, and died in September 1983.

Baudouin and his Spanish wife, Queen Fabiola de Aragón y Mora, whom he married in 1960, were to prove model parliamentary monarchs, though sadly they remained childless. The year of their marriage was overshadowed by Belgium's withdrawal from her vast African colony, the Belgian Congo which became independent as the Republic of Zaire; but their personal popularity grew as the reign progressed. They were talented and accessible; the Queen was a fluent linguist and widely travelled, the King admired as a photographer but always available to deal personally with his subjects' problems. Their modest lifestyle – for many years they were content with a six-room royal apartment in the Castle of Laeken – and their conscientious dedication to their royal duties endeared them to the people of Belgium, both the Flemish and the Walloon communities.

The serious-minded Catholic monarch would not abandon his convictions, even at the call of royal obligations. In April 1990 Baudouin 'took a holiday from the throne' to avoid having to sign a bill before the Belgian parliament legalizing abortion. As a man, he found the proposal in conflict with his personal principles; as a king, it was his constitutional duty to authorize the legislation. His ingenious way out of his dilemma was the kind of hypocritical compromise or fudge more usually associated with the British way of doing things. It was possible in part, no doubt, because a substantial proportion of public opinion in Catholic Belgium was opposed to the measure; in part because after a reign of some forty years the King enjoyed the deep respect of his people. For whatever reason, he was able to carry off an extraordinary manoeuvre which, if it could be categorized at all in constitutional

[223]

terms, would best be described as a twenty-four-hour abdication in favour of a republic, followed by an automatic unproclaimed restoration. That he could take such an action indicates the real authority residual in his office as king, as well as a confidence in himself as a decision-maker which would have been unimaginable at the beginning of the reign. Nevertheless, some months later, rumours were said to be circulating that Baudouin was considering abdication.

This was a confused episode in the public history of the Belgian monarchy. In a country where the privacy of the royal family is protected by law and press criticism virtually forbidden, Belgians learned little of the options under discussion, but it seems that both Phillippe, Baudouin's nephew, and Astrid, his niece, were possible candidates for the succession. Their father and king's brother, Prince Albert, does not seem to have been in the running. Habituated to a highly enjoyable lifestyle, he himself appears not to have been interested in the prospect of the staid respectability expected of the Belgian court. There were those among Belgium's elite who seem to have regarded him as little better than a playboy – some indeed muttered darkly about his having a love child.

When Baudouin died in 1993, his moving and majestic funeral procession was watched by hundreds of millions of television viewers all over Europe. Awarded an honorary doctorate in law by the University of Oxford in 1987 for his contribution to Europe, Baudouin's preferred company was intellectuals and scientists but for many of his compatriots he was the cement without which the country might well have fallen apart. Amid the communal and linguistic rivalries which constitute politics in this constructed nation of Flemings and Walloons, Baudouin was once described by a professor from the University of Liège as the only Belgian to escape the language 'hysteria'. He had admirers, too, among his fellow monarchs. It was said that the young Juan Carlos of Spain, like Belgium a kingdom of competing peoples and traditions, took him as a model of modern kingship. The fact that at the end

of the twentieth century the monarchy seemed to be the one secure institution in Belgium surely owed much to this unassuming
man who came to the head of his country's affairs after a period
of great turbulence and uncertainty.

The fact that the fifty-four-year-old Albert II did succeed to his
brother's throne, given the various rumours of the previous two
years, came as something of a surprise to many outside Belgium.
In addition to his evident delight in the luxurious royal yacht,
Albert II was also in his younger years a devotee of powerful mo-
torbikes. A kind of roving business ambassador for the Belgian
economy during his brother's reign, he was already au fait with
the mechanics of monarchy and had had the chance to meet
many of the leading figures on the royal circuit. His transition in
the business of the monarchy at home was not as smooth, but
then it is more demanding.

Sometimes considered the conscience of his country, the Belgian
sovereign bears a heavy responsibility. Soon after his accession,
Albert confronted a crisis of public policy and general public morale without precedent. The Dutroux case, in which child abuse,
incest and infanticide all seemed to be involved, shocked the conscience of the nation and diffused an atmosphere of anxiety. The
official investigations dragged on and public indignation
mounted as facts began to emerge which seemed to call into
question the integrity of the police. People even began to wonder
whether some members of the force themselves might not, in
some way, be involved in the world of sexual perversion being
uncovered and being connived at by their colleagues. In public
demonstrations which astounded Europe, some 200,000 people
carrying white flags and banners and emblems and flowers of
white processed silently through the streets of Brussels to demand
greater urgency from the authorities. The King himself came in
for criticism for not having intervened earlier, and in a democratic
show of solidarity with their troubled nation, in October 1996
Albert and Queen Paola took part in a televised debate on the
topic of child disappearances.

The heir to the Belgian throne, Prince Philippe of Belgium and Duke of Brabant, was born at Château Belvedere, Laeken in April 1960 and succeeded his father King Albert II as honorary president of Belgium's Office of Foreign Trade in 1993. Since that time he had led numerous trade missions – in 1998 to India where he was received by Prime Minister Atai Behari Vajpayee, and to Mexico where he met President Ernesto Zedillo, and in March 1999 when he headed a team representing some forty Belgian enterprises aiming to participate in a major development in Egypt, where he held discussions with President Mubarak. Essentially he was Belgium's roving ambassador and as such was required to keep himself au fait with the principal organizations of the UN, the International Monetary Fund and the World Bank. And of course as a European prince he maintained close contacts with the institutions of the Community. On the domestic front he presided over the National Council of Sustainable Development, and in all these positions he had regular meetings with ministers and senior administrators. All in all it is a classic profile for a senior royal at the turn of the millennium.

In his apprenticeship, so to speak, the Prince also followed the more traditional route for princes of the blood – a military career. After the obligatory secondary education for Belgian royals, in both French and Dutch academies, he began his university-level studies at Belgium's Royal Military Academy, becoming a qualified military pilot (clocking up some 300 hours, 50 of them solo between 1982 and 1988) and a paratrooper. In 1989 at the age of twenty-nine, he was promoted to the rank of colonel. Meantime, studies at Trinity College, Oxford and then Stanford University's Graduate School in California, where he took his masters in political science, filled out an impressive professional CV.

Nevertheless, as time went by, Philippe came to be known as the Unhappy Prince, unable to find himself a partner and future queen and perhaps a little less than brilliant. His younger sister Princess Astrid, President of the Belgian Red Cross and a lieutenant-colonel in the army's medical corps, sometimes seemed to receive equal billing in media coverage. By the constitution of 1993 the daughters of Belgian monarchs became entitled to accede to the throne. Her marriage to Archduke Lorentz of Austria Este in 1993 was enthusiastically received and, in due course, their children would take their places in the line of succession, ahead of their uncle Prince Laurente, a year younger than Astrid. Thus, with a Habsburg marriage, the sovereigns of Brussels maintained Europe's political and dynastic traditions, and even the admission of women to the succession could find a parallel in the eighteenth-century Pragmatic Sanction which enabled that great woman ruler Maria Theresa of Austria to fulfil her destiny. At any rate, the next generation of the Belgian dynasty was secured, even if not in the senior line.

Then in September 1999, all speculations about the future of the dynasty were transformed by the announcement of the engagement between Crown Prince Philippe and Madamoiselle Mathilde d'Udekem d'Acoz, daughter of an aristocratic Belgian Catholic family – twenty-six years old, a qualified speech therapist, vivacious, pretty, stylish and highly intelligent. The announcement seemed to have been rushed out to anticipate threatened press leaks, but the prime minister was happy to congratulate the couple with the government's concurrence in the royal assent to the match. The marriage was set for the first week in December. Mathilde was Belgium's ideal designer queen-to-be. With French and Flemish ancestry she spoke both languages, and after a succession of six foreign consorts, she would, if events took their expected course, be Belgium's first native-born queen. Suddenly, having succeeded in winning for himself such a partner, from being a rather sad dullard, Prince Philippe was revealed as a dark horse not to be underrated and the royal family leapt in the public esteem. In October the Prince and his bride to be embarked upon the round of *Joyeuses Entrées*, traditionally the ceremonial tour of the kingdom by which the royals introduced themselves to the people.

It was at this moment that a story broke which was calculated to cause maximum embarrassment to the royal family. The subject was a young Belgian sculptress in her early thirties living in London's Notting Hill, who was said to be an illegitimate daughter of King Albert. It seems that, no official denials came from the palace. Some remembered how, in the later years of the reign of his brother King Baudouin, there had been rumours that Prince Albert, as he then was, would stand aside from the succession. No satisfactory reason was given at that time. Perhaps the existence of a love child had been known to members of the establishment for some years. In the autumn of 1999 other rumours supported this idea. It was said that the news had been released to the author who made the allegation public, by members of highly placed Flemish adherents of the separatist movement bent on the destruction of the Belgian state. Certainly, while the Flemish papers carried features about the scandal – one even printed pictures of the young women, Mathilde and her fiancé's supposed half sister, side by side – the Francophone community accused them of royal scandalmongering in British media style while the French-language broadsheet press at first tended to downplay the story.

The circumstances of the disclosures were certainly suspicious. In general, the Belgian media as a whole respected the privacy of their royal family with an almost old-maidish discretion. In October 1999 a mine exploded in the staid grounds of the Laeken palace; one journalist called it an earthquake for the royals. For such a story, and such an old story, to break just as the dynasty was basking in enthusiastic public approval and looking forward to a secure future in the service of the country, not only deeply embarrassed the palace but also provided aid and succour to its enemies. The wedding of Crown Prince Philippe, Duke of Brabant, to Mathilde d'Udekem d'Acoz took place on Saturday 4 December. The civil ceremony, conducted by the Burgomaster of Brussels was held in the city's Town Hall. The Prince pledged himself with a Flemish 'Ja', the bride with a French 'Oui'. The weather was overcast that December day, but for many Belgians the millennial auguries for the conflict troubled country seemed set fair, the high-born young bride a symbol of reconciliation. She wore a simple form fitting ivory silk gown with a long-sleeved bodice with high winged collar, Snow White style, and long train. Her rich blonde hair was modestly swept back from her temples and a fine lace veil, secured by a circlet of simple design but encrusted with diamonds; the Prince wore the uniform of a senior air force officer. The guest list, which included representatives of all Europe's reigning royal families with Prince Charles, Prince of Wales there for the House of Windsor, included also the Crown Prince and Crown Princess of Japan and Princess Lalla Hasna of Morocco. The religious ceremony in Brussels' cathedral of Saints Michael and Gudul, conducted by the Cardinal Archbishop of Brussels, in the three official languages of Belgium French, Flemish and German, was enriched with choral works, outstanding among them music by the great Protestant composer Johann Sebastian Bach. Transmitted on all the major television channels, the event was a profoundly moving celebration of Europe's traditions and culture.

12

SPANISH SUCCESSION

Born in a Madrid clinic on 30 January 1968, some seven years before the death of General Franco, Spain's dictator, Prince Felipe of Borbón and Greece, was heir to the presumed successor to the country's throne, but would have no claim to the throne as such until his father should be formally accepted as heir by all interested parties and himself become king.

Alone among the heirs to Europe's monarchs regnant, Prince Felipe was born the son of a Pretender. Before he was ten years old the death of the Dictator had opened the way to the restoration of the monarchy, the institution's greatest triumph in the twentieth century, and he had been invested with numerous titles, among them Prince of the Asturias, traditionally that of Spain's crown princes. The only part of Spain to remain unconquered in the Moorish invasions of the eighth century, though much reduced in extent, the kingdom of The Asturias in the northwest corner of the country was the one from which the kings of Spain took their regnal numbers – as if the kings of England should be numbered from the kingdom of Wessex, the only one to survive the ninth-century incursions of the pagan Danes.

A visit to the province was among the Crown Prince's first official engagements and the following year, 1981, his father King Juan Carlos created him a Knight of the Golden Fleece. This chivalric order was founded in the fifteenth century by the dukes of Burgundy, then rulers of the Low Countries, into whose family the

House of Habsburg married, who furnished Spain with her kings during the sixteenth and seventeenth centuries. These and other titles and honours passed to the branch of the French Bourbon family who were inaugurated on the Spanish throne in the early eighteenth century.

The Spanish Borbóns were clearly adept at inheriting and practised in the art of continuity. Coming of age in 1986, Prince Felipe took the oath of allegiance to the constitution before a joint session of the Cortes (Spanish parliament). At the turn of the century this expert yachtsman and professional royal technocrat had fulfilled one important role for a man of his station – to provide gossip for the gossips with a succession of sensational girlfriends. But he had not discharged the possibly more important duty of acquiring a wife and starting a family. The Prince had always declared his intention to marry for love. His mother, the beautiful Queen Sofia, a royal lady with a will of iron, would not, it was believed, entertain any candidate not descended from a sovereign family to be found in the *Almanach de Gotha*. Since a prince of Spain who marries without sanction of the king loses his rights in the succession, a fully satisfactory outcome was not necessarily assured for the Prince. However, as the century came to its close, the outlook for the dynasty seemed perfectly secure, for in July 1998 the Prince's sister, Princess Elena, gave birth to a baby boy.

When talk turns to the prospects for monarchy in the twenty-first century and the possibilities of comebacks for the royals in waiting, sooner or later the example of Spain comes up. It is a telling precedent. The accession in November 1975 of Juan Carlos I of the House of Borbón as King of Spain in succession to the dictator General Francisco Franco y Bahamonde, marked the restoration of one of Europe's historic monarchies after a lapse of forty-four years. It surely gave hope to Simeon of Bulgaria, whose chancellery was actually in Madrid and who had been driven from his throne just thirty years earlier. The royal families of Romania, Yugoslavia and Italy, all in exile for a similar length of time, could look to the future with perhaps a little more optimism, while Leka of Albania, also resident in Madrid, could reflect that it was only thirty-five years since his royal parents had fled their country.

For the former King Constantine II of the Hellenes, the accession of his brother-in-law Juan Carlos, just two years his senior, had deep resonance. Some twelve months earlier, the right-wing military junta which had forced him from the throne in 1967 had itself been ousted from power, and there had been hope in Greek royalist circles of a restoration. Even as the new Spanish king was invested with the regal authority, the Greeks were in the throes of a referendum campaign on the future of the monarchy in their country. But the parallels between Spain and Greece were conflicting. Whereas Juan Carlos owed his reinstatement to the deliberate policy of General Franco, Spain's military dictator, the Greek Colonels had pledged themselves to the continuance of a republican regime. Republicanism was to triumph in Greece and there is little doubt that it had considerable popular support in Spain too in the dying months of the Francoist regime. However, the will of the old dictator and the vested interests of the establishment prevailed.

In some respects the Spanish monarchy has points of comparison with that of the UK. Both countries are constructed nations in so far as in both the crown rules a federation of peoples of different traditions, and in both countries the succession to the crown was a matter of European interest in the late seventeenth and early eighteenth centuries. But the differences are no less marked. The succession to the British crown was settled with a minimum of conflict after one battle and within the framework of the constitution, whereas the Spanish succession was the subject of a European war and settled by international treaty. During the nineteenth century, when Victorian Britain was at the height of her splendour, the Spanish royal house was torn by internecine rivalries, the Carlist Wars, in which regional separatism and ethnicity joined with dynastic politics. At the time, nobody could have imagined that the unprepossessing and fractious Spanish Borbóns would a century later provide their country with a king to unify the nation and buttress democracy. Yet that is what they did, and that is why events in

Spain over the period are relevant in any discussion of the future prospects for monarchy.

When King Juan Carlos I came to the throne, the political problems of a country emerging from forty years of dictatorship were compounded by demands for regional devolution in Catalonia and the terrorist violence of the Basque separatist movement, and he seemed destined for a troubled reign. It would have been quite in keeping with the traditions of both his house and his country. Many hopes were riding on the new young head of state. Francoists no doubt supposed that, as the chosen successor of the Caudillo, he would maintain the combination of political repression and social discipline which had characterized the old regime. Liberals, optimists and even former republicans persuaded themselves there were signs he would prove a champion of modern democratic monarchy.

It was not the first time a Spanish monarch had been looked to as a beacon of enlightened constitutionalism. Back in 1808, when Napoleon had occupied Spain and given its crown to his brother Joseph, the deposed King Ferdinand VII was sent a prisoner to Paris. Relatively unknown, he was for a time the focus of hope for Spanish liberals. Unfortunately, once restored after Napoleon's fall, he proved a ruthless and dull-witted reactionary in social politics and an irreflective radical in dynastic politics. Rebellions in South America ended Spain's empire there, while at home foreign troops kept Ferdinand on his throne. Without a son after four marriages, he allowed himself to be persuaded by an ambitious wife to change the bar on female succession in favour of his infant daughter the Princess Isabella, and as a result excluded his brother Don Carlos. What in the late twentieth century might be admired as 'politically correct' was, in the Spain of the 1830s, politically inept. Don Carlos was furious and when on Ferdinand's death in 1833 the three-year-old Isabella was proclaimed Queen as Isabella II, under the regency of the Queen Mother, the Carlists prepared for civil war. Their cause was a rallying point for other elements opposed to the Madrid government not necessarily for dynastic reasons.

[234]

The regency government for the young Isabella was generally supported by progressive political circles; the Carlists tended to be reactionaries, but they also attracted to their ranks Catalan and Basque separatists who hoped for concessions from a grateful pretender should he win the throne with their help. Declared Queen Regnant when only thirteen years old, Isabella was to intervene continually in the nation's political affairs while keeping public opinion agog with the scandal of her own private conduct. Catalans, Basques and Carlists contributed their ambitions to the turmoil while army factions also contested for the control of events.

In 1868, the Queen was deposed in a coup led by her former lover General Francisco Serrano y Dominguez who held office as regent for two years. He was followed by a constitutional monarchy voted by the Cortes who elected as king Amadeo I, of the Italian royal house. Faced with a second Carlist war, Amadeo discreetly abdicated when it seemed the Carlist cause had finally been defeated in the Catalan and Basque provinces. There followed Spain's first, short-lived constitutional republic. Then in 1874 the monarchy was re-established in the person of Isabella's son, the eighteen-year-old Alfonso XII, who entered Madrid to acclamation.

Ten years of royalist consolidation were tragically brought into question when in November 1885, just three days short of his twenty-eighth birthday, this capable and popular young ruler was struck down by tuberculosis. He left two daughters, a queen pregnant with a third child and a highly apprehensive nation. The succession was once more in question and the recrudescence of civil war possible. The admission of women had hardly been an unqualified success, and there was in waiting a third Carlist pretender, the exiled Don Carlos Duke of Madrid, who could expect to rally considerable support should the Queen's unborn child prove to be another girl. Accordingly when, on 17 May 1886, the word went out that the Queen had gone into labour, the ante-rooms of the palace filled with tense courtiers, many muttering their prayers for a male heir. At last the door of the Queen's chamber was opened and the prime minister emerged to make the momentous announcement – 'King Alfonso XIII is born' – his voice full of emotion.

The last time a baby had been born a king in Europe was in 1316 when John I 'Posthumus' of France was born in succession to his dead father Louis X. This birth had been surrounded in mystery and his death just five days later, welcomed by some court factions, was as mysterious. By contrast, the arrival of Alfonso XIII was welcomed with huge relief by the courtiers in the palace that day. The Duke of Madrid, being descended from a man, through the male line, still maintained the primacy of his own claim over the descendants of Queen Isabella, but the position of the court party was much more satisfactory now that the regency council was ruling in the name of an infant king. Shortly after the prime minister's announcement that day in May, the new-born child was carried into the salon on a silver salver in the awed silence of the waiting Spanish nobility and the diplomatic corps. Detached from the world by his personal arrogance and the rigidity of court etiquette – the Queen was not permitted to move, even within the palace, without being accompanied by two halberdiers – the King was wont to muse, in one of the best of royal jokes, on what it must feel like to be an heir apparent.

Stylish, witty and with a reputation as a playboy, Alfonso never had any doubt as to his right to rule. He assumed full powers on his sixteenth birthday. Spanish opinion was surprised and the Duke of Madrid was outraged, but on 17 May 1902 Alfonso was duly inaugurated with great pomp in the palace of the Cortes in the presence of the assembled members. Meanwhile the ancient flag of the Kingdom of Aragon fluttered under the sun of Barcelona.

It was a reminder that in some Catalan and Basque circles the Carlist cause, fragmented though it was into rival factions, still enjoyed support. At first, the teenage monarch enjoyed something of a honeymoon with the public. Evading his security guards he would make sorties on foot or by car in Madrid and its environs. Convention-bound courtiers as well as constitutional politicians frowned on such goings-on. By and large, it was the establishment view that a king should be content to occupy the throne and not try to occupy the whole of Spain as well. Sometimes, his walkabout style led Alfonso, accompanied by a few court favourites, to break away from the official party to let the people catch a closer sight of their king. His ministers felt snubbed at his preference for courtiers to constitutionally elected advisers. For his part Alfonso lost patience with the faction-ridden political class, which he considered obstructive to orderly government. In December 1904 he intervened in the proceedings of the national assembly to install an extreme rightist president of the senate who alarmed even conservative opinion. Over the next twenty years the King intervened on a regular basis, taking advice from politicians of his own choosing whether ministers or not, with little discernible effect.

He was the target of a number of assassination attempt at home and abroad. In 1905 he became the focus of serious controversy in England when news broke of his betrothal to Princess Victoria Eugenie ('Ena') Battenberg (later Mountbatten). The idea of an English princess and a granddaughter of Queen Victoria marrying a Catholic drew protests from Anglicans and nonconformist groups. But King Edward VII refused all petitions to withhold his consent and, as no vote of funds for her dowry was in prospect, the matter did not come up in Parliament. Spain's Catholic bigots were equally perturbed, even though the Princess had adopted the religion of her spouse. A few years before, a bishop had affirmed that the former Catholic Empire of Spain had been lost through masonic intrigue – and King Edward VII's sympathy for Freemasonry was well known.

The marriage was solemnized on 31 May 1906. As the royal procession returned through streets lined with cheering crowds, the scene suddenly exploded in screaming panic. A terrorist bomb had killed the horses of the royal carriage, spattering the bride's sun-dazzled dress with blood. Miraculously the King and Queen were unhurt. Alfonso, a veteran of such hazards, for whom it was 'all part of being a king' ran back down the procession to assure his family that all was well – possibly also to collect fragments of the bomb. Certainly such fragments were added to Alfonso's collection of murder weapons used in assassination attempts against him; the earliest exhibit was a poisoned feeding bottle he was to have succumbed to as a one-year-old. The Queen, used to the more leisurely pace of British royal progresses, nevertheless remained cool and continued with the scheduled programme of celebrations.

The following year, Catalan separatist demonstrations in the streets of Barcelona were put down with considerable brutality. The King attempted to lessen tensions and the following year, at an official ceremony in Barcelona, he responded to the mayor's address of welcome, delivered in Catalan, in the same language. Unfortunately it required more than such gestures to placate the activists. In 1909 a general strike in Barcelona degenerated into revolutionary violence and arson. Army intervention was followed by a two-month reign of government terror which caused a press outcry through Europe.

Two years later King Alfonso faced problems of another, somewhat less serious order. Used to being the only high-profile member of his family, he found himself upstaged among the gossips by his aunt, of all people. Rumours began to circulate at court that the Princess Eulalia, resident in France, was just completing a book which promised to be politically controversial. No doubt pleased to be in a position to discipline an aunt, Alfonso ordered her to halt publication or lose her royal privileges. But Eulalia simply ignored the directive, and the King thought better of his threat and withdrew it.

But he could not withdraw the blunder. True, Eulalia could go ahead without fear of reprisals from Madrid. But her English publishers knew better than to broadcast the fact. Instead the book, adorned with a wrap-around proclaiming 'The Book Forbidden by the King of Spain', enjoyed such soaraway sales that an American publisher congratulated her on co-opting the King's help in a brilliant piece of marketing. And the cause of all the trouble? The book's only political comments were some innocuous observations on the humane tendencies of socialist ideals. Far more worrying for the conventional establishment were the Princess's comments on the discrimination which women suffered. In one passage the Infanta seemed to equate marriage with legalized prostitution. Nevertheless, the only effect of the threatened royal ban was to ensure that such views got far wider currency than they could otherwise have expected.

In the 1920s Alfonso, whose government had kept the country out of the First World War, suffered severe criticism for rebel successes in Spanish Morocco which many attributed to incompetent interventions by him in military matters. In September 1923 the threat of a military coup, with the support of 'the garrisons of Aragon', by General Miguel Primo de Rivera forced the government to resign. The King appointed him prime minister but in fact, for the next seven years Primo de Rivera ruled Spain, under the King, with virtually dictatorial powers; the cabinet and ministries as such were abolished. Indeed, Alfonso is alleged to have introduced his chief minister to Victor Emmanuel, King of Italy as 'my Mussolini'. But unlike Mussolini, the General had no expansionist 'imperial' policy and no popular following – his Unión Patriotica, unlike Mussolini's Fascist Party in Italy, never carried much weight in national affairs. But the regime did suspend constitutional guarantees; many liberals emigrated while liberal politicians at home opposed the regime as best they could. Catalan extremists hated the King for his association with it. In May 1925, returning from a visit to Catalonia, the royal train was wrecked by terrorist action. Even so, at the price of civil liberties, Spain experienced a period of comparative calm and some stability.

As to the King, he continued with his high-profile lifestyle, maintaining a busy round of polo engagements, motor tours and involvement in the fashionable sport of flying. He was a keen golfer – one of Spain's first, in fact – and under the incognito of 'Duke of Toledo' at such fashionable resorts as Deauville in France he was also, according to the gossips, an active dancing partner of many beautiful women other than his wife.

The state of the country, however, despite ambitious plans for economic expansion, continued economically weak. Eventually his finance minister abandoned Primo de Rivera and as a last resort the dictator appealed directly to his brother officers by sending telegrams to all Spain's military garrisons, in which he indicated that unless they declared explicitly against him, he would remain in power. At this point the King intervened, objecting that the dictator held power by his appointment and not thanks to the army. The dictator retired to Paris where he died a broken man two months later.

King Alfonso attempted to conduct the government of the country along the lines of the fallen minister. However, the administrative structure of the country had been fatally weakened and, because many senior officers reckoned that he had treated Primo de Rivera in a shameful manner, he lacked the support of the army. Municipal elections on 12 April the following year persuaded the King, on the advice of friends in whom he had complete trust, to leave the country. On the eve of his departure he issued a solemn message of intent to the nation. It was clear, he said, from the election results that he no longer enjoyed the love of his people. He was equally confident that he could easily find means to sustain his royal authority 'against all comers', but he had no intention of plunging the country into fratricidal conflict. These measured and statesmanlike sentiments were followed by an obviously heartfelt but, to quote Hugh Thomas, 'cryptic' royal message of farewell. The King would 'deliberately suspend' his use of the royal prerogatives 'until the nation speaks'.

Republicans blamed Alfonso for a generation of misrule and considered his playboy lifestyle irresponsible. But it was part of the man. Impetuous on the polo field, Alfonso was also remembered for a gesture of courage exceeding even his steadiness under attack from terrorist bombs when, on a visit to the then impoverished western Spanish region of Las Urdes, he dared to shake the hand of one of its leper community. And he had much sadness in his own family. His wife was a carrier of the bleeding disease, haemophilia. The eldest and the youngest of the royal princes died comparatively young. The second son, Jaime Duke of Segovia, a deaf mute renounced all rights to the succession in 1933.

Alfonso had not formally abdicated and in the long term he no doubt hoped the monarchy would one day be restored. But it was not his wish to plunge the Republic and hence the nation into chaos. At first he disowned pro-monarchist agitators and encouraged all his supporters, army officers included, to back the republican regime 'in all patriotic policies'. Allegiance to the idea of Spain should come before that to any form of government, whether republican or monarchist.

Even when, in December 1931 he was tried *in absentia* by the Cortes and condemned to life imprisonment, he still held back from active participation in the insurrectionary schemes of the more passionate monarchists. With the defeat of the Republican government by the insurgency led by Franco, a long period of stability returned to Spanish policies – the stability of the oppressive order imposed the world over by one-party states.

King Alfonso, who had not abdicated, died in Rome in 1941. The standard-bearer of the conventional Spanish monarchist party became his son Don Juan de Borbón y Battenberg, Count of Barcelona, who lived in Estoril. Alfonso had officially designated him his heir, passing over Juan's older brother Jaime because of his debility. The chances of a royal return must have seemed slight. The Republican regime had been overthrown, after a civil war of such horror that no-one would contemplate reopening that apocalypse of hell in favour of a Borbón restoration. However, it transpired that Franco had a use for the institution of monarchy. Ruthless as well as capable, still in his forties and absolute master of the country, he had no son but had addressed the question of the succession with a highly ingenious formula. Clearly there was to be no question of a republic, and he had no intention of naming any of his colleagues as successors. But an open succession would be an open invitation to a return to political and social disorder. In 1947 he declared Spain to be a kingdom with himself as Regent, pending the choice of a king.

In some eighty years, since the time of Amadeo of Savoy, Spain had experimented with constitutional monarchy, a liberal republic, an absolute monarchy, a monarchy-dictatorship, a communist republic and an absolute dictatorship. It is hard to avoid the feeling that for Franco the monarch was before everything else a convenient tool, all the better for being conventional and traditional, with which to remove the question of the succession from the political arena. Thus the succession was vested in the family of the Count of Barcelona, whose credentials were impeccable to all except the Carlist minority. The Dictator had been careful not to designate either the Count or his nine-year-old son or any other member of the family. Such an acknowledgement could have been interpreted as presenting Spain with a more legitimate government than that of the Caudillo's own regime. Furthermore, so long as monarchists and the Barcelonas accepted him as arbiter of the country's future, they tacitly conceded his right to rule it in the present.

At the time, there were those who thought he would by-pass the Count, living in Estoril with his family, on account of the latter's liberal attitudes. In the event, the Count agreed that his son should be educated in Spain and be allowed to 'serve his country in a way appropriate to his rank and station'. The young man received a military education first in Madrid, with a personal tutor, then at the Spanish military, naval and aviation academies. By 1960, at the age of twenty-two, Juan Carlos held commissions in both the army and the air force and following a further meeting between his father and Franco, he was enrolled for a two-year course at Madrid University. It became increasingly apparent that he was being groomed for the succession in place of his father. The Count was to die in a clinic in Pamplona in 1993, happy in the success of his son who had displaced him in the succession and the Countess, the much loved mother of King Juan Carlos, died at her home, the Villa Giralda, in January 2000.

1961 was a notable year for 'Juanito', as he was known in the family. That summer he was a guest at the wedding of the Duke of Kent. Among the galaxy of royals who visited England for the occasion were King Paul and Queen Frederika of Greece with their daughter, Princess Sophia. She and the Spanish king in waiting were married in May 1962, their Athens wedding, under a royal blue sky, a fairy tale celebration of a love match. The following year Juanito and his bride set up home in the charming Zarzuela palace outside Madrid, formerly the summer palace of Spain's kings. Modest in comparison with the Royal Palace in the capital itself and heavily damaged during the Civil War, it had been restored for Prince Juan Carlos and has been his family's home ever since. The first child, Princess Elena was born in 1963, the second also a daughter, Princess Christina, in 1965 and the third child, this time a son Prince Felipe in 1968. The arrangements for his baptism were another step on the way to the formal adoption of Juan Carlos as the favoured successor. The ceremony was held in the state room of the Zarzuela Palace and was attended not only by the happy parents and their friends but also by the seventy-six-year-old Caudillo and, surely a more welcome guest for the family, by the child's great grandmother, the former Queen Victoria Eugenia who had been given a dispensation from the ban of exile for the occasion. She received an enthusiastic reception from the cheering crowds in the streets of the capital and her death the following year marked a break with the days of the old monarchy.

On 22 July 1969, Juan Carlos was formally presented to the Cortes by General Franco with the title, Prince of Spain. For some years past, the Prince had been attached to various government ministers, and it was supposed that the ageing dictator was grooming a successor who would continue in the oppressive and autocratic ways of his regime. No doubt those close to Prince Juan Carlos knew that this was a fond hope, but outside the intimate circle few gave much for the chances of a return to democratic constitutionalism after Franco's death. On 20 November 1975 it was announced that the dictator had died peacefully in his bed. Two days later Juan Carlos I was proclaimed King of Spain. The succession appeared to be settled, and yet many people were dissatisfied. For Carlists, the new king was merely the latest in a line of usurpers. But majority monarchists must also have been uneasy. After all, this highly personable and qualified thirty-seven-year old, an Olympic-class yachtsman and karate black belt, as well as holding serving commissions in the armed forces, was where he was by the grace, not of a legitimate succession – that still lay with the Count of Barcelona, designated by the last king regnant, Alfonso XIII – but by that of General Francisco Franco y Bahamonde. Liberals were distrustful and extremists on the Right suspicious. The King's advisers were said to be dedicated to the reintroduction of democracy. As for separatists in the Basque country or in Catalonia, they saw nothing in the new dispensation to offer them hope. After all, this king, as head of state, retained many of the considerable powers of the dictator. There was no guarantee that they, or indeed any other malcontents, would hold back from violence.

The following year, 1976, was one of mixed omens. The new cabinet, headed by Spain's youngest twentieth-century prime minister, favoured democratic progress. The King gave a speech advocating democracy and calling for national commitment to working together. There was an amnesty for political prisoners, and in July the Cortes passed a law legalizing political parties once again. Liberals jibbed at wording designed to exclude the communists. In September five Basque terrorists were executed, a further setback to liberal ideals. However, in 1977, in a carefully worded statement, the Count of Barcelona formally let it be known that he renounced his claim to the succession in favour of his son. For majority monarchists, the throne was legitimized and was no longer a Francoist fiefdom; for democrats, too, the news could only be good – the Count would hardly now have accepted the new reign if he was not satisfied, either through his own judgment or through confidential assurances, that the King's objective was genuine liberalization. It would soon become plain that, despite the contradictions inherent in his unique position in history, the young King was looking to a genuine democratic society for his country.

But what is the 'country' of a king of 'Spain'? For a few million of his 'subjects' such a country was a polite fiction with no reality outside the drawing rooms of the establishment bourgeoisie of Old and New Castile. Catalan and Basque separatist demonstrations continued and in 1976, on a visit to the Canary Islands, Juan Carlos was the target of an assassination attempt. Two years later disgruntled paramilitary activists attempted to kidnap the entire cabinet in the hope of blocking the onward march of the King's now obvious determination to drag his fractious countrymen into alignment with the received conventions of political discourse. On 27 December 1978, in military uniform but with Queen Sofia wearing a day dress seated at his side and with their twelve-year-old son and heir Prince Felipe – an inspired image of the formalities of power wedded to the conventions of civility – Juan Carlos I signed a new constitution for his subjects. This, while containing provisions to protect the privacy and dignity of the head of state which to a London journalist would seem positively draconian if applied to his dealings with the House of Windsor, has allowed Spaniards of whatever religion, language, tradition or ethnicity to live with a hopeful ambition for peace and mutual respect.

However, the right wing remained a dangerous factor in Spanish politics for some years. The group of malcontent military and paramilitary officers, who had hoped to restore the tradition of military interventions in Spanish politics, were to prove a dangerous augury of things to come. In October 1980, three days before the scheduled national elections, plans were discovered for a military coup which involved the isolation of Madrid by military units and the imprisonment of the King – an undoubted tribute to his democratic credentials. Three colonels were arrested. The malcontents did well to target Juan Carlos, as became apparent during the sensational events which electrified Europe over the twenty-four hours of 23–24 February 1981.

In January the government, coming under attack for what the Right construed as more liberal policies towards the Basque problem and the social measures such as relaxation of the divorce laws, the prime minister had resigned. His left-of-centre successor failed to gain the necessary overall majority to confirm his appointment in a vote of the Cortes on 10 February. A new session was convened for the 23rd when a second vote would be taken. As the deputies began the formalities of the ballot there was a commotion at the entrance of the chamber and armed Civil Guards broke in on the session, firing warning shots. As deputies cowered behind their desks, the leader of the assailants, Lieutenant Colonel José Antonio Tejero Molina, advanced on the president of the Assembly and held him at gunpoint. The deputy prime minister was manhandled out of the way when he attempted to challenge Molina, who then mounted the rostrum, an armed Civil Guard in the seats behind him covering the assembly with his carbine. Members were told that they were to await the arrival of 'a competent military authority' (apparently the deputy chief of staff of the army) who would arrive shortly to initiate the establishment of a new government.

An astonishing vigil now began, during which the bulk of the nation's deputies and the entire cabinet found themselves being held hostage under the muzzles of their own guardians of the peace. Outside Spain, people apprehensively kept their radios tuned for news of developments. Was this violation of the democratic process at the very seat of its authority an omen of a return to the anarchy and civil war of fifty years before? Above all, what would the King do? Would he indeed be free to do anything?

For it was soon learnt that a detachment of armoured vehicles from the Madrid garrison had appeared at the buildings of the state radio TV stations and ordered them to stop broadcasting, while another detachment had positioned itself outside the King's residence. The aim was surely intimidation, but for a moment pessimists wondered whether the intention was to protect the King from a possible counter coup. For it now became known that to the south, in the extensive military district of Valencia, General Milans del Bosch had declared a state of emergency and ordered tanks to patrol the streets of the city as a precaution against 'the power vacuum' in Madrid – and all this, he said, on orders from the King himself. With the government ministers held hostage in the parliament building and a leading military commander telephoning colleagues and subordinates, supposedly with royal authority, to enforce martial law to save the country, some wondered whether

Franco's protégé had in fact turned his coat or might at least be persuaded to do so. They did not know their man.

The instant he was alerted to events in the Cortes, the King, in his constitutional position as head of the armed forces, summoned the joint chiefs of staff committee and gave them the direct order to maintain the constitution. Then in a marathon telephone session (strangely reminiscent of de Rivera's telegrams) he contacted all the army's district commanders throughout Spain with orders to take instructions only from the JCSC; following this he contacted the under-secretaries of state to take over the running of day-to-day administration of civil affairs. The JCSC ordered all military and police units without specific duties to remain in their barracks, and the Madrid armoured units (whose failure to cut the telephone wires at the palace had made possible the royal counter-coup) obeyed, as did those blockading the broadcasting stations. They resumed transmissions and at 1 am in the morning of 24 February the King, wearing the uniform of commander-in-chief of the armed services appeared on Spanish TV to report to the nation on his action over the past few hours and, with a clear message for those insurgents still holding out, concluded with the solemn assurance that the crown would not tolerate actions which aimed to disrupt the democratic process by force. For a charismatic moment the distinction between the Crown, as the institution of monarchy, and the King, the person of the monarch, so important in the normal constitutional procedures of government, was fused into a single identity in the handsome, serious and determined face of a man verging on middle age but in the prime of his personal vigour and in the panoply of a power and authority vested in him by the will of a recently free people.

For all its emotional drama, the royal broadcast was a short one. The uprising was by no means over, and the outcome was even now not certain. After all, such events were hardly an aberration in Spanish history. The tanks remained in the streets of Valencia and the Civil Guard still kept its guns trained on its hostages in the Cortes building. If they were hoping for support they were to be disappointed, and if they were contemplating violence their moment had passed. Whether as members of the armed forces or of the Civil Guard trusted with the defence of the legally established order, they could hardly justify their actions in defiance of that order when disobeying their commander-in-chief. Nevertheless four tense hours were to pass before, at just after 5 am on the 24th, the streets of Valencia reverberated to the rumble of tanks returning to barracks. Even after the last of them had been counted in, Madrid still held its breath. Molina, having perhaps a stronger hand in the capital with the lives of the government members literally in the sights of his men's carbines, held out before the mesmerized eyes of millions of European television viewers – the cameras had been in the chamber at the outbreak of the insurgency – until just before noon.

To outsiders his obstinacy seemed pointless in a lost cause as well as endangering the lives of the hostage politicians. In fact, as soon as the latter were once again at liberty, the King convened the leaders of the main parties to spell out measures for the normalization of national life, warning them that nothing should be done to antagonize the armed forces at this juncture. The next day, 25 February, the Cortes endorsed the premiership of Calvo Sotelo and over the next month the leading rebels were rounded up and indicted. The public came to realize how close a call it had been. Thirty-two army officers were named and one prominent civilian. But during the course of the investigations it became obvious that many more, both military and civilian, had been implicated and that Molina had, perhaps, had some justification for his obstinacy. He and the ringleaders could hardly escape arrest and, in due course, imprisonment, but the authorities judged it expedient to turn a blind eye to hundreds more.

By the clarity with which he analyzed the 1980 insurgencies, the firmness and adroitness with which he handled the developing crisis, and the foresighted tolerance with which he directed government policy after the event, Juan Carlos surely ranks as twentieth-century Europe's most distinguished holder of the office of monarch. In Spain, the involvement of the monarchy with the business of government seemed to extend to that most political of activities – identification with popular, sometime populist, gestures of concern for the public good. Early in 1998, the province of Estramadura suffered catastrophic flooding which made hundreds of families homeless and left twenty-one people dead. At the funeral ceremony in Badajoz the royal government was represented by Prime Minister Aznar, but the royal family was also present in the person of the heir to the crown, Prince Felipe. The two joined in expressing condolences to the victims' families.

Under Juan Carlos the Spanish monarchy was an integral player in the constitution. The King's hands-on approach to his job and his centrality in Spanish political life was promoted in many ways. At the grass-roots level the approval ratings for the monarchy are boosted by an annual school competition: 'What does a king mean to you?' Children are encouraged to express their ideas about the monarchy and about their King in poems, drawings and paintings. Every year, during the Christmas holidays, the national winner gets to visit the King in the Zarzuela Palace. An exercise which in late twentieth-century Britain would be scouted as egregious royal propaganda or exploited by pro-republican teachers, in Spain was presumably accepted and approved for what it was – straight palace PR.

But then promoting the image and the standing of the restored monarchy was considered to be important. Unpretentious in style, the tall handsome King had from the start had an air of confidence and authority. Easy in his dealings with people of all walks of life, he had a clear sense of the dignity due himself as King of Spain. Early in his reign, when Paris liked to look upon itself as the patron and sponsor of Europe's new boy in constitutional democratic politics, President Valéry Giscard d'Estaing invited the young monarch to drop formalities and call him Valéry. Politely ignoring the invitation the King continued to address his guest as Señor Presidente – the republican head of state could hardly avoid the word *Majestad* after that. And yet as the authors of the book from

[249]

which this anecdote comes tell us, Giscard was taken aback by the familiarity His Majesty showed towards his opposition party leaders, shaking hands with the communist one along with the others. Abashed, the President from the land of Fraternity had to follow suit, commenting as he did so, 'I had to come to Spain for my first handshake with a communist leader!'[23]

Royal involvement in the country's political agenda is not confined to the domestic scene. For years relations between Spain and Castro's Cuba were strained: under Franco because the regime was communist, under Juan Carlos because of the estimated 600 political prisoners in the island republic's jails. Then in October 1998 the kaleidescope took a twist. The wearing of funny costumes is an occupational hazard of monarchy so that when, during the course of the Eighth Ibero-American Summit in Portugal in 1998, King Juan Carlos found himself required to don the robes, cape and wide-brimmed hat of the Oporto Confraternity of Wine for his initiation into the brotherhood, he no doubt took it in his stride. However, the fact that a fellow initiate was the aging communist Fidel Castro of Cuba may have been rather less than welcome. The King was said to share a taste for fine Havana cigars with the communist dictator and now he was obliged to clink glasses with him. But the year before, at the Venezuela summit, Juan Carlos had spoken in forthright terms about the moral values of democracy in Latin America – with Castro an apparently attentive listener. Compared with the generally anodyne speeches of Elizabeth II to a conference of Commonwealth heads of state, this was a foreign policy statement of position which in Britain would come, if at all, from the foreign secretary.

On 4 October 1998 the royal family assembled in the grand state apartment of the Zarzuela Palace where Felipe Juan Froilan de Todos los Santos, son of the Infanta Elena and her husband Jaime de Marichalar, was to receive the sacrament of baptism at the hands of the Archbishop of Madrid. The baby having been born in mid-July, the ceremony was thought by some traditionalists to have been somewhat delayed and the official reason – that the diary of

[250]

the heir to the throne, the Prince of Asturias, was fully booked before that date – prompted others to suggest that an apprentice king should be able to organize his time better. Originally the ceremony had been planned for the chapel and the gardens of the palace but on account of the weather the ceremony took place in the grand state apartment of the palace, decorated with tapestries by Goya. On the morning of the christening the court officials had set up a temporary altar, complete with statues of the Virgin Mary and Christ carefully moved from the little chapel. The baby, third in line to the throne after his uncle and mother, weighed in at 6.5 kilos and measured 62.5 cm. A sizeable infant he was, to his mother's disappointment, at the age of two and a half months, too big to wear the faldon, the traditional christening robe of the Borbóns.

With his thirtieth birthday that same year as his nephew's arrival, the Prince of the Asturias had inevitably found himself the focus of media attention, but only of the kindest and most flattering kind. His father regarded him as the best qualified of Europe's crown princes – and who among Spain's media were going to disagree? Some voices were raised in the more serious press about the level of sycophancy towards the palace which the coverage of the celebrations revealed. One commentator mused that perhaps the royal family itself should be concerned at the unhealthily flattering consensus across the media – as if anybody or any institution ever worried about having too good a press – and least of all the monarchy's media managers. One felt that the Borbóns' press office was doing a more professional job than the Windsors'. But they faced a much more docile opposition. In fact the palace-press relationship in 1990s Spain was about where things stood in Britain in the 1950s. As then in Britain, so now in Spain there seemed to be a tacit understanding among newspaper editors and TV producers to be friendly to the royals. Some with long memories saw lingering traces of the mentality of Franco's Spain in the eagerness to flatter power. Would criticism be construed as unpatriotic? It seemed inconceivable to a British observer that the family of Juan Carlos I or the King himself might ever suffer anything so heavy as the mild, good-natured anti-royalist satire of the BBC's *That Was The Week That Was* of the 1960s – let alone the grotesqueries of *Spitting Image* or the venomous malice and disingenuous constitutional philippics turned on the House of Windsor by the British print and electronic media in the 1980s and 1990s.

And yet Spain, of course, was not a generation clear of Franco's shadow, so perhaps the country's media considered that a wrecking job on the monarchy of the kind Britain's journalists had launched against their royals could be unproductive in a dangerous kind of way. Even so it was remarkable that, unlike any other monarchy in Europe, the Spanish seemed spared virtually all serious criticism or even scrutiny. Even details of the civil list, elsewhere generally discussed in parliament and the figures involved a matter of public knowledge, were little debated. By and large, Spaniards knew as much or as little about their royals as the press office at the palace wanted them to know.

As for Prince Felipe, it was known that at the helm of his yacht *Aifos* he shared the King's passion for sailing; that like his father he was tall and handsome; that his girl friends were spectacular – in the spring of the year 2000 the press began to rumour that the Prince had been bewitched by an alluring twenty-four-year-old Norwegian model – that he had had a top flight education starting with a year at Canada's elite Lakefield College School; that he was reckoned a star pupil in his Spanish university and military academy; and that when in 1986 at the age of eighteen he took his oath as heir to the throne, neither the Crucifix nor the Gospels were involved, as being unsuitable oath-helpers for the heir to a secular state. That may be so, so far as his public duties are concerned. His private life was to be more religiously correct. For years it was said that the love of his life was the daughter of a divorced aristocrat. It was also said that Queen Sofia would not tolerate the idea of his marrying a divorcee or the daughter of one.

During 1999 two events outside Europe raised the profile of monarchy as an issue. The deaths of King Hussein of Jordan and of King Hassan of Morocco meant the elevation of two young men, both in their early thirties, to the rank of sovereign. In Spain, at least, once the colonial power in Morocco, this may have fed the increasing interest of Felipe, Prince of the Asturias, in a greater independence of identity. Increasingly active as his father's deputy – it was he who represented Spain at Hussein's funeral in the spring of 1999 and at the investiture of South Africa's President Mbeki, Nelson Mandela's successor, in June.

At the beginning of that year he had joined the procession of young European royals on study tours of EC institutions, spending time at the court of justice in Luxembourg and the Central Bank in Frankfurt. In the last year of the century Prince Felipe was being entrusted with increasing responsibilities, and he let it be known that he wished to set up his own domestic establishment. Still living in the family apartments in the Zarzuela Palace, his ideal was a custom-built modernistic residence within its extensive grounds. The alternatives were a wing of the Pardo palace made over as his exclusive residence or perhaps the renovated Quinta palace, the residence of his father during his years as Franco's 'heir'. Generally admired for his thoughtful and methodical attention to his responsibilities, though like his father with something of a reputation as ladies' man, the Prince seemed determined to be something more than a deputy figurehead. By increasingly entrusting the monarchy's official engagements in the autonomous communities to his heir, King Juan Carlos demonstrated his confidence in the Prince's abilities in one of the most important domains of the country's political life.

And there were symbolic gestures too. A straw in the wind was a matter of royal heraldry – to republicans a field barren of significance, to monarchists often symbolic of great meaning. It was disclosed that the royal house had asked Madrid's Royal Academy of History to prepare suggestions for elements suitable for incorporation into a personal coat of arms for the prince. The choice will have to be carefully made, for shields, like pictures, tell a story. Finally, it was noted that the King approved the rapid promotion of the Prince, already a middle-ranking officer in the air force and the navy, to the rank of general in the army. For the most part, Spain's military high command cheerfully concurred in the decision. In a country where the army has always been a central institution, such promotion which in other monarchies is merely a part of the conventional flummery of royal status, carries significance not only for the personal career of the Prince but also for the institution of monarchy itself. In the year 2000 it seemed reasonable to predict that in Spain at least the monarchy was assured of a useful life well into the third millennium.

13

LORDS OF THE ROCK

———•◦•———

On Saturday 22 January 1999, a love match joined two of Europe's oldest sovereign families – the German House of Hanover, once monarchs of a now defunct kingdom, and the House of Grimaldi, lords of a rocky enclave on France's Riviera coast for more than 700 years.

The marriage of Princess Caroline of Monaco to Ernst August Prince of Hanover and Duke of Brunswick on that unseasonably warm and bright winter's day was an event rich in relevance for Europe's royal dimension, both past and present. Following the requirements of the Royal Marriages Act 1772, which provides that all members of the House of Hanover may marry only with the authorization of the monarch of Great Britain, the Prince had first to seek the permission of Her Majesty the Queen Elizabeth II. However Ernst August might, but for the acceptance of female succession to the British crown, himself be wearing that crown. Like the Queen he is descended from George I, King of the United Kingdom and Elector of Hanover; but while she descends from Victoria, he is a descendant of Ernest Augustus, Duke of Cumberland, the younger brother of Victoria's father. This tall and ferocious-looking German-born prince of England was hated in England for his supposed debaucheries – his bedroom was lined with mirrors – his fiery temper and his political ruthlessness. Some people seriously believed that he would plot the death of Princess Victoria to achieve the throne and stop the chance of liberal reforms. His descendant is not thought to be so bloodthirsty, though he has reportedly been accused of violent assault on more than one occasion.

Notorious for his reactionary politics, the Duke of Cumberland was yet capable of the proto-politically correct gesture in advance of his time. Speaking on the Adultery Bill, which would have denied the right of guilty parties to remarry, he argued that since 'so few men are inclined to marry the women they seduced, it would be unfair to deprive the females of this last hope'. This, says Roger Fulford in his book *Royal Dukes*, 'was the only occasion that I have been able to discover, on which the Duke allowed even a faintly liberal sentiment to pass his lips'.[24] As a soldier he was a vicious disciplinarian even by the standards of his day but brave, too, to match his elegant six foot of 'English gentleman'. Monstrously scarred by a sabre wound which had cost him his right eye in the French wars, his sword shattered, he parried his adversary's thrust and, as the Frenchman prepared for the blow to finish him off, lifted the man bodily off his horse and rode with him across his saddle bow back to the British lines.

Since the Hanoverian succession law effectively barred women, when Victoria's uncle William IV of Great Britain and I of Hanover died in 1837, his niece succeeded him in Britain and his younger brother Ernest Augustus (who, priding himself as an Englishman, preferred the English version of his name) took the crown of Hanover. One of his first acts was to rescind the country's liberal constitution, introduced by his brother four years earlier. Ernest Augustus considered the mildest republicans rank rabble-rousers, though according to his extreme Tory principles he governed Hanover conscientiously and was rewarded by a statue in his honour dedicated to 'The father of his country from his faithful people'. But enlightened despotism was out of vogue. The wave of revolutions which swept across Europe in 1848 did not pass Hanover by, and the king was forced to restore some elements of liberalism to retain his throne. Nevertheless his tradition of patriarchal autocracy was continued under his amiable but equally stubborn son and successor the blind King George V who sided with the reactionary Austrian empire against Prussia in the struggle for supremacy in Germany during the 1860s. Prussia's triumph meant the end of the kingdom of Hanover, though the family did not abandon its claim to the throne and retained its numerous properties. In 1946 those of its possessions in East Germany were nationalized by the communist regime. The Hanovers' legal battle to recover them after the fall of that regime, was complicated by the fact that in the 1930s Ernst August V, had expressed admiration for Hitler. In the summer of 2000 legal arguments decided the German administrative court to block restitation of an important Hanover property in Magdeburg.

In the 1860s, while the Hanovers lost their kingdom, the Grimaldis of Monaco lost half their national territory. They survived, but theirs is a qualified sovereignty. By the terms of international treaties and protocols the succession to the throne must be approved by the French government and the Prince's domestic and 'foreign' policy must respect the political, military, naval and economic interests of France. One can see the entire principality from vantage points round the palace. Within this perimeter, the authority of Prince Rainier III was virtually absolute for most of the second half of the twentieth century.

With an area of just under 200 hectares Monaco is, in the rankings of Europe's five enclave statelets, somewhat larger than Vatican City is almost thirty times smaller than the hilltop Republic of San Marino and seventy times smaller than the Principality of Liechtenstein. In this company the 495 square kilometres of the diarchy of Andorra – ruled jointly the Spanish Bishop of Urgel and the French President (who in this case takes on some aspects of royalty) – seems positively gigantic. But Monaco contains some of the world's most valuable real estate, with banks, finance houses and luxury tourist traps congesting the bay and rising even from its waters in projects of major land reclamation. The bay is dominated by the famous 'rock', actually a plateau promontory about 600 metres long and 200 wide surmounted for centuries by a fortress, the medieval structure having being 'modernized' in the sixteenth century.

Obscure in its origins, the coastal settlement of the Monoecos tribe was known to the ancient Greeks and Romans as a haunt of pirates. Arab Saracen corsairs made it one of their numerous bases on the Mediterranean coasts of Europe, but it was not until its occupation by the Grimaldis, a leading family of the commercial republic of Genoa in the year 1297, that it began to edge its way into mainstream European history. For millennia its destiny lay to seaward. Even when its medieval rulers extended their territories along the coast to Roquebrune and Menton, communication was maintained by sea, apart from a mule track along the cliff tops.

It was in the fourteenth century with Charles 'the Great' that the Grimaldis began to make their mark. A mercenary captain in the endless wars that plagued Europe, Charles numbered among his employers the king of France, then engaged in the early stages of the Hundred Years War with England. With a flotilla operating out of Calais he was one of the privateers in French pay who ravaged the south coast of England. Next we find him active in the Mediterranean nominally in league with the Christian Knights Hospitaller on the island of Rhodes. From his stronghold of Monaco he was able to levy protection money on the merchant ships passing within his range, and he also extended his territory by acquiring Roquebrune and Menton. All this time he was in theory a representative of Genoa; in fact he was playing the part of a sovereign prince. He increased the population of his inhospitable domain by offering tax concessions on land and property to prospective settlers.

Midway between the French and Italian worlds, the Seigneurs, or Lords, of Monaco intermarried with Italian as well as French nobility. The link with Genoa was finally broken in February 1489 when Lambert Grimaldi, the 'Sieur Grimault de Monique' won a promise of protection from the king of France in exchange for a simple pledge of loyalty and support. Forty years later, France's rival, the Habsburg Emperor Charles V who was also King of Spain and had lordships in Italy, paid a three-day state visit to Monaco on his way from Spain to Rome. For more than a century Monaco became in effect a Spanish dependency, its princes subject to the commander of a Spanish garrison.

This situation was terminated in 1641, with a mixture of cunning and bravado, by Honoré II, lord of Monaco. At Peronne in northern France he negotiated a secret agreement which would restore his sovereignty, earn him a decent annual allowance and guarantee French protection in exchange for his doing nothing to harm the interests of France. On his return home, having feasted the Spanish troops until they were drunk, he and his men forced them to quit the fortress. The Treaty of Peronne remained the basis of Monaco's independence until the overthrow of the French monarchy in 1792. Honoré II was created a member of the French peerage with the title Duc de Valentinois; he also adopted the style of 'Prince' rather than 'Lord' of Monaco, though it was only with his grandson Louis I, who ruled from 1662 to 1701, that the letters patent for that title were granted.

This Louis aimed to mimic Louis XIV, *le roi soleil*, within the confines of his micro state. His wife Charlotte, daughter of the Duke of Gramont, had other ideas. Spending the minimum amount of time there required to conceive and deliver their five children, two boys and three girls, she lived most of her married life at the court of the great Louis and was for a time his mistress. But 'Madame de Monaco', as she was known, made other reputations for herself in this ambidextrous environment where the men pursued one another, as well as the women, while the women indulged what was called the Italian taste, as well as more conventional infidelities. It appears that on her appointment as lady-in-waiting to the Duchesse d'Orléans, Charlotte proposed to initiate her mistress into a more liberal interpretation of that term than convention usually allowed.

In fact Charlotte found adventure where she could. She died a horrible and lingering death from a wasting disease which left her disfigured and repellent. The sententious and smug court *memoiriste*, Bussy-Rabutin, was delighted. In his opinion, given the life she had led, the condition of the Princess of Monaco was of more value to the reform of morals at court than a sermon from the fashionable Jesuit preacher Bordaloue. And when we remember that the porcelain manufacturers of the day turned out specially designed little intracrural pots called '*bourdaloues*' for the use of ladies not wishing to be caught short during his interminable sermons, we can see what a powerful homily Madame de Monaco's sufferings could have offered the piously inclined.

The eighteenth century saw a decline in the fortunes of the dynasty. Antoine I, a huge figure of a man known to his contemporaries as Goliath, badly weakened the finances with extravagant schemes to improve the fortifications and with his passion for music. He maintained his own opera/ballet and spent his days making music in the 'grand casino', a pleasure palace he had built by the shore. Nearby a *petit casin* was reserved for his mistresses, among them the ballet dancer Elisabeth Dufort who gave him a son, Antoine Grimaldi. His wife produced only daughters. The eldest, Louise Hippolyte, would no doubt succeed him in the principality where there was no Salic law to impede her, but the family would lose its recently granted and valuable French peerage unless the French king could be persuaded to make exceptional concessions. After much manoeuvring, Antoine succeeded in marrying Louise to a major French nobleman Jacques de Goyon Sire de Matignon (who took the name of Grimaldi as required by a family succession ruling of the fifteenth century) and in persuading Versailles to create a new ducal peerage of Valentinois for Louise and her descendants. Louise succeeded her father but died in the same year (1731), to be followed by her husband Jacques I. This man, having ensured the ultimate succession of his fourteen-year-old son Honoré III, returned to his Paris mansion, the Palais Matignon, now the residence of the French prime minister, leaving the administration of the principality in the hands of his dead wife's bastard half brother Antoine Grimaldi, who continued to administer the place for most of the rest of the century since Honoré, following his father's example, left for Paris as soon as he was able.

[260]

There, his love life was an extraordinary saga even in the age of Casanova, the Venetian adventurer. In fact, for a time the two men were after the same actress. By way of distracting the Italian, Prince Honoré offered to introduce him to a duchess. The young, virile but also snobbish Casanova could not resist the prospect. Only when it was too late did he discover that the noble woman was neither exceptionally beautiful nor in any sense young, and the only way for him to evade her eager advances was to pretend he was infected with a venereal disease. He never forgave the man who set the trap.

The Revolution in France, by abolishing the feudal and seigneurial rights of the French nobility, cost the princes of Monaco dear in lost revenues from the French possessions they had acquired under the Treaty of Peronne. Technically a foreign potentate, Honoré III claimed compensation and no doubt to his surprise, the Constituent Assembly passed a decree in his favour. But no indemnity was ever paid and, resident in his Paris mansion at that time, Honoré thought it wiser to maintain a low profile in view of the revolutionaries' cull of the French aristocracy. The fact that his second son Joseph joined the emigrés hardly improved his standing; and then the revolutionary army in the Nice region sent a battalion to occupy Monaco. Local activists formed a commune which announced the deposition of the Prince and the accession of the principality, which at that time included Menton and Roquebrune, to the Republic. The National Convention in Paris thereupon formally annexed the territory and, with the obsession of the politically correct, abolished the name 'with its unacceptably monastic emphasis' and renamed it Fort Hercules from supposed classical and, of course, pagan associations. The authorities of the Alpes Maritimes department sold off Grimaldi assets to swell their own coffers, while in Paris 'Citizen' Grimaldi sought to placate the Revolutionary regime with donations to its defence arsenal.

It did little good. As the father of an emigré 'criminal'. Honoré was thrown into prison for a year while his daughter-in-law joined the thousands of others judged guilty by association, condemned to death for having wanted to escape so as to be able to assassinate the members of the committee of public safety. George Orwell's Thought Police had nothing on these brave champions of liberty. There was, it must be admitted, an elegant Revolutionary logic about the proceedings. Since murderous thoughts against the tyrants were the only rational as well as the only remaining re-source left to their victims, it could in reason be assumed they were guilty of them. Along with twenty-four other women, one of them a seventy-two-year-old (nothing ageist about the incorruptible judges), Françoise Thérèse de Choiseul-Stainville Grimaldi-Monaco prepared to mount the tumbrils of death. The other Grimaldis managed to evade the guillotine.

Prince Honoré III died a year after his release from prison, to be succeeded by his eldest son Honoré IV, a depressive recluse, oblivi-ous to the sordid scrambles for place and favour which constituted the politics of the Napoleonic empire. But the Grimaldi were peers of France and some were willing to flatter for favours from the imperial regime. Françoise's husband Joseph, returning from exile, was appointed to a number of sinecures while his nephew Honoré Gabriel (the future Prince Honoré V) became an equerry in the household of the Empress Josephine, remaining with her after her divorce. Unfortunately he seems to have embezzled funds to help his parlous family finances and was recalled to his regiment on Napoleon's orders.

With Napoleon's fall in 1814 Joseph moved into action to re-store as far as possible the family fortunes in Monaco. Exploiting his contacts, he secured the restoration of the Grimaldis as sover-eigns of the territory as it was before 1792 – that is, including Menton and Roquebrune. On 1 March 1815 his nephew, the young Prince Honoré, recognized as regent for his hypochondriac father, riding in an expensive coach he could hardly afford the hire of, rattled into Cannes escorted by two gendarmes en route to take up the administration of the restored principality. Unfortunately, unknown to him as to the rest of the world, only days before Napoleon had escaped from exile on Elba and landed at Fréjus just a few kilometres away. The outlook seemed bleak for the princes of

Monaco when, after Waterloo, the Congress of Vienna settlement made the principality a mandate of the kings of Piedmonte-Sardinia and all hope of compensation from France for the territories lost to the Revolution disappeared. A royal garrison was installed along with a new currency, new taxes and revived feudal obligations.

To all intents and purposes Monaco had fallen to the status of a dependency en route for integration. When in February 1819 Honoré's father drowned in a river accident in the Seine, people supposed that it would not be long before his son's title too would be submerged beneath the waves of history.

Nevertheless, client state though it might be, the Monaco which Honoré V passed on to his son, the fifty-six-year-old Prince Florestan I (ruled 1841–1856), still included Menton and Roquebrune within its frontiers. Florestan proved another absentee monarch, preferring the life of a cultivated man of leisure in his Paris mansion. The mood in the little principality was excited by the revolutionary goings-on among its Italian neighbours. Just as the Italians wanted rid of the Austrians, so Menton wanted to be free of the administrative interference of Monaco. Unrest continued until 1860. In that year the newly emerging kingdom of Italy ceded Savoy and the county of Nice to France, on the condition that the populations concerned agreed to the transfer. The territories of Menton and Rocquebrune were included and voted overwhelmingly for French nationality. The ruler of Monaco received compensation of four million francs for the loss of a third of his territory and its revenue potential. There seemed to be nothing that the new Prince, Charles III, could do and once again the pundits wrote off 'this charming orangerie' of a principality, to use the words of Alexander Dumas, author of *The Three Musketeers*. But even as the ink was being dried on the Franco-Monégasque accord of February 1861, events were (literally) in train which were to transform the topography of the French Riviera. A railway was in the planning.

The primitive access to these coastal settlements, none more so than the cragbound bays of Monaco, had always been a handicap for local landowners hoping to exploit their assets. However the princes, as sovereign rulers, could accord such terms and privileges as they wished to hopeful entrepreneurs. Various projects were considered in discussion with financial advisers from Paris. It seems to have been Prince Charles III himself who decided on the jack-pot solution of a gambling club or gaming house which should also have the appeal of the fashionable German spa towns such as Bad Homburg. Charles had the venue, the seaside villa Bellevue at Condamine; he had the name, the Société des Bains de Mer; and he had a couple of financial entrepreneurs. They opened for business in April 1856 but found they lacked the final essential ingredient of commercial success – customers.

The only means of transport, an ancient diligence (stage coach), took four hours to do the twenty-mile journey from Nice. It carried twelve passengers. The first train ran on 19 October 1868; it carried 346 passengers. Forty years later more than a million visitors spent time in the principality. The success was due not merely to the railway but also to the commercial genius of a Monsieur Blanc who, according to the Ninth Edition of the *Encyclopaedia Britannica*, having been asked to leave Bad Homburg where he had begun his career as a gaming impressario, saw in the sovereign territory of Monaco (little bigger in extent than the casino and its attendant support facilities, hotels, restaurants and the like) the ideal platform for his self-promotion into the high society of the demi-monde and Europe's fringe nobility. He had secured a fifty-year lease on the exploitation of Monaco's Société des Bains de Mer (SBM) in April 1863, five years before the railway line was opened but seven years after it had been first projected.

Prince Charles had driven a shrewd bargain with the entrepreneur, requiring that he provide running water for the new town of Monte Carlo, gas lighting for the palace, town hall and other public buildings, rubbish collection and disposal, various subsidies to help the port, and much else besides. With the guarantee of such investments and revenues, Charles, like his medieval predecessor Charles 'the Great', was able to attract residents with the lure of virtually tax-free living. He inaugurated a gold coinage bearing his portrait, created orders of nobility, issued his own postage stamps and by these means ringfenced Monaco's sovereignty against the threat of creeping integration into France. Three years after the opening of the rail link to Nice, Monsieur Blanc and his company were in a position to advance a loan of nearly five million francs to the French government for the building of the Paris Opera, designed by Nicholas Garnier. Not long after Monte Carlo was to have its own Opera Garnier to match its soaring reputation among the world's pleasure seekers.

Of course Monaco had enemies – chiefly among its neighbours. As early as 1867, one year after the magnificent steamer *Charles III* had begun coasting between Nice and Monaco, the French senate received a petition signed by nearly 1,000 Niçois complaining of the threat to the moral health of France posed by the gambling at Monaco. Another objector proposed that the Republic get an independent valuation of this 'wicked little territory' and acquire it by compulsory purchase. A government report, however, concluded that all sovereign governments were masters in their own house and in international law Monaco was absolutely independent. The fact was that too many of the world's important people enjoyed the pleasures of Monte Carlo for anyone to consider infringing them. Furthermore Charles, seen by some as the patron devil of gambling, won favours even from Rome. At a time when popular anticlericalism was encouraging hostility to the Church in France, Monaco welcomed religious foundations. A grateful papacy elevated Monaco to the status of a bishopric.

Prince for thirty-three years, Charles III had reversed the odds on his country's future. His marriage to Antoinette-Ghislaine de Mérode had linked the Grimaldis to one of the families of the former Holy Roman Empire, but it was thanks to an innate business instinct that he had restored the princely dynasty to the kind of revenues needed to maintain its pretensions. When he died in 1889, an inaccessible anachronism from Europe's feudal past had become the continent's most up-to-date and opulent society venue; chronic insolvency had been transformed into a per capital prosperity to match that of the world's major economies; the principality's sovereign status was more secure than at any time since the French Revolution; and, however questionable some might find the morality of its economic miracle, Monaco had a bishop.

The principality's wealth provided the resources for his successor, Albert I (1889–1922), called 'the Magnificent', to indulge his passion for oceanography. With a programme of scientific patronage on the grand scale, he established Monaco as a world leader in the discipline. His first marriage to a daughter of the Duke of Hamilton produced an heir to the title, Louis II, but ended in divorce after ten acrimonious years. He named two of his yachts *Princess Alice* after his second wife. A convinced pacifist, Prince Albert hoped his friendship with the German Emperor Wilhelm II might influence the course of world affairs. He was disappointed. However, in 1912 he was enthusiastically received on a visit to the US in his capacity as an oceanographer. He was received at the White House by President Warren Gamaliel Harding whose week-long poker sessions (boot-leg but top quality alcohol served by the First Lady) gave Washington's 2001 Pennsylvania Avenue the kind of bizarre reputation only to be matched eighty years later. Visiting dignitaries were, of course, not invited to such parties but Harding must surely have itched to discuss the main business of his presidency with one whom America's Sunday press described as 'boss of Monaco's Casino'. Instead, the ageing Prince was honoured with awards and honorary degrees.

Albert also enriched the territory with its beautiful gardens, drove the tunnel under the rock, and constructed the magnificent underwater oceanarium. He was also the first prince to institute any form of representative bodies, promulgating a constitution which he devised in consultation with French advisers – the concessions were slight and the administration of all aspects of the government remained in the control of the ruler. At about the same time, a treaty of friendship and protection with France stipulated that Monegasque policy should not conflict with the political, military or economic interests of France.

On Albert's death, his son became Prince as Louis II. A lifelong bachelor he nevertheless acknowledged an illegitimate daughter, Charlotte, whom he legally adopted in 1919 when she became 21 and whom he recognized as heir apparent. The following year she married Count Pierre de Polignac who on the eve of his marriage took Monegasque nationality and adopted the family name of Grimaldi as required by a fifteenth century constitutional ordinance. When the couple divorced some eleven years later, the two children, Antoinette and Rainier, remained with their mother and when, in 1944, Princess Charlotte renounced her title, Prince Louis II formally designated his grandson Rainier, then aged twenty-one, Crown Prince.

The 1920s were among the most brilliant years in the history of Monaco, for the glitter and luxury of the casino was matched by the more substantial cultural season at the Opera, home for a time to Diaghilev's *Ballets Russes* and then to the ballet company of Colonel de Basil. During the Second World War, first the Italian and then the German army occupied the principality; the casino remained in business and the opera house management put on various shows featuring such stars as Maurice Chevalier. After the war international celebrities such as the Duke of Windsor and the President of France, and film stars such as Errol Flynn and Marlene Dietrich returned to the place. But Monaco's prosperity was not what it had been. In the early 1950s the principality was rocked by rumours of a banking scandal and bankruptcy. In January 1957 Prince Rainier III suspended the constitution and prorogued the councils, established by Prince Albert I in 1911, for an indefinite period.

The fairy-tale marriage of the Prince to the American film star Grace Kelly flooded the media. The daughter of an Irish-American millionaire, who had begun life as a bricklayer, she was at the peak of her career when she came to make Alfred Hitchcock's film *To Catch a Thief* in Monaco in 1955. The year before she had received an Oscar for her performance in *Country Girl* while the following year she would appear, fittingly enough, in *High Society*. Meanwhile, by her wedding with Rainier III of Monaco she had become queen, so to speak, of high society itself. It was six years since the death of his father had brought Rainier to the throne, but it was only after his marriage, many observers felt, that he began to take his job as ruler seriously.

Over the next forty years he was to develop the economy to such good effect that the casino and the tourist trade came to be displaced by banking, industry and real estate as the main sources of the principality's prosperity. He faced opposition from a minority of his subjects for his autocratic methods, and the councils demanded the right to participate in financial and other policies. But only the most minor participation was accorded to them. Yet the early 1960s transformed Monaco. World economic conditions boomed with new money, and as France's colonies won a degree of autonomy, millions of dollars worth of expatriate investments were flooding back to Europe looking for safe and friendly financial havens. Monaco benefited along with the secretive banking worlds of Liechtenstein, Luxembourg and Switzerland. Hundreds of companies and commercial organizations of one kind or another were licensed to set up in the principality, while the banks of Monaco received deposits of billions of francs. During this decade too the once delightful aspect of the statelet was transformed into an opulent concrete ghetto, as high-rise apartments and stunted skyscrapers elbowed out the wedding-cake architecture of earlier generations.

The economic implications of this booming economic enclave, coupled with the minimal taxes and financial regulations which it enjoyed, prompted the French government to seek new accords. These introduced somewhat harsher tax regimes on French expatriate residents, and customs regulations were agreed. The chief minister of state in the four-man government council was until the 1990s a senior French civil servant chosen by the sovereign prince from a list submitted by Paris. But the prince's powers are little infringed, and successive French presidents acknowledged the independence of Monaco as a sovereign state at the bar of international law. Its legation in Paris enjoys the status of an embassy and while it is not actually a member of the UN it participates as an equal member of various organizations and committees. Much to the delight of Crown Prince Albert, in the 1990s it was awarded its own international telephone dialling code.

In 1997, during the 700th anniversary celebrations of the Grimaldis' presence on the rock, Prince Rainier gave a firmly upbeat estimate of the dynasty's future. The Monégasque dream, he said, was a reality which was not about to evaporate with the millennium. Even so, some commentators in the continent's royalist press – of which, incidentally, there is a surprising number of titles – had been hinting that he was undecided about his successor.

While headline writers trumpeted a dispute over the succession, the royal family spoke in terms of Albert's experience and preparedness for the job. Even in his late thirties the Crown Prince could seem ambiguous on the question. But since his father had taken up the government at the age of twenty-six, it was difficult to believe that the candidate's qualifications could be seriously in doubt. It is true that, in terms of effective decision-making, Monaco's sovereign has real powers. The territory is minuscule but the authority of the prince within his borders verges on the absolute. Rainier compared its government to running a great company – and in a company the word of the president or managing director tends to be final. The days of the casino/festival culture were long past. The four- or five-man cabinet tended to hold its weekly meetings round a modest boardroom table in Prince Rainier's spacious office under his chairmanship. Having heard their views, the Prince made the decisions, usually the following day.

Rainier once remarked that his son was too soft-hearted, implying that his qualifications lacked the one essential ability – that of saying No. And Albert himself once admitted to that most unprincely of vices – unpunctuality. But while he might have been apprehensive about the responsibilities that would one day be his, in a fortieth-birthday interview with the magazine *Point de Vue*, in response to a direct question about his views on the long-term future, he said that while renunciation was always in theory possible, he had never considered such a course because it would have unacceptable consequences for the principality.

In fact, many commentators believed that the real issue between father and son was not the question of professional competence but rather the heir apparent's failure to find himself a wife. In Rainier's view, Monaco was not destined to become the fiefdom of an old bachelor while his son, who freely joked about being Europe's most eligible marital prospect, admitted to a regular postbag of would-be brides – 'touching' letters usually with photograph attached. Any successful candidate would of course require not only the love and affection of the Crown Prince but also the constitutional approval of his father. There was no doubt that Rainier would be delighted at the prospect of a daughter-in-law and still more delighted at the prospect of a grandchild (Albert mooted the ideal family at two boys and two girls). But according to him, his father had not made his marriage a precondition of his succession. In fact, without a change in the principality's succession law, such a condition could not be enforced. Then, in an interview with the Italian newspaper *Corriere della Sera* on the occasion of the wedding celebrations of Prince Charles de Bourbon-Sicilles and Camilla Crociani, Albert of Monaco, asked when it would be his turn for the wedding stakes, laughingly replied that he did not believe in marriage.

Whether after this he remained Europe's most eligible bachelor, he surely became its most intriguing one. Although a child of the 1960s (Albert was born in March 1958), on his own assessment in an interview with *Paris Match* he was never overtly rebellious as a teenager – no long hair, perhaps a brief flirtation with cannabis, the occasional slam of a door to signify dissent from parental authority. Things can change. In that same interview, to celebrate his fortieth birthday on 14 March 1998, Albert observed that his wife, like himself, would not have a purely ceremonial role but would be closely involved in the business of government. It was eight months later that he calmly announced his opposition to the very idea of marriage. Albert has a reputation for indecisiveness but he denies this. A good listener, he likes to hear all sides of a question before taking a decision, but once it is taken he holds to it. In his birthday interview he explained that he had been born under the sign of Pisces and that Pisceans, while they might sometimes seem to be dreamers and perhaps give the impression of being uncertain of their direction, in fact knew where they were going and in the end achieved their objectives one way or another.

In fact, Albert's destiny as sovereign prince seemed assured at the turn of the millennium. Certainly his training began early. He was inaugurated into the ceremonial aspects of the princely life as a child. At the age of six, something of a Christopher Robin figure in his gloves and cap à la English prep school, he solemnly declared Monaco's electric railway open. He remembered the stagefright, but with a yearly calendar of more than 300 official engagements it is doubtful whether the forty-year-old could find time for nerves. In addition there were financial and business dossiers to examine and assess and negotiating skills to master and the plans for the large-scale engineering works on the port installations, the opening of an underground railway station as well as large-scale schemes to extend the principality's territory and the port of the Condamine still further into the bay with facilities to accommodate modern cruise liners. The state of Monaco, having no public debt and enjoying a budget surplus, aimed to finance the works.

After an officer training course in the French navy, Prince Albert completed his higher education in the US with a degree in political science, German and art history at Amherst College, Massachusetts. He followed this with a period working in a New York bank and in real estate, returning to help in the management of Monaco plc with a well-adapted portfolio of qualifications. Bilingual in French and English, thanks to his beloved mother and the family's English nanny, and with good German – Europe's largest language community – and a passion for IT, he is well placed to take his country to a leading position in the competitive field of communications.

[271]

In the summer of 1999 he launched the Monaco website which, while it carries news and information on the country and the dynasty, is chiefly preoccupied with Net commerce offering secure trading in luxury goods and apartments. His fascination with IT is one reason why the principality is fully wired up with fibre optic cabling to meet the new millennium. It is said that the tragic death of his beloved mother, when he was twenty-four, in a car crash as she descended the steep coast road, changed his outlook on life and turned him towards a more serious interest in the Principality's affairs. He did not lose his love for life or his passion for sport – he was a member of the 1992 Monaco Olympic bobsleigh team – but he also participated in his country's UN delegation.

As to the Principality's image overseas, the future seemed to be in good hands. Although it lacked the luxury of an independent foreign policy, it proved as pragmatic and unswayed by ethical considerations in these matters as its neighbouring republic and mentor. No doubt Prince Albert's state visit to China in June 1999 was arranged in conjunction with the French foreign ministry, but his imaginative conduct of the visit was surely his own.

Travelling by a scheduled Air France flight, the Prince was received with the protocol of a head of state and had a thirty-minute meeting with the Chinese president Jang Zemin. Albert displayed a sureness of touch in international relations which many a greater power might have envied. In a later press interview he claimed, as stereotyped diplomacy required, that the personal high points of his trip had been an informal discussion with a peasant family and the delights of Chinese cuisine. But it was in a more formal context that Monaco's roving ambassador (he had visited more than sixty-five countries) achieved a diplomatic stroke approaching genius. By convention, of course, such state exchanges are occasions for talk of Peace and Friendship, but Prince Albert ensured that Monaco would be remembered in China with special esteem when he traced the ideogrammes for the two words in a fluent, free-hand calligraphy under the watchful eye of a master calligraphist. Traditionally, skill as a calligraphist had been a major attribute of China's rulers from imperial times to Mao Zedong. A Western statesman prepared to risk his reputation in this highly conventional field of expression not only paid a delicate compliment to the values and traditions of the People's Republic; he also by implication made a statement about his own fitness for the honours due to a head of state.

EPILOGUE

In a referendum held on 6 November 1999, the Australian electorate, by a majority of 54 to 46 per cent voted in favour of the country remaining a constitutional monarchy. Few imagined that this was a vote in favour of HM Queen Elizabeth of the House of Windsor. But equally no commentator was prepared to recognize it for what it was – a triumph for the institution of monarchy as such. Buckingham Palace issued a statement to the effect that Her Majesty had taken notice of the outcome, declared her intention to accept it and her willingness to continue to serve the people of the country as their head of state, but observed that the matter lay with the decision of the Australian people. It seemed that she and her advisers recognized that the issue would no doubt be raised again in the future, though many Australians questioned whether this would be in their lifetimes. In fact, in the weeks running up to the referendum, opinion polls had shown upwards of 70 per cent of the population wishing to change to a republican form of government. How then did it come about that on the day of decision, in a vote in which, as required by Australian law, all eligible to vote took part, a decisive majority rejected the republican proposal in favour of the monarchist status quo? Even a modest proposal that the national holiday celebrated as Queen's Birthday should be renamed 'Heritage Day' did not meet with favour.

Most commentators agreed that the explanation for the republican setback lay in the referendum proposal itself. In other words,

Australians rejected not the principle of republicanism but the practical republican model proposed in the question on the voting form. The choice offered was between the continuation of the existing constitution, in which the Queen is head of state while her residual functions in that capacity were exercised by a Governor General of Australian nationality proposed by Australians and approved by the palace on advice, and a republic in which the president would be elected not by the people but by the parliament. And that was the problem. For decades, Australians had viewed their politicians with cynical distrust. The idea that these man and women would be the people to choose the head of state seemed preposterous – to such an extent, indeed, that many self-proclaimed republicans declared their intention to vote the monarchist option. Whatever might be the shortcomings of the Royals, their impartiality in Australian affairs seemed assured while the quirks of hereditary succession could hardly be influenced by political horsetrading. In principle, it seemed that the majority of the Australian electorate would have sympathized with the preference said to have been expressed by the Duke of Edinburgh for hereditary peers rather than political appointees in the upper house of the British parliament because he would rather its members be chosen by God than by a prime minister.

In fact, for any democratic politician capable of self-questioning, the Australian referendum was a heavy indictment; for Australians are not alone among the world's electorates to distrust their political class. Maybe it is for this reason that the republican movement in Canada, were Queen Victoria's Birthday is still listed as a public holiday, has still to win majority support. Of the other fourteen Commonwealth countries who have the Queen as head of state, some observers regard republican opinion in New Zealand as among the most vigorous.

In Britain itself, while the overwhelming majority of the population supports the monarchy, confusion is fostered by a media and government establishment discontented, it would seem, with the country's centuries' long tradition of political stability, for whom 'change' is the watchword and 'modernity' the mantra. They attack, as if unique to it, aspects of the British regime which in fact are found elsewhere. The Royal Marriages Act of 1772, which requires members of the royal family to receive the sovereign's approval before they marry is paralleled in the constitutions of Denmark, Sweden, the Netherlands and Spain with requirements that royals have permission from the monarch or from parliament or from both, on pain of losing their rights in the succession for themselves and their descendants. In Denmark, Sweden and Norway moreover the constitution requires the sovereign to be of the Protestant religion, though most British commentators imply that Britain is unique in this requirement also.

Republican views in Britain, which resulted in the execution of King Charles I in 1649 and media vilification of the House of Hanover in the 1820s and 1830s, and which for a brief period in the 1870s seemed to threaten the position of Queen Victoria herself, were enjoying something of a media resurgence in the 1990s. Above all the demand was for a monarchy with a 'more modern' image. Exactly what benefit this might confer was difficult to understand. Governed by a monarchy, in the eighteenth century the United Kingdom led the world into industrial revolution and in the twentieth century, still governed by a monarchy, built the world's first working electronic computer and, under Francis Crick, revealed the structure of the DNA-RNA double helix which opened the way to the genome revolution of the year 2000.

Carping on the sometimes outmoded archaisms of monarchy, while it may be irrelevant, is not new. On a state visit to Italy, Hitler fretted at being obliged to ride through the streets of Rome in a horse-drawn carriage musing aloud in the King's hearing as to whether the royal house had heard perhaps of the automobile. Mussolini, who was to be ousted by the king he failed to depose when he had had the chance, and who was engagingly cognisant of his junior role in the Nazi-Fascist Axis fumed that after the war he would 'tell Hitler to do away with all these absurd anachronisms in the form of monarchies'.[25] The Führer would have willingly complied.

[277]

In the 1930s and 1940s a number of German royals who refused cooperation with the Third Reich joined the victims in the concentration camps. Crown Prince Rupprecht of Bavaria at first chose exile rather than live under the Nazi regime, his second wife Princess Antonia of Luxembourg was sent to Buchenwald where her health was permanently broken by the regime of harsh treatment verging on torture.

In its ceremonial trappings the Third Reich was, in fact, a rare instance of republican modernity. For Ruritanian folderols are not the exclusive preserve of monarchy. France's Republican Guard is regularly to be seen at the Presidential Elysées Palace complete with antique sabres, breast plates and plumed helmets, while the President of the National Assembly is daily escorted to his place by flunkies in old fashioned fancy dress uniforms. The French are, perhaps, more solicitous of the stability of the institutions of the Fifth Republic (dating from 1958) than the British are of a constitutional monarchy with its two party system rooted in the late seventeenth century which provided the world with the model for safe, constitutional opposition to government. At the opening of the twenty-first century, under the presiding genius of Queen Elizabeth II, the British monarchy should feel confident for its future – even that ardent Scottish Nationalist Sir Sean Connery has admitted to being as proud of the knighthood conferred on him by the Queen (in Scotland as well as England, be it remembered) as of his Hollywood Oscar. But in the year 2000, it was the Queen Mother rather than her daughter who was focus of the major royal event.

On 11 July 2000, St Paul's Cathedral was the setting for the solemn Service of Thanksgiving in Her Majesty's one hundredth year. Known world-wide as the 'Queen Mum', she was honoured not only by national dignitaries and of course by Britain's royal family, but also by many royal personages from Europe. On 19 July the streets of London and Horseguards Parade witnessed the most astonishing parade of popular enthusiasm commemorating Britain in the twentieth century to honour this most popular of royals – a show which occupied no less than ninety minutes of air time on

French television. The other celebrations, such as a reception held by the City of London in Her Majesty's honour were covered by photo features in the continental society journals, as were the festivities on 4 August the day itself. No doubt there was surprise in countries like the Netherlands, where Queen's Day is a national holiday, that this was not declared a national holiday by the British government. There was surprise in Britain itself. Such celebrations, of course, have little 'practical' effect, but it is hard to contest their importance in the world of symbols and emotion so important in the human experience of life and so preëminently the preserve of monarchy in the political arena.

The year had its fair quota of royal events, major and minor. The Bourbon prince, Louis Alphonse Duc d'Anjou, to some 'Louis XX' of France was inaugurated with great ceremonial into the ranks of the Knights of St John of Malta. In February, crowds thronged the cathedral of Porto for the baptism of Diniz of Portugal, the third child of the Duke and Duchess of Braganza of Portugal's former royal house. The Duke is still of interest to royalty watchers, even though his ancestor Manuel II, the last king to rule Portugal, was driven out of Lisbon by revolution in 1910. Various representatives of Europe's Catholic royal families attended, among them the heir to the Belgian throne Prince Philippe Duke of Brabant and his wife Princess Mathilde, the venerable Comtesse de Paris, widow of the former Orléans claimant to the crown of France, accompanied by her grandsons the Dukes of Vendôme and of Angoulême, and a Habsburg Archduke.

That same month, at the other end of Europe, Queen Margrethe of Denmark and Prince Henrik were on a visit to England (their second) as guests of their good friends Queen Elizabeth and the Duke of Edinburgh. On the agenda, of course, a state banquet in St George's Hall, Windsor Castle. It was impressive enough as befits such affairs, but some of the better informed guests may have reflected that the Queen's revenues had become subject to more rigorous financial scrutiny than almost any other of Europe's reigning sovereigns. In 1990 the Civil List was frozen at £7.5 million a year agreed by parliament on the expectation of a high inflation rate in the coming years. Inflation being much less than anticipated and the Palace organization's practising strict economies combined to produce a balance in hand of several million pounds. The savings could perhaps have been put towards a replacement of the royal yacht *Britannia*, so treasured by the Queen but decommissioned in 1997, the government having refused to finance its refurbishment. In fact, in July 2000 it was announced that, thanks to these reserve funds so thriftily accumulated, the civil list would be frozen at the figure of £7.5 million for a further decade – perhaps the only case in history of a revenue frozen for twenty years.

The Danish monarch, who designs many of her own clothes, had packed a resplendent wardrobe for her visit to her British cousins, including a luxurious velvet gown adorned with pearls and diamonds and a luxurious natural fur coat. The Queen, whose great height makes her an imposing figure, does not apparently feel intimidated by the hectoring guardians of contemporary puritanism. Criticisms by Swedes and by fellow Danes of her 'excessive' smoking are not taken kindly, and it was reported that, in response to the animal rights' protests provoked by that fur coat, her entourage let it be known that Queen Margrethe was accustomed to dress as she pleased. It showed, no doubt, a regal indifference to fashionable sensibilities, but it struck a blow for what was once a democratic right.

In many of its aspects, in fact, Denmark's monarchy seems to be even less 'modern' and much more splendid and formal than does Britain's. It was rumoured that, soon after becoming prime minister, Tony Blair had proposed to drop his weekly audience with the Queen. Such meetings had taken place every Tuesday evening, when parliament was sitting and the monarch was in London, for as long as anyone could remember. Mr Blair, however, who also rarely appeared in the Commons, was apparently too busy. Under pressure, he agreed to spare the monarch some of his time. Things seem to be different in Denmark. According to the brochure *25 ans de règne*, published in 1997 for Margrethe II's twenty-five years as Queen, her prime ministers have what amounts to a constitutional obligation to keep her informed, presenting a report every Wednesday. Margrethe of Denmark still enjoys the use of the state-funded royal yacht the *Danebrog*, the court chamberlain still carries a gold key of office while, observing a tradition dating back to 1746, grades of the nobility, ministers of the crown and senior civil service still form five classes. Perhaps still more significant in this age of broadcast media, Queen Margrethe's New Year television message is given preferential billing in the schedules and was prologued by scenes of the palace square and the ceremony of the changing of the guard.

The celebrations for the Queen's sixtieth birthday in April 2000, signalled a notable manifestation of the historic pomp of monarchy which was also marked by popular affection and enthusiasm. During the two official days of festivity, she received countless bouquets and birthday presents brought to the Amalienborg Palace by private citizens, as well as deputations from town councils and professional bodies. At midnight, the crowd packed the palace square. Within the palace, the Queen presided over her birthday banquet. The King of Sweden was seated on her right, Prince Philip Duke of Edinburgh on her left at the chief of the numerous separate tables which accommodated the many guests, who had been officially welcomed by Prince Henrik the Prince Consort. Each of the other tables was presided over by a king or a queen. The music of trumpets, horns and drums heralded the entry of Queen Margrethe and punctuated the banquet with occasional fanfares and airs.

For the Scandinavian monarchies, 2000 was marked in May by a unique millennial celebration, to coincide with the inauguration of an exhibition of Washington's Smithsonian Institution, 'The Vikings: The North Atlantic Saga'. This recalled the adventures and achievements of the Norsemen whose 'Vinland' is generally credited as the first European settlement on the North American continent. In May, President and Mrs Clinton hosted a banquet at the White House at which King Harald and Queen Sonja of Norway, Crown Princess Victoria of Sweden and Prince Joachim of Denmark were the principal guests. Perhaps less cause for celebration in the

[281]

case of Norway's royal couple was the fact that, during the year, Crown Prince Haakon made public a romantic commitment to a beautiful young commoner who was an unmarried mother and who was said to have had connections with the drug scene.

In July, Sweden and Denmark celebrated the completion of one of the world's greatest engineering achievements, with the opening of the Öresund road, bridge and tunnel transport link, carrying traffic via the artificial island of Peberholm across the Sound between Copenhagen and Malmö. Naturally, the two royal couples led the celebrations at the opening ceremony, the Queen of Denmark and the King of Sweden and their consorts Prince Henrik and Queen Silvia embracing one another and the two queens throwing their bouquets into the waves.

In late February-early March Portugal had again been the focus of monarchist interest, though for a sad occasion, when the death was announced at her home in Estoril of Queen Ioanna of Bulgaria, widow of King Boris III, at the age of ninety-three. The chief mourners at the funeral ceremony held in the church at Estoril were her son King Simeon II, together with Queen Margrita, and his sister Princess Marie Louise of Bulgaria, while the nine pall bearers were the dead Queen's nine grandchildren. Heading the list of the numerous other mourners, royal and noble, was King Juan Carlos of Spain, who had known the Queen and her family during his days as king in waiting and whose own mother, the Countess of Barcelona, had died some two months earlier. With him was Queen Sofia while the Duke and Duchess of Braganza, as head of the former royal house of Portugal and friends also of the dead Queen and her family, were also present. Two days after the Estoril funeral, the body having been flown to Italy, Queen Ioanna daughter of King Victor Emmanuel III of Italy and sister of his successor King Umberto II, was, at her own wish, laid to rest in the Church of Assissi where, some sixty years earlier, she and King Boris had been married. Following the stipulation of the Italian government, the ceremony was restricted to the immediate family – children and grand children. Since the con-

[282]

stitutional law which banned the head of the House of Savoy from entering Italy was still in force, the aim was no doubt to insure against Queen Ioanna's nephew, Prince of Naples the son and heir of King Umberto II, and who had attended the Estoril funeral, from anticipating a dispensation to enter the country.

In fact, a public opinion survey conducted by the Italian weekly magazine *Oggi* showed an almost unanimous response in favour of the Savoys being permitted to reside in Italy. By any reasonable interpretation of European Community laws, the denial of the right of free movement to a European citizen must be unacceptable. Numerous moves had been made to get the legislation repealed. In March 2000 a British MEP initiated a vote in the European Parliament at Strasbourg but without success. The Prince himself had made petition. The European Court of Human Rights was expected to deliver its opinion before the end of the year.

In the Netherlands 2000 was an important epoch in the royal calendar, being the twentieth year of Queen Beatrix's reign. In neighbouring Luxembourg the year was to mark the beginning of a new reign. The celebration of the country's National Holiday of 23 June was an emotional occasion, as it was the last official public engagement for Grand Duke Jean and Grand Duchess Josephine Charlotte. The formal abdication of the Grand Duke was to take effect on 28 September when he was to be succeeded by his son Prince Henri. The event was to be celebrated by three days of festivities and the new Hereditary Grand Duke would be Prince Guillaume, son of Grand Duke Henri and his wife Grand Duchess Maria Theresa. So far as is known, republicanism has a very low profile in the politics of Luxembourg and the continuation of the monarchy in that country seems assured.

The same seemed to be true of Monaco where the formal abdication of Prince Rainier, speculated on for many years, seemed to be brought measurably nearer by two major operations in the winter of 1999–2000 which had greatly weakened his health. But the atmosphere in the principality was somewhat febrile thanks to a number of factors. Observers felt that Prince Rainier was increasingly reliant on Hereditary Prince Albert who seemed also to be evincing a strengthened seriousness of purpose and sureness of touch in the business of the state.

Nevertheless there were events which tended to tarnish the image of Monaco. In February, the sensational death of an international banker in an arson attack on his heavily guarded luxury apartment in the principality sparked speculation of possible Russian 'mafia' involvement, while a 400-page report by two French *deputés* called its banking regulations into question and even implied the connivance of the government in Paris at certain questionable practices. From time to time, all three of Europe's monarchical mini-states have been targets of similar suspicions. In a press interview before his accession, Henri of Luxembourg was careful to emphasize that his country's banking laws were rigidly framed against the possibility of money laundering. Like those of Monaco and Luxembourg and, if it comes to that of the Republic of Switzerland, the banking system of Liechtenstein had also been criticized for what some commentators considered its less-than-stringent financial procedures. But, for a time in mid 2000, it seemed the French media had declared open season on Monaco. One article sought to probe the reality of Prince Rainier's personal fortune, proposing an estimate of some ten billion francs. The Prince's minister of state charged that such speculation was simply a measure of the contemptuous indifference journalists could show when dealing with small states.

In fact, this was not entirely fair to the French media which for some months had been conducting investigations into the affairs of their own country's petroleum giant ELF-Aquitaine. Press and television articles and documentaries claimed to expose the systematic accumulation of a slush fund, by a concealed minimal surcharge at the pumps of ELF petrol stations. The billions of francs thus raised produced massive cash reserves, said to be held in Liechstenstein bank accounts. The money was, the journalists claimed, destined principally for the benefit of certain African heads of state and while there was no suggestion that HSH Reigning Prince Hans

Adam had any knowledge of the funds in question, the French researchers discovered evidence which satisfied them that France's own head of state at the time, the late President François Mitterand, did. The full accusation against him was that a substantial amount of these funds, illegally raised by the Republic's national petroleum company and siphoned off into the banking system of a foreign monarchy, was used on the President's directions to provide secret funding for the campaign which ensured the reelection of his friend and political ally Germany's president, Helmut Kohl. Thus, whatever the political importance of Europe's mini-monarchies may or may not be, their financial sectors may, perhaps, make them key players in a concert of Europe where money rather than tradition is the theme.

Speaking in London in 1960 Otto von Habsburg advanced the view that palaces and crowns were no more 'than top hats to presidents'. A number of currently reigning monarchs were inaugurated without coronation. Those in exile have lost their regalia but still have sizeable bodies of admirers and supporters in their home countries as well as among expatriates. There were numerous examples of the persistence of such pro-monarchist sentiments during the millennium year. King Constantine II of Greece, Queen Anne Marie were the centre of an enthusiastic crowd when they celebrated Easter in London's Greek Orthodox Cathedral. At about the same time, King Michael of Romania in his eightieth year and Queen Anne, were welcome visitors among the large majority of the republic's citizens when they celebrated the feast in Bucharest. The Romanian government had restored a number of royal properties confiscated during the communist era. In Bulgaria, where the post-communist regime has made similar restitutions of real estate King Simeon II, while he no longer has a throne, plays an active if undefined role as adviser and icon in the life of his countrymen and women. These are the ties of loyalty and affection which could yet lead to the reintegration of the royal element into some countries' constitutions. As to those European monarchies still in place, one would like to think that, dormant in the royal DNA lurk the genes of cynicism and opportunism which marked the rule of princes in the days of their glory and today seem to have engineered themselves into the chromosomes of the democratic politicians who have succeeded them in the genealogy of power.

But there are surely better grounds for royal optimism about the prospects for the future. Interviewed by Alan Hamilton for *The Times* at the time of her state visit to the United Kingdom in February 2000, HM Queen Margrethe of Denmark was asked whether she thought the continent's monarchies would still exist a century thence. 'I don't see why not, she replied, they are responsible people and have young people who are also responsible.'

Even so, it must be said that at times, royals can be every bit as slippery in their behaviour and hypocritical in their attitudes as their subjects. Like all public figures they depend for their survival on the oxygen of publicity, yet they are jealous of their privacy. As long ago as 1912, King Ferdinand of Bulgaria described photography as 'not a profession but a disease' and he would have found many to agree with him in the chancelleries of modern Europe. Even official portraitists can be liable to sanctions. In 1991 it was reported that King Baudouin of the Belgians had blocked the introduction of a new bank note series because the portraits of himself and Queen Fabiola, approved by the authorities, made them appear too old.

So what conclusion, if any, can we come to? Perhaps the last word should go to Ken Livingstone, who in May 2000 became the first Mayor of London to be elected by its citizens since the Commune of 1191 and who was dubbed *roi de Londres* by the French newspaper *Le Figaro*. A noted republican, but also a skilled professional politician, he surprised some observers by his willingness to share photo opportunities with the Queen and with the Queen Mother. He would have to be an obtuse as well as graceless candidate for popular approval who ostentatiously snubbed the House of Windsor in the year of the Queen Mum's one hundredth birthday celebrations but in any case, as Mr Livingstone cheerfully admitted on a BBC radio programme, the royals were going to outlast his years in office. Apparently, he reckoned that common sense as well as common courtesy required a policy of friendly cohabitation. It would be unwise for any one to predict the early demise of monarchy in Europe. If this book has shown anything it may have conveyed something of the institution's considerable ability to adapt.

NOTES

QUOTATION SOURCES

* = text translated from French or Spanish by author

1 *Royalty Digest: Journal of Record,* (Old Knowle, Frant, Kent, December 1992) p. 170

2 Toland, John, *Adolf Hitler* (Ballantine Books, New York, 1977), p. 374

3 *Balansó, Juan, *Los Reales Primos de Europa* (Planeta, Barcelona, 1992), p. 219

4 Davies, Norman, *Europe: a History* (Pimlico, London, 1997), p. 645

5 *Deslot, Thierry, *Geraldine d'Albanie: reine du pays des aigles* (Edition BOC & C, Puteau, n.d.), p. 10

6 Hindley, Geoffrey, *The Royal Families of Europe* (Lyric Books, London, 1979), p. 153

7 Ibid. p. 107

8 Ibid. p. 156

9 Ileana of Romania, *I live Again,* (Gollancz, London, 1952), cited *Royalty Digest,* October 1991, p. 105

10 *Roumanie, Michel de, *Le Règne inachevé: conversations avec Philippe Viguié Desplaces* (Paris, 1992), p. 38

11 Ibid., p. 68

12 *Ibid., p. 183

13 Cobban, Alfred, *A History of Modern France,* Volume 2: 1799–1945 (Penguin, Harmondsworth, 1961), p. 149

14 *Chiappe, Jean-François, *La France et le roi de la restauration à nos jours* (Perrin, Paris, 1994), p. 507

15 *Ibid., p. 607

16 Cobban, Alfred, *A History of Modern France*, Volume 3: 1871-1962 (Penguin, Harmondsworth, 1965, p. 195)

17 *Hvidt, Christian, *25 ans de règne* (Le Ministère royal des Affaires étrangères de Danemark, Service de l'Information, Copenhagen, 1997), p. 7

18 *Ibid., p. 16

19 *Point de Vue*, semaine 23–29 juin, 1999 ("Point de Vue", Paris, 1999), p. 73

20 Hindley, Geoffrey, *The Royal Families of Europe* (Lyric Books, London, 1979) p. 116

21 Ibid., p. 134

22 The account of King Leopold's swearing in ceremony and of the early part of his reign is mainly based on Pascal Dayez-Burgeon's *La reine Astrid ...* (Paris, 1995)

23 *Cernuda, Pilar, Lose Oneto, Ramon Pi & Pedro J. Ramirez, Todo un rey (E.Y.E., Madrid 1981) p. 36

24 Fulford, Roger, *Royal Dukes* (Collins, Fontana Books, London, 1973), p.207

25 Galloway, Peter, *An Uneasy Cohabitation... 1922–1943*, Royalty Digest September 1998, p. 266

BILBIOGRAPHY

The Almanach de Gotha: Genealogy, Volume 1 (London, 1998)

Appleby, John T., *England without Richard 1189–1199* (G. Bell & Sons, London, 1965)

Aron, Robert, *Léopold III ou la choix impossible* (Plon, Paris, 1977)

Balansó, Juan, *Los reales primos de Europea* (Editorial Planeta, Barcelona, 1992)

———— *Los diamantes de la corona* (Plaza Janés, Barcelona, 1998)

Barnett, Anthony, *Power and the Throne: The Monarchy Debate* (Vintage, London, 1994)

Bethell, Nicholas, *The Great Betrayal: The Untold Story of Kim Philby's Biggest Coup* (Hodder & Stoughton, London, 1984)

Brégeon, Jean-Joël, *Les Grimaldi de Monaco* (Criterion, Paris, 1991)

Carpenter, Clive, *The Guinness Book of Kings, Rulers and Statesmen* (Guinness Superlatives, Enfield, 1978)

Cernuda, Pilar, Lose Oneto, Ramon Pi & Pedro J. Ramirez, *Todo un rey* (E.Y.E., Madrid, 1981)

Chapman, Hester W., *The Tragedy of Charles II* (Jonathan Cape, London, 1964)

Chiappe, Jean-François, *La France et le roi de la restauration à nos jours* (Perrin, Paris, 1994)

Cobban, Alfred, *A History of Modern France, Volume 2 :1799–1945* (Penguin, Harmondsworth, 1961)

————Volume 3: 1871–1962 (Penguin Harmondsworth, 1965)

Davies, Norman, *Europe: A History* (Pimlico, London, 1997)

Dayez-Burgeon, Pascal, *La reine Astrid: histoire d'un mythe* (Criterion, Paris, 1995)

Deakin, F. W., *The Last Days of Mussolini* (Penguin Books, Harmondsworth, 1962)

de Badts, Chantal, *Les Dix Princes héritiers des familles régnantes d'Europe* (Collection Petit Gotha, APB, Paris, 1999)

de la Bastide, Guy, 'Bavière d'hier et d'aujourd'hui' *Revue de psychologie des peuples* (CNRS, Caen, 18e année 2, 2e trim., 1963)

Delorme, Philippe, *Louis XVII – La vérité, sa mort au Temple confirmé par la science* (Pygmalion, Paris 2000)

Deslot, Thierry, *Géraldine d'Albanie, reine du pays des aigles* (Edition BCG & G, Puteau n.d.)

Douglas, Walburga, *Otto von Habsburg -Ein souveräner Europäer* (Baier, 1997)

Duverger, Maurice, 'Les Monarchies républicaines', *Les Monarchies, POUVOIRS, Revue française d'études constitutionelles et politiques* N°78 (Seuil, Paris, 1996)

El Gammal, Jean, 'Les Courantes Monarchistes sous la IIIe République' *POUVOIRS* N° 78 (Paris, 1996)

Empatz, Erik, Editor in Chief, *Les Joyeux de la couronne: le tour du monde des monarchies* (Les Dossiers du Carnard enchainé, Paris, 1999)

Encyclopaedia Britannica Book of the Year

Fenyvesi, Charles, *Royalty in Exile* (Robson Books, London, 1981)

Fox Davies, Arthur Charles, *A complete Guide to Heraldry* (T.C. and E.C. Jack, London, 1929

Foyer, Jean, 'Les Querelles dynastiques aujourd'hui'. *POUVOIRS* N°78 (Paris, 1996)

Fulford, Roger, *Royal Dukes* (Collins, Fontana Books, London, 1973)

Gauthier, Guy, *Les Aigles et les lions: histoire des monarchies balkaniques* (France-Empire, Paris, 1996)

Government Information Service, The Hague, *The Royal House* (The Hague, 1999)

Groueff, Stéphane, *Crown of Thorns* (Madison Books, Lanham, Md, London, 1987)

Hindley, Geoffrey, *The Royal Families of Europe* (Lyric Books, London, 1979)

Hvidt, Kristian, 25 *ans de règne* (Service de l'Informatioin ... des Affaires étrangères, Copenhagen, 1997)

Judd, Denis, *Eclipse of Kings: European Monarchies in the Twentieth Century* (Macdonald and Jane's, London, 1976)

[292]

Kreins, Jean-Marie, *Histoire du Luxembourg* (Presses Universitaires de France, Paris, 1996)

Lagerqvist, Lars O. and Nils Åberg, *Kings and Rulers of Sweden - a Pocket Encyclopaedia* (Vincent Publications, Stockholm, 1995)

Longford, Elizabeth, *Elizabeth R: A Biography* (Weidenfeld and Nicholson, London, 1983)

Mack Smith, Denis, *Italy and its Monarchy* (Yale University Press, New Haven, London, 1989)

Miguel, Pierre, *Les Derniers Rois de l'Europe* (Robert Laffont, Paris, 1995)

Morby, John E., *Dynasties of the World* (O.U.P., 1989)

Nourry, Philippe, *Juan Carlos: un rey para los republicanos* (Editorial Planeta, Barcelona, 1986)

Opello, Walter C., *Portugal from Monarchy to Pluralist Democracy* (Westview, Boulder, Oxford, 1991)

d'Orléans, Jacques, *Les Ténébreuses Affaires du Comte de Paris* (Albin Michel, Paris, 1999)

Paris, Isabelle, comtesse de, *Mon bonheur de grand-mére* (Robert Laffont, Paris, 1995)

Pinson, Koppel S., Modern Germany: *Its History and Civilization* (The Macmillan Company, New York, 1954)

Potter, Jeremy, *Pretenders* (Constable, London, 1986)

Prebble, John, *The Lion in the North: One Thousand Year's of Scotland's History* (Martin Secker & Warburg, London 1971)

Robert, Hervé, *L'Orléanisme* (Paris, 1992)

Roumanie, Michel de, *Le Règne inachevé: conversations avec Philippe Vigué Desplaces* (Paris, 1992)

Royalty Digest: Journal of Record (Old Knowle, Frant, Kent, December 1992–)

Shakespeare, Nicholas, *The Men Who Would Be King* (London, 1984)

Sencourt, Robert, *Heirs of Tradition* (Carroll & Nicholson, London, 1949)

Spada, Antonio, *Ordini dinastici della Real Casa di Savoia decreti reali* (Grafo, Brescia, 1985)

The Statesman's Year Book (Macmillan, London, 1864 et seq.)

Taylor, A.J.P., *English History, 1914–1945* (OUP, Oxford, 1965)

Thomas, Hugh, *The Spanish Civil War* (Penguin Books, Harmondsworth, 1965)

Toland, John, Adolf Hitler (Ballantine Books, New York, 1976)

Uboldi, Raffaello, *Juan Carlos : La España de ayer, hoy y mañana* (Plaza y Janes, Barcelona, 1985)

Van der Kiste, John, *Northern Crowns : The Kings of Modern Scandinavia* (Sutton Publishing, Stroud, 1996)

Van der Kiste, John, *Kings of the Hellenes* (Sutton Publishing, Stoud 1994)

VOX special edition, *The Belgian Dynasty* (SID, Brussels, 12 November 1997)

Ward, S.G.P., *Wellington* (Batsford, London, 1963)

Warren, Raoul de, et Aymon de Lestrange, *Les Prétendants au trône de France* (L'Herne, Paris, 1990)

Warren, W.I., *Henry II* (Methuen, London, 1973)

Wilson, Edgar, *The Myth of British Monarchy* (Journeyman Press, London, 1989)

Ziegler, Philip, *Mountbatten: the Official Biography* (Collins, London, 1985)

INDEX